CULTURESHOCK!

A Survival Guide to Customs and Etiquette

CAMBODIA

Peter North

GRAPHIC ARTS®
BOOKS
Portland, Oregon

Marshall Cavendish
Editions

Photo Credits:
All photos by or from the author except pages x, 3, 8, 11, 13, 62, 64, 113, 120, 125, 138, 165, 201, 220–221 (Alex Drummond); pages 22, 162, 171 (Larry Horner); pages 58, 69, 141, 145, 192, 203 (Louise Horner); pages 12, 77, 150, 180, 185 (Jill Richards) and pages 85, 159 (Amy Sholtz). ▪ Cover photo: Age Fotostock/Angelo Cavalli

All illustrations by TRIGG

This edition published in 2005 by:

Marshall Cavendish Editions
An imprint of Marshall Cavendish International (Asia) Pte Ltd
1 New Industrial Road, Singapore 536196
Tel: (65) 6213 9300, fax: (65) 6285 4871.
Email: te@sg.marshallcavendish.com
Online bookstore: www.marshallcavendish.com/genref

and

Graphic Arts Center Publishing Company
P.O. Box 10306, Portland, Oregon 97296-0306
United States of America
Tel: (503) 226 2402
Website: www.gacpc.com

Please contact Graphic Arts Center Publishing Company for the Library of Congress catalogue number

ISBN 981-232-901-3 (Asia & Rest of World)
ISBN 1-55868-927-3 (USA & Canada)
ISBN 1-904879-79-9 (Europe)

Printed in Singapore by Times Graphics

ABOUT THE SERIES

Culture shock is a state of disorientation that can come over anyone who has been thrust into unknown surroundings, away from one's comfort zone. *CultureShock!* is a series of trusted and reputed guides which has, for decades, been helping expatriates and long-term visitors to cushion the impact of culture shock whenever they move to a new country.

Written by people who have lived in the country and experienced culture shock themselves, the authors share all the information necessary for anyone to cope with these feelings of disorientation more effectively. The guides are written in a style that is easy to read and covers a range of topics that will arm readers with enough advice, hints and tips to make their lives as normal as possible again.

Each book is structured in the same manner. It begins with the first impressions that visitors will have of that city or country. To understand a culture, one must first understand the people—where they came from, who they are, the values and traditions they live by, as well as their customs and etiquette. This is covered in the first half of the book

Then on with the practical aspects—how to settle in with the greatest of ease. Authors walk readers through how to find accommodation, get the utilities and telecommunications up and running, enrol the children in school and keep in the pink of health. But that's not all. Once the essentials are out of the way, venture out and try the food, enjoy more of the culture and travel to other areas. Then be immersed in the language of the country before discovering more about the business side of things.

To round off, snippets of basic information are offered before readers are 'tested' on customs and etiquette of the country. Useful words and phrases, a comprehensive resource guide and list of books for further research are also included for easy reference.

CONTENTS

FOREWORD

A few years ago, the outside world knew little about Cambodia. In 1975, the Khmer Rouge communists staged a successful revolution and the borders were closed to foreigners. Few people entered the country and even fewer got out. There were disquieting rumours of social upheaval in the country, but very little hard news. Only gradually, over the next 20 years, did the borders reopen.

In the last few years, this picture has changed completely. In 2002, the Cambodian government dubbed 2003, 'Visit Cambodia Year'. The country opened its doors to the world, and the world dropped in for a visit. Once best known for the award-winning movie, *The Killing Fields*, Cambodia is now better known for its splendid ruins at Angkor Wat. Cambodia has now established itself as a must-visit country on the South-east Asian tourist trail.

From the point of view of the visitor, Cambodia has many attractions. With its amazing history, both ancient and modern, its natural beauty, friendly people, this small and fascinating country has much to offer, whether you visit to snap photographs, to start a business or to disseminate aid in its various forms to a deserving poor.

Along its path to the present day, Cambodia's recent history has been filled with long periods of anguish and despair. Even before the Khmer Rouge began their reign of terror, Cambodia was already torn by conflict, despite the efforts of its one-time king-turned prime minister, Norodom Sihanouk, to maintain the country's neutrality and peace.

Sihanouk is probably Cambodia's best-known contemporary political figure. Few leaders in the present world have presided over such tumultuous times. The second half of the 20th century in Cambodia saw the defeat of European colonialism, the rise of communism, the South-east Asian war with America, the takeover of Cambodia by the communist Khmer Rouge, and their subsequent defeat by the North Vietnamese army. During this march of history, Cambodia was at war with itself and with foreign powers for the better part of 30 years.

Since then, the focus of global disputation has shifted from South-east Asia to the Middle East. The major force driving geo-politics in the first decade of the new millennium is no longer the competition between the econo-political ideologies of communism and capitalism, but the contest to control diminishing resources such as oil. By the end of the 20th century, South-east Asia, including Cambodia, has largely become a zone of peace and prosperity, perhaps even the 'oasis of peace' which Sihanouk sought for most of his life.

Cambodia is still rundown, recovering from its exhausting history. The recipient of much aid in recent years, the country still cannot stand on its own feet. The resources of the outside world—people, talents and funds—are still needed to help the old nation rebuild and the new nation emerge. Cambodia appreciates its visitors. In whatever capacity you come to Cambodia, you are sure to be welcome in this very friendly country. 'Visit Cambodia Year' may have ended at the end of 2003, but many Cambodians would like to make 'Visit Cambodia Year' a permanent fixture.

ACKNOWLEDGEMENTS

Many people provided information, anecdotes, suggestions and viewpoints for this book. I would like to take the opportunity here to offer my collective thanks.

As little as 20 years ago, Cambodia was essentially a closed country still emerging from two decades of war in which it was a mostly unwilling participant. Scars of this conflict still show. Where one perhaps might have expected lingering hostility towards visitors from previously belligerent countries, I instead found in Cambodia openness, friendliness and helpfulness, which at times was just a little bit overwhelming.

To the Cambodians I have met—taxi drivers, business owners, street beggars, agricultural labourers, politicians, kids selling newspapers and media people—thanks for your stories. To members of the expat community in Cambodia, thanks for your stories too. To the photographers listed in the photo credits section, thanks for your photos. The neat green countryside, the extraordinary Angkor ruins and the spontaneous Cambodian smile you find wherever you go makes Cambodia a very photogenic country.

My thanks to all. And my very best wishes for the future to Cambodia, the country.

MAP OF CAMBODIA

THAILAND

LAOS

CAMBODIA

PHNOM
PENH

VIETNAM

GULF OF
THAILAND

SOUTH
CHINA
SEA

Cambodia's smile.

CAMBODIA AT FIRST GLANCE

CHAPTER 1

'If a tiger lies down, don't believe
the tiger is showing respect.'
—Cambodian Proverb

BACK TO THE FUTURE

At the close of the 13th century, the mighty Khmer Empire centred at Angkor Wat in present day Cambodia, stretched from the Bay of Bengal to the South China Sea. It included much of present-day Malaysia, Laos, Cambodia, Myanmar and Vietnam. Cambodia's power had reached its zenith. The country was prosperous and advanced. Irrigation water from a network of canals nourished the rice paddies. People planted and harvested their crops by hand and drove oxen to plough the fields. Barefoot monks in saffron robes at temples in each village supplied the community its inspiration, culture, administration and education.

At first glance, it might seem little has changed. The Cambodian country is still a predominantly agricultural society. The bulk of the population lives in the countryside. Crops are sown and harvested largely by hand. Saffron-clad monks mingle with the population. Even the smallest village is sited near a temple.

Such a state of affairs might suggest little has disturbed the tranquillity of Cambodian life for centuries. Nothing could be further from the truth of course. Anyone with a passing knowledge of South-east Asian history has heard of the killing fields, the Khmer Rouge, the Indo-Chinese wars of the 1960s and 1970s and a landmine problem that persists till today. Within the living memory of many of its inhabitants, Cambodia has been one of the most traumatised countries

Harvesting the rice crop.

on the planet. Only in the past few years has Cambodia returned to the relatively peaceful conditions that prevailed centuries before.

While the culture shock experienced by expats is the principal theme of this book, Cambodia in recent years has experienced its own culture shock at a level seen by few other countries. In the space of less than two generations, Cambodian culture has been trashed to an extent barely imaginable by people from more fortunate countries. Just about any Cambodian you meet can recount the death of a family member in some battle conducted on Cambodian soil.

Visitors experiencing culture shock from the minor inconveniences of modern-day Cambodia can take heart from the coping skills of Cambodians themselves. To their great credit, the Cambodian people are extraordinarily warm, friendly and obliging to their visitors, even to those from previously belligerent nations.

But the scars of war, both physical and psychological, remain. Cambodia has neither forgotten nor completely recovered from its troubled past. Perhaps to remind itself and the rest of the world that this must not be allowed to happen again, Cambodia has preserved the killing fields and detention centres that operated during the dark days of the Khmer Rouge—even turning them into tourist attractions.

RECENT HISTORY: A THUMBNAIL SKETCH

A country is the product of its history. An underlying theme of its history in the last few hundred years has been Cambodia's failure to make peace with its neighbours and countries further afield. No sooner had Cambodia rid itself of one meddling foreign influence than another made its presence felt. Over the past few centuries, the French, Japanese, Thais, Chinese, Russians, Americans and Vietnamese have all manipulated Cambodia one way or the other for their own ends.

Cambodia's recent history perhaps commenced in 1863 when the French colonised what they viewed as a backward country. French colonial rule lasted until 1953 when Cambodia gained its independence. For a little more than a decade after that, the country enjoyed a period of prosperity.

But in the 1960s, the war clouds were gathering across the border in Vietnam. Prince Sihanouk, then Cambodia's prime minister, tried to keep his country out of the escalating war in Vietnam, declaring his country neutral and describing Cambodia as 'an oasis of peace'.

This turned out to be wishful thinking. Cambodia's problem was location. In the 1960s, the country lay at what was the border between the communist and capitalist world: to its east was communist North Vietnam; to the south capitalist South Vietnam; to the west capitalist Thailand; to the north the small and ostensibly neutral country of Laos.

Capitalism and communism waged war in Cambodia from the late 1960s until the country fell to the Khmer Rouge communists in 1975. Khmer Rouge rule lasted until the regime's former allies, the Vietnamese, invaded from the east to remove the Khmer Rouge from power. A Vietnamese backed administration took over in 1979, but that wasn't the end of the fighting. The Khmer Rouge retreated to bases on either side of the Thai border from which they continued their attacks on the Cambodian civilian population.

In all, Cambodia spent over 30 long years at war with itself and with the international community. These long decades of war shattered the country's infrastructure, devastated its economy, destroyed its agriculture and killed millions of its citizens. All military activity in Cambodia finally came to an end in 1999 when the last remnants of the Khmer Rouge laid down their arms after the death of their leader Pol Pot.

After that, peace returned to Cambodia.

THE COUNTRY

Cambodia is situated entirely in the tropics, lying between latitudes 11° to 15° north. Tucked between Laos, Thailand and Vietnam, Cambodia is the third smallest country in South-east Asia after Singapore and Brunei. At 181,040 sq km (69,900 sq miles) Cambodia is slightly larger than England and Wales combined. The country is roughly square in shape and measures about 580 km (360 miles) from east to west and about 450 km (280 miles) from north to south with the capital, Phnom Penh, near the centre. To the south, the approximately 440 km (273 miles) of mostly unspoiled coastline looks onto the Gulf of Thailand.

The countryside features stretches of magnificent tropical rainforest, in some places, neat villages tucked between green paddy fields in others. Covering about half the country's area, the Mekong alluvial plain in the centre of the country is ringed by low mountains and hills. In the south-west, are the Elephant (Damrei) Mountains. To the west, the Cardamom (Kravanh) Range spills across the Thai border. To the north, on the border with Laos and Thailand, a string of hills about 500 m (1,600 feet) high rises to the Dangrek Mountains. To the north-east, the Annamite Cordillera Range runs along the border with Vietnam and up into Laos. To the south, the flatlands merge into the Mekong delta of southern Vietnam.

This mixture of hills and plains—some tropical, some temperate—produces a variety of landscapes. Different authorities estimate that forests still cover 30–50 per cent of the country. Forest type varies with terrain and climate. To the south, the evergreens of the tropical rainforests of the Elephant Mountains give way the mangroves along Cambodia's coast on the Gulf of Thailand. Towering forests of broadleaf hardwoods grow in the Cardamom Mountains in the west and the Dangrek Mountains in the north. Forests in the north-east, near the borders with Laos and Vietnam, feature bamboo, jungle vines, palm trees and ground plants.

In contrast to the forests that fringe its borders, the Mekong delta region at the heart of the country is Cambodia's food bowl. Flying into Phnom Penh's airport in daytime, a patchwork of different shades of green passes under the wings. From the air, the neatness, order and harmony of the Cambodian countryside—with irrigation channels, embankments and neat rows of palms encircling the paddy fields—is picture perfect, like a postcard of rural France.

Seen at ground level, soil appears mostly as various shades of red—the characteristic red dust of the dry season and red mud the consistency of thick soup in the wet season. The Cambodian countryside is at its most attractive in November. The wet season has just ended and the heat of the dry season has not yet arrived. The weather is dry and warm, with plenty of water about. The sun glints off the rice paddies that stretch between stands of sugar palms, and the greenery of the countryside is at its greenest.

Climate

The south-west monsoon drives the rhythm of life in South-east Asian countries from Thailand to Vietnam. As the northern hemisphere summer builds, the Asian land mass heats up. Hot air rising behind the Himalayas, in places like the Gobi Desert, draws cooler moisture-laden air from the Indian Ocean over lands from India to southern China. Towards the end of April, moisture level in the atmosphere rises. Occasional showers presage the coming monsoon. Sometime in May, the cooling rains arrive.

The monsoon runs from May to October, with the balance of the year relatively dry. Within these two seasons a further distinction can be made based on temperature. The first four months of the monsoon season, May to August, are the hot-wet season, with September to October the cool-wet season. Likewise, the first three months of the dry season, November through January, are the cool-dry season, with February to April the hot-dry season.

During monsoon season, heavy rain falls in short bursts almost every afternoon. As the season runs its course, water levels rise in paddy fields and rivers. Roads are cut. Low-lying towns with their houses built on stilts become islands and people use boats to get around.

In November, the monsoon begins to shut down. For the balance of the year, north-easterly winds bring dry weather and the surface water evaporates or drains away. The driest place in the country with annual rainfall of about 1,200 mm (47 inches) is the north-central region between Phnom Penh and the northern border with Thailand. The wettest spot is in the Cardamom Mountains with an annual average of around 5,000 mm (197 inches).

The peak time for tourists is the cool-dry season, when the weather is at its most pleasant. At this time of the year, night-time temperatures may fall to around 15°C (59° F) and Cambodians may complain about the cold snap! Though Cambodia lies in the tropics, you may need to don a light overcoat at night in the mountain regions during the cool season. By contrast, touring in April at the height of the hot-

Siesta time in Phnom Penh.

dry season can be an ordeal. Temperatures peak at around 40°C (104°F). The air is still and precious few clouds dot the burnished blue sky. Humidity is high but the rain stays away. An oppressive heat envelopes the country.

May is the start of the ploughing season when the ground is prepared for the monsoon rice crop. The rural population, man and animal, work siesta hours. Oxen can be seen pulling the plough from dawn to late morning. Midday is time to take a rest in the shade if you are an agricultural worker, or to wallow in irrigation channels of the paddy fields if you are an ox. Overheated temple aficionados visiting the splendid ruins at Angkor are advised to follow a similar timetable. During the hot season, the best times for temple viewing are early morning and late evening.

IN THE COUNTRYSIDE

The majority of Cambodians are country dwellers living a simple life. Cambodia is a country of limited resources, where a dollar will stretch further than in most places. Agriculture is predominantly based on rice. Other crops include corn, sesame, durian, mango, cashew nuts, pepper, chilli, tobacco and tapioca.

The modern age has touched Cambodian agriculture only lightly. Much hard work is still done by hand.

Mechanical assistance, where it exists, is often the product of improvisation. Cambodia has adopted a recycling culture, using whatever second hand parts and materials can be scrounged from somewhere. In agriculture, Cambodia has developed an ingenious line of tractor/trailers made from second-hand axles, transmissions, motors and transmissions from a variety of expired vehicles. The Cambodians' use of whatever meagre resources that come their way to improve their lot is a tribute to the indomitable spirit of this country and perhaps an inspiration to those of us from more privileged lands.

Despite the new range of Cambodian made tractors-trailers, for the most part, agricultural practice has not changed greatly from the past. Across Cambodia, oxen and not tractors are still the most common method of ploughing the rice paddies. In fact, the Cambodian word for tractor is *go yuan*, meaning bull machine.

An Odd Couple

Oxen are picturesque beasts, sometimes attended by herons that ride on their backs. Oxen and herons share a symbiotic relationship. The heron obliges the ox by picking out the ticks from its ears. The ox obliges the heron by providing a breeding ground for its food supply. To the ox, the heron is a pest control service. To the heron, the ox is territory. "Get out", the heron might screech in heronese to other herons that may try to muscle in on this tranquil scene. "This is my ox."

Architectural styles of Cambodian buildings have evolved to suit the warm and humid monsoon climate. Houses are designed for ventilation but not insulation, with plenty of openings, both deliberate and inadvertent, through which air can flow freely. Houses are commonly built on stilts of logs to provide flood protection as well as a cool shaded area beneath for animals and people in the hot season.

Common building materials are the products of the forest—wood, bamboo, thatch and straw. Judging by the number of motor scooters and pushbikes that appear on the roads loaded with thatch, roofs made from this material are maintenance intensive. Tiled roofs, a more recent innovation, are also common. Alternative building materials may also be used when available. Cambodia is a society that wastes little and recycles whatever is at hand. Packing cases, plastic sheets and iron sheeting may be favoured over traditional palm materials, particularly in urban shanty towns. While making no claims for architectural awards, a packing-case structure may be more rainproof and draughtproof than one built from palm fronds.

Water, Water, Everywhere

In Cambodia, water provides work, sustenance, transport and leisure. Few Cambodians live far from a large river or a substantial lake and many live in homes that float on lakes and rivers. They wash their clothes and themselves in the water beneath their houses. They splash about, have fun and punt themselves around in anything that floats. Fishing, whether commercial or recreational, is a major activity.

Central to Cambodia's geography and way of life is the Mekong River, which flows across the northern border from Laos and through a wide alluvial plain in the centre of the country before exiting at the southern border with Vietnam. This mighty waterway is the longest river in South-east Asia and one of the ten largest rivers in the world. A number of its tributaries are major rivers in themselves.

Cambodia's most unusual geographical feature is South-east Asia's largest lake, the Tonle (pronounced Ton-lay) Sap, which means freshwater lake in Khmer.

Getting around—Cambodian-style.

Geologists believe Tonle Sap Lake was formed by a massive asteroid strike about 770,000 years ago that scarred the landscape with an elongated crater around 100 km (62 miles) long. Into this large new hole in the ground flowed streams from the surrounding hillsides, forming the Tonle Sap Lake that now provides Cambodia with much of its livelihood.

Tonle Sap Lake connects to the Mekong by a 120-km (75-mile) long channel. This waterway is identified by a number of different names. Some maps and guidebooks call it the Tonle Sap, some the Tonle Sab, and others the Tonle Sap River. In this book, the lake is called Tonle Sap Lake, while the waterway from the lake to the Mekong is called the Tonle Sap River.

The Tonle Sap River has one unusual, perhaps unique, feature. It flows in different directions at different times of the year. As a result, Tonle Sap Lake periodically fills and empties. The lake is at its shallowest in May, at the end of the dry season, when it might shrink to an area of around 2,500 sq km (975 sq miles).

Laundry facilities at Tonle Sap Lake.

About this time, the Mekong rises from an influx of melt water from the Himalayas as well as from monsoon rainfall in the Mekong's vast catchment area. From May to October water from the Mekong fills Tonle Sap Lake from the south while various streams around its banks also add water to the lake. By the end of the wet season the lake may expand to over 10,000 sq km (3,900 sq miles) in area. Trees and shrubs lying on the foreshore of the lake will become inundated so only their tops can be seen.

Around November, the rain abates, the level in the Mekong falls and Tonle Sap Lake starts emptying, returning its waters to the Mekong and providing downstream rice farmers with a steady supply of water for most of the dry season. This natural phenomenon regulates floodwater, nourishes the fertile alluvial plains to the south with irrigation water, and is enormously important to Cambodia's primary industries of fishing and agriculture.

Tonle Sap Lake is Cambodia's major source of freshwater fish with about 60 per cent of the country's total catch drawn from its waters. Based on weight of fish taken per square kilometre of water area, Tonle Sap Lake is the richest fresh water fishing ground in the world. The Mekong is also a major source of fish. Traditional fishing methods using nets suspended from bamboo poles have changed little over the centuries. As well as netting fish,

Fishy Business

Based on the weight of fish taken per square kilometre, Tonle Sap Lake is the richest freshwater fishing ground in the world.

Cambodians also tease eels from the bottom of water courses using rakes on long poles. Fish paste made from tiny fish called riels, and sometimes referred to as Cambodian Cheese, is a major protein source.

Houses in low-lying areas are built on knolls, if available, with construction on stilts offering additional clearance from floodwaters in the wet season. Some communities are built entirely over lakes and rivers, particularly around Tonle Sap Lake. Lakeside living at Tonle Sap is complicated by a shoreline that may move with the seasons by as much as 50 km (31 miles) and water levels that might rise and fall by 7 to 10 m (23 to 33 ft). One of two solutions is adopted. You can build your structures on stilts or you can build on pontoons. Under the second method, entire villages are floated, including houses, shops, schools, hospitals and even a Catholic church.

A floating church on Tonle Sap Lake.

Floating Homes

Tonle Sap Lake is famous for its fascinating floating villages, with houses built on flotation tanks, often empty oil drums. Alternatively houses fixed to terra firma are two-storied affairs with slideable wall panels that are moved up or down depending on the season. In the wet season the upper floor is occupied, and in the dry season the lower floor.

In such villages, traffic moves by canoe. Vendors bring their produce to each home where it is transferred from canoe to customer by baskets tied to a length of rope.

Conditions in these watery settlements are cramped. But people still manage to keep pigs or other animals. While solutions to the problems of living over water are ingenious and make interesting discussion points for visitors, inhabitants may see the rising and falling waters as a nuisance in their daily lives. The Cambodian government is presently relocating many lake dwellers to villages on dry land.

A CLOSED SOCIETY OPENS UP

The majority of foreigners who visit Cambodia come as tourists. The other major source of visitors is employees of Non-Governmental Organisations (NGOs). From a Cambodian point of view, tourism is a relatively recent phenomenon. In its darkest hours, when Cambodia was at war with itself, its neighbours and some of the world's largest military powers, the few visitors the country attracted were a handful of thrill seekers and mercenaries. After Cambodia fell to the Khmer Rouge communists, even the thrill seekers stayed away

Limited travel to Cambodia resumed after the Vietnamese takeover in 1979, with the arrival of international observers, reporters and personnel from various international aid agencies sent to help in the reconstruction. But Cambodia in the 1980s was still a dangerous place to travel as the Khmer Rouge and the central government fought a sporadic civil war that spanned two decades. In addition, scattered across Cambodia and lying in wait for the unwary, were millions of landmines and thousands of unexploded bombs. The rigours of a country that was dangerous, difficult to travel, hot and at times uncomfortable, held little appeal for most tourists.

Though Pol Pot died in 1998, aspects of his rule were harder to remove than the man himself. During their three years in power, the Khmer Rouge expended much of their energies destroying the accomplishments of the society the regime replaced. Buildings and infrastructure were demolished, intellectuals murdered and institutions destroyed, all in the name of glory for the regime. Since the demise of the Khmer Rouge, fixing roads, bridges, utilities and communications systems laid waste by decades of war, re-educating the population, reassembling family life and recreating social institutions have imposed enormous burdens on the impoverished country and hampered the travel plans of Cambodia's visitors. At the time of writing, repairs to Cambodia's infrastructure are underway, but not complete.

The Tourist Tide

With fuel-efficient planes, aggressive competition between airlines, cheap fares and government handouts to the tourist industry, tourism has been one of the late 20th century's boom industries. Travel, particularly air travel, has never

Angkor Wat—Cambodia's national icon.

been more affordable. No destination on the planet is beyond the reach of an industry that seeks to satisfy its customers with new experiences supplied from the widest possible range of tourist attractions.

These days, Cambodia is well and truly on the tourist map. Cambodia is an attractive country to visit from a number of viewpoints: it has a rich history; its people are friendly; its countryside is easy on the eye; and prices are low.

In the first few years of the 21st century, tourism has been Cambodia's fastest growing industry. Tourist arrivals were around 330,000 in 2000, rose about 40 per cent in 2001, nearly doubled in 2002, but dipped slightly in 2003, probably due to the SARS epidemic that swept through Asia that year. In 2004, the authorities estimated around one million tourists visited Cambodia—a ratio of nearly one tourist per ten citizens—one of the highest figures in the world.

The country's most widely known attraction is Angkor Wat, South-east Asia's most extensive temple and one of Asia's most elaborate ancient man-made structures. Angkor Wat, near the town of Siem Reap, is the largest of hundreds of temples and other structures built over several centuries in

what is present-day Cambodia. The monuments of Angkor, the administrative and economic centre of the ancient Angkor Empire, stand testament to Cambodia's finest hour.

After the Angkorean period, Cambodia experienced a long decline characterised by invasions of various outside powers. The Cambodian urban landscape reflects the country's various historical influences. Its towns are a mixture of indigenous shanty style homes, soaring traditional Khmer buildings and architecture of the French colonial period. In Phnom Penh, elegant Khmer buildings, classic colonial architecture and sweeping boulevards convey the decayed elegance of a once grand nation.

While Cambodians in Phnom Penh and Siem Reap have grown accustomed to tourists, Cambodia's rural population outside these two main venues is still fairly innocent of the tourist phenomenon. If you venture into the backwoods, particularly to the rugged jungle-draped hills and mountains of the country's north-east, you may be something of a novelty. Those who stray off the beaten track, and those that stay on it, are equally likely to get a friendly reception.

One danger cannot be overemphasised in Cambodia. Those who wish to get in touch with Cambodia's rural roots should remember to observe widely posted precautions regarding landmines before succumbing to an urge to wander into the countryside for a pleasant Sunday stroll. The golden rule of safe travel in Cambodia is to tread a path that someone else has trodden before you. If you see muddy footsteps along the levee banks in the paddy fields, you should be pretty safe. Fields in which people are actually working, planting or harvesting rice are also likely to be free of mines. But you can never be absolutely sure which area is mine-free and which isn't. Even well-trafficked areas may be suspect. Deep seated, still active mines lying dormant for years may pop to the surface any time, in particular after periods of heavy rain.

THE LAND AND ITS HISTORY

CHAPTER 2

'When the elephants fight, ants should stand aside.'
—Norodom Sihanouk quoting a Cambodian
proverb to justify his country's neutrality

EARLY SOCIETIES

Remains recovered from coastal areas of Cambodia are of a hunter-gatherer society from around 6800 BC. Carbon dating of pots found in caves at present-day Battambang suggests that the first settlement was a cave-dwelling society that existed around 4300 BC. These are the earliest settlements that have been established from fossil records.

Cambodians domesticated pigs and water buffalo fairly early and established permanent farming based on rice and root crops. The first evidence of domestic animals comes from around 2000 BC. Bronze artefacts date from about 1500 BC and iron from about 500 BC. Like many early cultures elsewhere in the world, Cambodia's earliest religious ideas were based on animism that afforded humans, animals, plants and even rocks and rivers with spirits. Animism has proved to be a persistent belief. The idea that good and evil spirits are out and about in the community lives on in Cambodia today.

Creation Myth

Cambodia's creation myth describes how the country originated from a union between the princess of a serpent king and an Indian Brahman named Kaundinya. As dowry, the king presented the couple with a new territory called Kambuja—the source of both the names Cambodia and Kampuchea.

Around the time of Christ, Indian traders crossed into China through the Mekong delta area, bringing not only goods but also aspects of their own culture including languages and religion. Hinduism was Cambodia's first formalised religion, introduced by Brahman priests who accompanied Indian traders. Indian influence, both Hindu and Buddhist, later appeared in the everyday life of early Cambodia, for example in clothes such as turbans, eating with spoons, carrying goods on the head and wearing skirts rather than trousers.

Indian religions became a driving force. The first temples built in Cambodia were Hindu-inspired. Statues of Hindu gods like Ganesh (represented as a man with up to six arms and the head of an elephant) and Vishnu (represented as a man with four arms) can be seen in many of Cambodia's temples.

Communal rules of early Cambodian society were in some ways similar to the feudal system of medieval Europe: people belonged to a village; they may have been free to grow their own rice, but they were also obliged to serve their overlords in public works and war.

The borders of Cambodia waxed and waned over the years, as national borders tend to do. From the 6th to 8th centuries, Cambodia was a patchwork of competing village states similar to the localised cultures of Africa and Europe at the time. Most of the population was located on the Mekong river system, living in agricultural communities based on irrigated rice. Cambodia, at that time, was not one country in the modern sense but a loose aggregate of associated settlements. The boundaries of the country could not really be defined, since they depended on the shifting allegiances of outlying communities.

The Angkor Empire

During the first decade of the 9th century, Cambodia coalesced into a more coherent political entity under a uniting king, Jayavarman II. Then, as now, community activities were centred on temples—also called *wats* (from Thai), or *pagodas* (from Sanskrit or Tamil). Temples served not only as the focus of religious beliefs, but also as centres of local administration and literacy. As in Europe at the time, the priests were the record keepers. Numbers of slaves, inventories of temple treasures and dimensions of rice fields and orchards were written on media such as palm leaves and animal hides and kept in temple archives.

The Angkor Empire's glory days were from about AD 800 to 1400. A series of kings in this 'Angkorean Period' expanded Cambodian influence over much of present-day Thailand, Vietnam, Burma and Laos. Early Angkorean kings worshipped Hindu gods like Siva and Vishnu. Temples of Hindu influence proliferated from the 9th century onwards, mostly built in a general area covering about 300 sq km (116 sq miles) around present-day Siem Reap. Succeeding kings constructed new towns, moving the Empire's capital a number of times within this region.

Angkor or Angkor Wat

Confusion sometimes surrounds the word 'Angkor' because this centre of the Empire's power is sometimes named Angkor Wat which, strictly speaking, is a temple in a region with many temples from the same period. That the word *angkor* comes from the Sanskrit word for city and *wat* is the generic word for temple probably adds to the confusion.

The best known temple in Cambodia is Angkor Wat, 'the largest religious building in the world' according to *A History of Cambodia* by David Chandler. The massive structure was built by King Suryavarman II, who ruled from 1113 to 1150. The temple was first dedicated to Vishnu. Subsidiary structures were dedicated to other Indian gods. Apart from its primary purpose as a religious edifice, Angkor Wat served as a political monument to honour the economic and political power of a powerful king during his lifetime and as a tomb to house his remains after his death.

Another striking construction project from the Angkorean period is Angkor Thom (meaning 'Big City'), which was, at various times, the administrative centre of the empire. Angkor Thom was sacked by the Cham invasion of 1177 and reconstructed by King Jayavarman VII (1181–1219), serving as his capital. A walled city laid out to a square plan 3 km (1.9 miles) wide by 3 km long. Its population, inside and beyond its walls, has been estimated to have been from three quarters of a million to one million, making it one of most populous cities in the world at its time.

Bas-reliefs in Angkor's many temples preserve accounts of the times. As well as depicting scenes from the empire's

History in stone bas-reliefs at Angkor Wat.

endless warfare, bas-reliefs of people in neck chains driven by overseers with whips show that slavery was common at the time. Temple building was a major industry in which slaves from defeated tribes were employed in large numbers. Bas-reliefs show slaves employed in tasks like cutting stone in quarries and hauling and erecting stone blocks. Slaves were also engaged in less arduous tasks as musicians, dancers and record keepers—the equivalent of modern-day clerks.

The Accounts of Chou Ta-kuan

A principal source of information of 13th century Cambodian life was Chou Ta-kuan, the assiduous Chinese record keeper and Chinese envoy to the Cambodian court. Chou Ta-kuan's records, despatched back to China, provided a vivid description of Angkor's day-to-day activities. He wrote about the economy, social structure, dress, cultural activities and festivals. He also gave details of the grand temples he came across in the kingdom, including Angkor Wat still in pristine condition nearly 200 years after its construction. The accounts of Chou Ta-kuan describe Angkor as a developed, prosperous civilisation.

Jayavarman VII's reign has been acknowledged by some historians as the peak of the Angkor Empire. Angkoreans built religious and political monuments of extraordinary scale and complexity, practised irrigated agriculture, obtained their water supplies from long distances from point of use, built substantial towns and developed systems of interconnecting roads. At the time, the structures of Angkor were as technically advanced as anywhere else in the world. During this period, an enormous number of temple building projects were underway at Angkor and elsewhere, some as far away as present day Sihanoukville.

While the king's building projects symbolised the might of the Empire, they also contained seeds of the Empire's decline. History has shown that rates of monument building for many empires tend to reach a peak just before an empire's collapse. Like many major public works projects making political statements, Angkor's massive building projects impoverished its constituents, consumed its resources and weakened the Empire.

After the death of Jayavarman VII, a series of weaker kings followed and over a long period, the power of the Angkor Empire gradually declined. In 1431, Angkor fell to the Thais. The Thai invasion brought to an end an empire that had lasted over six hundred years.

AFTER THE ANGKOR EMPIRE
Cambodia's Expanding and Contracting Borders

After the fall of Angkor, Cambodia's fortunes continued to decline. The Thais nibbled away at the western borders while the Chams did the same in the east. From the 17th century until the French arrived in 1860, Thais and Vietnamese battled each other sporadically for influence over the Cambodian court. Overlaying this split of power was the European influence first felt from Spanish traders pushing up from the Philippines. Though Cambodia was no Eldorado, it offered useful products of timber, precious metals and gemstones. China, Japan, Arabia, Portugal, Holland and Britain also traded into Cambodia.

In the early 17th century, the Cambodians lost an important piece of territory to Vietnam when the Vietnamese succeeded in taking over Saigon along with the lower Mekong delta—an area still held by Vietnam today. The Cambodians also lost a stretch of coast on the Gulf of Thailand, that appears today as a sliver of Thailand pushing into Cambodian territory from Thailand's south-eastern provincial capital of Trat. Cambodia's access to the sea was reduced to its current 440 km (275 miles) stretch of shoreline, around the present seaside town of Sihanoukville. Resentment regarding this annexation and other territorial disputes still rankles, particularly towards the Vietnamese.

But for the French, Cambodia, under siege from all directions, would probably have ceased to exist as a separate nation sometime in the 19th century. Like the Indian traders hundreds of years before, the French saw Indo-China as a pathway into southern China. The 1858 conquest of Da Nang by an armada of French ships marked the start of French control over Vietnam and the decline of Vietnamese influence over Cambodia. A few years later in 1863, under a treaty signed by King Norodom, France took over Cambodia. Later, the French extended their power further north and east, forming the Union of Indo-China that combined territory in present-day Vietnam, Cambodia and Laos under one administration. The French-introduced postal system issued postage stamps for the region under the designation 'Indochine'.

When the French arrived in Cambodia, the town of Oudong, 37 km (23 miles) north of Phnom Penh, had been Cambodia's capital since 1618. But the French based their operations at Phnom Penh, which subsequently became the capital, and remains so today. Like other European powers, the first rule of French colonialisation was to run the colonies at a profit. Under French treaties, Indo-China received French protection (from notional enemies but not from the French) in return for timber concessions and mineral exploration rights.

The Cambodian ruling elite suffered little under French administration and the Cambodian monarchy lived a comfortable existence of puppet rule. The Chinese merchant class also prospered as French trading with Europe was good business for Chinese merchants. But the rural population was as exploited as it had always been by one ruler or another.

The French funded the cost of their administration in Cambodia from taxes on rice, salt, opium, alcohol and various lesser crops. The French were assiduous tax collectors, ruthlessly imposing taxes on those who could least afford to pay them. Taxes were collected in cash and if that wasn't available, forced labour. When they reinvested in the colony at all, the French spent the taxes they collected on infrastructure, such as roads and rail that enabled them to plunder the colony more efficiently.

World War II and the Aftermath

After King Norodom died in 1904, puppet rule in Cambodia continued with the next three kings hand-picked by the French. Now and again, simmering unrest of the peasant community boiled over into overt hostility. Riots, when they occurred, were brutally repressed.

During World War II, when the Japanese controlled much of South-east Asia, the Vichy French maintained its tenuous rule over Indo-China by declaring its support for the Axis powers. Thailand, France and Japan shared an uneasy alliance in South-east Asia, with the Japanese exercising the real power behind the scenes.

In 1941, Cambodia's King Monivong died. Instead of installing Monivong's son, Prince Suramarit, who was next in line, the French skipped a generation and selected Suramarit's 19-year-old son, Prince Norodom Sihanouk, who they thought could be easily manipulated. As things turned out, this was a major strategic error by the French. The young prince turned out to be far from the shy and retiring individual the French thought he was. Instead, Sihanouk became an adept and wily politician who kept his head while those about him were losing theirs.

The reputation of the French in Indo-China was irrevocably weakened by World War II, in which, from a Cambodian perspective, the French appeared to change sides three times. At the outbreak of war, the French were the enemies of the Axis powers. When France fell to the Germans, the

Vichy French of Marshal Pétain became reluctant allies of the Japanese. After the D-Day invasion of Normandy in 1944, the French role in Cambodia became even more confused. Indo-China was still under the thumb of the Japanese while back home, the Vichy government had been overthrown. The coup de grâce for French respect came in 1945, when the Japanese jailed Cambodia's French administrators. They remained in jail until Japan surrendered to US forces several months later.

When France returned to Indo-China after the war to pursue its neo-colonial aspirations, its reputation as an invincible European military power had been shattered beyond repair. Communist resistance to the French, centred in Vietnam, spilt over the border into Cambodia. In addition, the Thai government was also active in supporting anti-French guerrillas. By 1952, according to French intelligence, less than a third of Cambodian territory remained under the control of the government in Phnom Penh. As the French struggled to maintain influence in their Indo-Chinese colonies, their involvement in Indo-China became increasingly unpopular at home.

For his part, Sihanouk directed his energies against French rule by opposing unpopular French reforms. Sihanouk abolished the Gregorian calendar introduced by the French in favour of Cambodia's traditional lunar calendar. He also defeated the proposal to Romanise the Khmer language, retaining instead the traditional Sanskrit-based alphabet that is still in use today. At the same time, the French increased their unpopularity by implementing insensitive nit-picking changes that inflamed the passions of the local population. These measures included arresting prominent Cambodian nationalists and renaming the streets in Phnom Penh after French national heroes.

Sihanouk tirelessly travelled his kingdom, promising his subjects that the French would be removed. Outside the country, he lobbied the world for his country's independence. As French-held territory around him crumbled, Sihanouk took over personal control of the nation. In June 1952, he dismissed the government and declared himself sole ruler.

French rule in Cambodia ceased on 9 November 1953 when Cambodian independence was declared.

INDEPENDENT RULE

Sihanouk loved to be loved. He enjoyed being the focus of attention and had acquired a taste for leadership. However, under a constitutional democracy, it was the prime minister who exercised real power. The monarch could not be both prime minister and king at the same time. To overcome this problem, Sihanouk hit on a radical solution that probably would have occurred to no one but him. In June 1952, he abdicated the throne and replaced himself as king with his father, Prince Suramarit, whom the French had overlooked 14 years before.

Sihanouk then hit the campaign trail as leader of the party he formed—Sangkum Reastr Niyum or the People's Socialist Community Party (SRN). Sihanouk toured the countryside on whistle-stop tours addressing thousands of peasants and hearing their grievances. Widely revered for delivering the country from the French, the community granted Sihanouk hero status. Six months later, the SRN won every seat in the National Assembly and Sihanouk became prime minister in an election marred by accusations of vote rigging and political violence.

Typical of Cambodia's leaders for centuries, Sihanouk tried to tread an intricate path that avoided offending powerful external powers while at the same time kept strong internal factions on side or off-balance. Sihanouk had to fend off the communists, keep the peasants from revolting, placate the army and maintain the co-operation of his own bureaucrats. Sihanouk displayed his considerable political skills in dealing with these competing pressures. As prime minister, Sihanouk retained widespread popular support, but he employed a fair degree of brutality to retain his power—rigging elections, purging the emerging communist party and intimidating political opponents, some of whom mysteriously disappeared. Though he was prime minister and the leader of his party, Sihanouk led his country in the manner of a king. He ignored advisers and went his own way, working 18-hour days for weeks on end to handle his self-imposed workload, meeting thousands of his constituents in the process. He travelled endlessly throughout Cambodia and his constituency loved it. Sihanouk's impassioned speeches and quirky dramas earned from his peasant subjects an affection that endured for decades.

For a few years after Sihanouk's election, Cambodia prospered. The country was at peace, and Sihanouk traded on a personality cult that extended both inside the country and into diplomatic missions as far away as Europe and North America. This style failed to win complete acclaim. According to his critics, Sihanouk's medieval treatment of his subjects set the stage for the tragedy that befell the country a decade and a half later.

After the French were kicked out, the United States took over as the Western colonial power in South-east Asia. The US declared its enemy to be communism, a force that knew no national borders. Communist-inspired independence movements were in train throughout the area. Communists fought installed regimes, with various degrees of success, in Vietnam, Laos, Malaysia and Cambodia itself. Gradually the United States and Cambodia found themselves on a collision course.

CAMBODIA AND THE VIETNAM WAR

In his role as prime minister, the countries Sihanouk most feared were the bastions of capitalism in the region—Thailand and South Vietnam - which both supported America's war against the communists. Immersed in a sea of rising conflict, Sihanouk opted for neutrality, the same failed policy of appeasement Cambodia had practised for over a hundred years. But what were the alternatives for a small strategically-situated but militarily weak country?

To maintain Cambodia's neutrality Sihanouk rejected US aid in 1963, something the country could ill afford, and made his anti-US feelings widely known. Sihanouk correctly believed that the North Vietnamese would win the war and that the Americans would eventually depart South-east Asia. He saw that his country's future lay in forging a peaceful alliance with Vietnam, its historically powerful neighbour. Though Sihanouk had suppressed Cambodia's own communists a few years earlier, Cambodia adopted increasingly socialist policies, nationalising banks and commercial institutions.

Cut off from US financial aid, support for Sihanouk from Cambodia's institutions—the army, the bureaucracy and others in government—wavered in the late 1960s. In 1970, while on a political mission abroad, Sihanouk was ousted from power by his own army.

Sihanouk's number one general, Lon Nol, took over as head of state and promptly sentenced Sihanouk to death in absentia. But Sihanouk had put himself beyond Lon Nol's reach and the sentence was never carried out. By this time Sihanouk had developed a warm relationship with Chinese leader, Chou En-lai, and set up a government-in-exile in Beijing. Supported by the Chinese, Sihanouk continued to orchestrate his resistance campaign against Lon Nol from afar. Meanwhile, back in Phnom Penh the new government declared Cambodia a republic, putting paid to more than a thousand years of Cambodian monarchy.

Culture shock reigned across South-east Asia as nations that little understood each other's viewpoints gathered to conduct the Vietnam War. That Cambodia aspired to be neutral was incidental. Belligerent nations pursued their own agendas and national borders were ignored. The Ho Chi Minh trail, through which the North Vietnamese supplied its forces in South Vietnam, cut through the porous border with North Vietnam. South Vietnamese and American troops poured into Cambodian territory across the border with South Vietnam. The United States conducted bombing raids on suspected North Vietnamese positions in Cambodia. Under air and surface attack, Cambodia became a full-scale battlefield for someone else's war.

The United States never declared war on Cambodia. The

Just a Game

William Shawcross in his book *Sideshow* relates an incident that took place in 1973 during a truce with Vietnam, just as bombing in Cambodia was at its height. A US official explained to the author that 'bombing the Cambodians was the only game in town'. It was as if war was a game and the US Air Force needed to be bombing someone to keep itself occupied.

massive bombing of Cambodia was a secret war between a million Cambodian peasants and US President Richard Nixon and his right-hand man, Secretary of State Henry Kissinger. Even the US Foreign Relations Committee was kept in the dark over the bombing of Cambodia. US B-52 pilots based in Guam and sworn to secrecy, filed false flight plans and were refuelled in mid-air. To the north, the equally defenceless country of Laos received similar treatment. Cambodian villages across the entire countryside were hit, in particular those in the south-east on the border with Vietnam.

US bombing delivered psychological terror to most of the rural population. There were no warnings and no provocation. B-52s flew so high they were invisible and inaudible. Their 30-ton cargoes of 500-pound and 750-pound bombs fell faster than the speed of sound. The peasants of Cambodia knew the world's most powerful military force was attacking them only when the ground started exploding around them.

Even today, Cambodia's poorest provinces in the south-east, near the border crossing to Vietnam at Bavet, have yet to recover from this pummelling. Over four years from the late 1960s, the US dropped 150,000 tons of bombs on Cambodia, about 50 per cent more tonnage than was dropped on Japan during World War II. The massive damage inflicted on Cambodia by third parties conducting wars on its territory was given little coverage in the foreign media either at the time or later. US contemporary history of the Vietnam wars passes off the bombing as barely worth mentioning. As William Shawcross describes it in a book of the same name, to the United States Cambodia was merely a 'sideshow'.

US bombing of Cambodia divided the country. Rural areas under bombardment from the B-52s became increasingly hostile to the Americans and sympathetic towards the communists. Cambodian cities by contrast were not bombed and remained under the control of the United State's anti-communist ally, the Phnom Penh government of General Lon Nol. A vicious civil war broke out between the countryside (supported by the North Vietnamese army) and the cities (supported by the United States). The war concluded in April 1975, two months ahead of the fall of Saigon, with victory to the Khmer Rouge communists.

THE KHMER ROUGE REVOLUTION

In the early 1950s, the leaders of the later communist revolution in Cambodia, including the nefarious Pol Pot, had been students in Paris. There they joined the French communist party, which was then at the peak of its power. The communist movement in Cambodia started in the 1960s when these young communists returned home to foment rural discontent. In the process they formed the Communist Party of Kampuchea (CPK). Sihanouk disparagingly termed the CPK the 'Khmer Rouge' (Red Khmer) and the name stuck.

Cambodian communism received a boost in 1970 when General Lon Nol deposed Sihanouk. Whatever his faults, Sihanouk was regarded in the countryside as the god-king for his role in delivering the country from the French. By contrast, Lon Nol had no support whatever.

The Khmer Rouge exploited Sihanouk's name as a rallying call to revolution. So did North Vietnamese army cadres who recruited fresh Khmer Rouge troops from the community under the banner 'Let's do this for Sihanouk'. While Sihanouk languished in exile in Beijing, pro-Sihanouk riots broke out in rural towns back home. Saturation bombing of the countryside by US planes played its part in driving the rural population into the communist camp.

The war between the Khmer Rouge-North Vietnamese alliance and Lon Nol's forces raged for five years. Civilian casualties were massive. The Khmer Rouge encouraged the people to rise against Lon Nol. When they did so, they were slaughtered in thousands by Lon Nol's Cambodian army. When Lon Nol gave North Vietnam 48 hours notice to pull its troops out of Cambodia, the North Vietnamese responded by slaughtering more thousands of Cambodians, civilians and soldiers alike. Gradually, amongst the mayhem, the bombs, and the blood of the innocent, the CPK took over the countryside and encircled Phnom Penh— the last piece of Cambodian territory the government controlled.

When Phnom Penh fell to the Khmer Rouge in 1975, liberated citizens cautiously welcomed their liberating force of black clad columns of unsmiling soldiers. Such was the cultural division between city and country that few of the onlookers who lined the streets realised that the rebel soldiers—largely teenagers recruited from oppressed rural areas—viewed city dwellers as enemies of the revolution who needed to be 're-educated'. This realisation wasn't long coming. Within a day of taking over the city, the Khmer Rouge proceeded to implement one of the most massive social reconstruction experiments of all time, leading directly and indirectly to the death of a million or more Cambodians.

Spreading a story that the US was about to bomb Phnom Penh and claiming it was for the people's own protection, they compelled all citizens to evacuate the city. Given two hours' notice, people were evicted from homes, hospitals or wherever they happened to be. Possessions the evacuees could not carry were left behind. The sick and others who could not maintain the pace of the march were casually killed. The surviving evacuees were then forced at gunpoint to walk miles to new slave labour camps in the countryside where the Khmer Rouge proceeded to turn Cambodia's city dwellers into the regime's new peasant class.

The Khmer Rouge saw this huge untrained agricultural labour force as a resource to repair agricultural infrastructure damaged by years of war. People were allocated to certain areas of the country at the whim of officials of the revolution. Once there, they were prohibited from travelling anywhere else. Outside the country, the movie *The Killing Fields* is the most widely known account of this period in Cambodian history.

Cambodia has had more than its share of stern taskmasters. But little in history before or since has matched Cambodia's bloodbath during the years of the Khmer Rouge when an estimated 20–30 per cent of its population were killed and many of the rest half-starved. Day after day the victims of the Khmer Rouge saw sights and experienced privations that were the stuff of horror movies.

Expendable

A widely quoted saying during the Khmer Rouge reign summed up the prospects of the nouveau peasant class created by the revolution: 'Keeping you is not profitable to us. Discarding you is no loss.'

Return to Ground Zero

One of the remarkable aspirations of the Khmer Rouge was to return the country to 'Ground Zero' and 'Time Zero' of the Dark Ages. From its first day in power, the new regime abolished what it saw as the trappings of the bourgeoisie—money, markets, schools, Buddhism and private property. As institutions were eliminated, books burned and icons destroyed, the culture and hierarchies of 2,000 years of feudalism were shattered in a single moment. The new regime turned society upside down. Peasants became overseers and the urban middle class became peasants. Rural people ruled their urban leaders. The younger generation ruled the old. Students ruled their teachers. The ignorant ruled the knowledgeable. Parents lost their children and children lost their parents. A generation of orphans was created.

One side effect of relocating people across the country was to screen the regime's activities from the outside world. Before it assumed power, the Khmer Rouge claimed that the CIA had agents equipped with radios planted in towns all over Cambodia. If it really existed, this network was completely destroyed by the mass evacuation of Cambodian cities. Whatever radios agents possessed were left behind in the evacuation. After the Khmer Rouge completed its takeover, Cambodia became an information vacuum. Not that the world was paying a great deal of attention to Cambodia at this moment in history. The South-east Asian war had run down, pressures in the Middle East were building, and Cambodia had become a backwater.

Books such as *First They Killed My Father* by Loung Ung and *Stay Alive, My Son* by Pin Yathay are intensely personal accounts of these extraordinary times by captives of the Khmer Rouge. Both authors were from middle-class Cambodian families taken from their homes in Phnom Penh, force-marched into the countryside, stripped of their possessions and identities, then brutalised and starved.

Loung Ung's account is particularly gripping since she was just five years old at the time Phnom Penh fell and her book describes the next four years of her life. By the time she reached nine, Loung Ung had seen her father killed, battled starvation for four years, watched her mother die of overwork and malnourishment, been spattered by the brains of her best friend who was shot standing beside her and narrowly escaped rape at the hands of a

Vietnamese soldier whom she disabled in a knife fight. The story of extraordinary brutality of the Khmer Rouge regime was told through the eyes of a child who, in other societies, would have been attending primary school.

As the years of the brutal regime unfolded, the Khmer Rouge social experiment failed in the most spectacular fashion. The rulers of the new order were thoroughly incompetent. They exterminated what talent they had by executing anyone smarter than they were, which was just about everyone else. Middle-class people with urban lives suffered the most. At best they were conscripted as agricultural labourers. At worst they were executed. In particular, the Khmer Rouge victimised people they considered professionals—teachers, doctors, administrators, monks, engineers and even anyone who possessed a pair of reading glasses.

Mysterious Angkar

The mysterious being which directed the affairs of the Khmer revolution was called 'Angkar', a collective noun for the Khmer Rouge political apparatus. All land, and all the produce from it, belonged to Angkar, to be distributed as Angkar saw fit.

An Uphill Task

In his book *Stay Alive, My Son*, Pin Yathay, an engineer forced to work as a labourer under the Khmer Rouge, recounted how the teenage supervisors of his work crew decreed the construction of irrigation projects that would require water to flow uphill. If he pointed out this design flaw, Pin Yathay knew he would be executed. So the slave labour force built the irrigation ditches as instructed, and not even incantation of Angkar's awesome powers could persuade the water to flow along them.

Under a regime in which the foolish ruled the intelligent and the ignorant ruled the enlightened, the results were devastating, nowhere more so than in agriculture. By the time the Khmer Rouge came to power, US bombs and various ground wars between varied combatants had destroyed much of Cambodia's delicate centuries-old irrigation system. Thousands of slave labourers, mostly from the cities, were set to work in the countryside fixing damaged irrigation channels and building new ones.

But in a society in which knowledge and intelligence were grounds for execution, such plans were doomed to failure. Workers and their supervisors were equally inexperienced in construction projects. As irrigation projects failed countrywide, not only did people starve, oxen starved too. A generation of draft animals perished along with Angkar's people.

HOW THE KHMER ROUGE SELF-DESTRUCTED

The principal ally of the Khmer Rouge was China which had, for centuries, been an enemy of Vietnam, with which both China and Cambodia shared borders. In the 1970s and 1980s, Vietnam was seen by China as an ally of the Soviet Union, China's rivals in the communist camp. China's strategy in Cambodia was to use the Khmer Rouge to preoccupy the Vietnamese army. The Chinese provided the Khmer Rouge arms for this purpose and the Khmer Rouge obliged by attacking Vietnamese villages across the Cambodian-Vietnamese border. In the end, this was a suicidal policy by the Khmer Rouge and typical of their erratic leadership.

Child Soldier of the Khmer Rouge

In her autobiography *And First They Killed My Father*, Loung Ung described how, as an eight-year-old girl, she was conscripted into the Khmer army. As part of her training, she was given a wooden model of an AK-47 automatic rifle and told to bayonet straw dummies set up in a field while yelling "Death to the Vietnamese!"

Loung Ung and the other reluctant, half-starved conscripts did as they were told. But instead of viewing the straw dummies as Vietnamese, the conscripts visualised the dummies as their captors. While she poked holes in straw dummies and cried "Death to the Vietnamese", in her heart Loung Ung was thinking "Death to the Khmer Rouge!" or "Death to that Khmer Rouge officer over there!"

The Khmer Rouge believed their own publicity that their army would be a match for the Vietnamese and marched their army to the border to teach the Vietnamese a thing or two. But the Khmer Rouge were boxing well beyond their weight in picking a fight with the Vietnamese. They could not possibly match the battle-hardened Vietnamese forces which had defeated all comers in the various wars of the period—the United States, the French and even the Chinese.

Initially, the Vietnamese responded to the Khmer pinpricks on their border villages in a fairly restrained manner, capturing Cambodian territory and taking hostages who were groomed for future political leadership of a Cambodian government sympathetic to Vietnam. But towards the end of 1978, the Vietnamese had enough and decided to rid themselves of this troublesome neighbour, entering Cambodia with an army of more than 100,000.

Some of the under-aged recruits the Khmer Rouge had pressed into armed service greeted the invaders as liberators. Others put up fierce resistance. But the outcome was never in doubt. With vastly more firepower and battle experience, the Vietnamese took 17 days to defeat the Khmer Rouge army and take over the country. Casualties to the North Vietnamese numbered about 10,000. The number of Khmer Rouge soldiers killed remains unknown.

On 7 January 1979, a day since declared a national holiday (Victory Day), the North Vietnamese army entered Phnom Penh. What was left of the Khmer Rouge hierarchy avoided capture by boarding helicopters and trains and fleeing to western border regions.

As head of the new government the Vietnamese installed Heng Samrin, a Khmer Rouge military leader who had defected to Vietnam in 1978 and had been groomed for leadership. Heng Samrin was one of many Khmer Rouge commanders who lost his enthusiasm for the rebellion after Pol Pot's excesses. To acknowledge its liberation from the Khmer Rouge, the new government rechristened the country the People's Republic of Kampuchea.

AFTER THE KHMER ROUGE

Even though it all came to an end over 35 years ago, the terrible reign of Pol Pot has left scars on Cambodia that are still healing. Pol Pot's first measure on assuming power had been to attack the basic unit of Cambodian society: the family. The Khmer Rouge destroyed families by tearing them

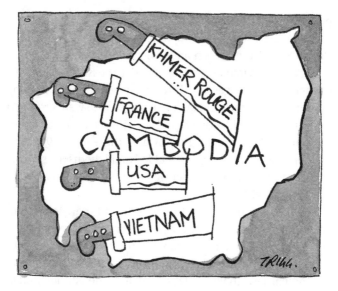

apart, firstly from their homes, and secondly from each other. Some families managed to stay together as they were herded across country by the Khmer Rouge army. Others weren't so lucky: children, parents, husbands and wives were separated and sent to collective farms across the country. Once there they were forced to stay out of contact with their family members. Up to the last days of the Khmer Rouge, no one knew, including Pol Pot himself, how many of their family members were dead or alive.

When liberation came, courtesy of the Vietnamese army, the first thing most of the population tried to do was recreate their families by returning to homes from which the Khmer Rouge had torn them. The new Vietnamese rulers allowed the people freedom to come and go as they pleased. Almost overnight the survivors of the Khmer Rouge criss-crossed the countryside en masse searching for missing family members.

In the first six months of its rule, this mass migration posed an enormous problem for the Heng Samrin regime. Vietnam conquered Cambodia in January 1979, after the dry season rice crop had been planted in November but before it was harvested in February. With people preoccupied with returning home, much of the 1978–1979 dry season rice crop was never harvested and much of the monsoon season crop of 1979 was never planted.

By the middle of 1979, when Cambodia had opened up to the world a little, relief agencies headed by the United Nations and many NGOs, such as Oxfam, believed Cambodia faced a massive short-term food shortage. Relief agencies were astonished at the degree to which physical infrastructure, roads, irrigation systems, hospitals and entire towns had been destroyed. The bulk of the population appeared to be dying on its feet through lack of food, clothing and medicine. In early 1979, aid agencies estimated that, unless something was done, half the four million or so Cambodians thought to have survived the Pol Pot regime would die of starvation by Christmas of that year.

The Khmer Rouge and the preceding Indo-Chinese wars had devastated Cambodian agricultural production. In the 1950s and 1960s, Cambodia had been a significant exporter of both rice and fish. Between 1969 and 1970, before US bombing began, rice production had reached its peak of 3.8 million tons (tonnes). Ten years later, it was down to about 650,000 tons and Cambodia had to rely on rice imports to feed its people. Likewise between 1969 and 1979, fish catch was estimated to have fallen by more than 90 per cent.

With Cambodia facing the possibility of imminent starvation, what ensued was another unseemly display of international politics in which the hungry and ill-treated people of Cambodia were again the victims. A central issue was the political and military position of Thailand. For centuries, the two strongest powers in South-east Asia were Thailand and Vietnam, two countries without a common border. Cambodia was a buffer zone wedged between them. After Vietnam's lightning invasion of Cambodia, the Thais viewed the shrinking buffer zone with alarm as the remnants of the Khmer Rouge were pushed into positions along the Thai border. Before them, as they headed west, the Khmer Rouge herded somewhere near a million Cambodia citizens.

The irrepressible Vietnamese army had conquered most of Cambodia in just over two weeks. Stories started to circulate in the Western press of the Vietnamese army 'gobbling up the rest of South-east Asia'. The 'domino theory' received another run in the media. The Chinese, the only real ally of the Khmer Rouge, were also obsessed with Vietnam's military prowess.

The West aligned itself with the Khmer Rouge, a movement it had been fighting for the previous twenty years. As far as the West was concerned, the Khmer Rouge, being militarily less significant, was a lesser evil than the Vietnamese. As remnants of the Khmer Rouge arrived at Cambodia's western border, the Chinese and an alliance of nations including Thailand and the USA, took steps to support them.

This left the problem of the refugees—the unfortunate Cambodians, the customary meat in the sandwich of international politics in this region. Even as vast numbers of refugees arrived at the border, Thailand hadn't quite figured out what to do with them. On one occasion the Thai army force-marched 45,000 refugees over a 200-metre-high cliff face, where they fell to their deaths. On another they were forced back into Cambodia across a heavily mined section of the border. But for the most part, they were accommodated in hastily-constructed refugee camps inside the Thai border.

When the Thais realised the refugee influx contained significant numbers of Khmer Rouge soldiers, attitudes towards the refugees changed. The Thais were keen to have the Khmer Rouge around to fight off the Vietnamese army when it arrived at their border. What to do with the refugees then became a matter of cost.

The United Nations and Western aid agencies came to the rescue with funds. But corrupt members of the Thai army discovered they could hijack the supplies meant for refugees and sell them at a profit on the open market. Refugee camps received only a fraction of the aid supplies. Moreover, much of this went to the Khmer Rouge cadres installed by the Thai army as camp administrators. Genuine refugees received the little that remained.

Malnutrition was not the only problem faced by refugees. Khmer Rouge cadres and Thai soldiers serving as camp administrators delivered brutal beatings and other forms of mistreatment. The camps were also exposed to occasional shelling by Vietnamese forces in Cambodia. Aid agencies could do little to change anything.

Meanwhile in Phnom Penh, aid agencies were facing problems getting help to the Cambodian community—the new Cambodian government had withheld permission to land their shipments of food and medical supplies. The sticking point with the Vietnamese was that Western nations still recognised the Khmer Rouge as Cambodia's legitimate government. Since both the United States and China were supporting the Khmer Rouge, the Vietnamese feared that Western aid agencies could be running covert operations inside Cambodia with the object of reinstalling the Khmer Rouge regime.

As a result, aid agencies were given limited access to Cambodia and no authority to distribute supplies when they arrived. In addition, many of the supplies that made it into Cambodia were stolen and used to feed the occupying troops or officials of the Cambodian government. Ordinary Cambodians in Thai refugee camps and within the country itself missed out.

Aid agencies were aware of the inequities of the food distribution system, which they could do nothing to fix. They battled on as best they could, pressing the Vietnamese to accept the aid and continuing to lobby governments of the international community. Gradually, the situation improved. Both sides made concessions. After a while, more food aid reached the people through various routes and the starvation worries eased.

Cambodia in the 1980s

As things turned out, the 1979 fears of mass starvation were exaggerated as predictions of food shortages were based on expectations for the rice harvest. But Cambodia is a country of lush vegetation and high rainfall, in which plenty of edible things grow apart from rice. Bananas, nuts, coconuts and other natural foodstuffs could be harvested from the countryside while pondweed, going under the name of 'morning glory', made an excellent substitute for spinach. Eating the fruits of the forest would have been enough to earn a death sentence from Khmer Rouge cadres doling out the food entitlements. Nature's bounties belonged to the state, which insisted that perfectly edible fruit should fall to the ground and rot while its citizens starved. In Pol Pot's Cambodia, people were publicly disembowelled for eating so much as a wild banana. Under the new government, while waiting for the rice crop to grow, people could once more dine in nature's kitchen.

With seed supplied through international aid agencies, Cambodia repaired its agriculture. Recovery in rice production started in the 1980 growing season, with rice harvest more than doubling from the previous year. The crop faltered in 1981 when the monsoon was erratic but improved steadily in ensuing years. Overseas aid diminished once the spectre of mass starvation dimmed. During the 1980s, aid agencies had countries in Africa to keep from starvation. Cambodia received little government financial help other than aid from Russia.

The new government moved cautiously, reintroducing the institutions that Pol Pot had demolished—markets, money, religion, education, the right of association and freedom of movement. Collective agriculture, instituted by Pol Pot, was dismantled and farmers returned to their traditional methods.

Despite mounting evidence of its genocide, the Western powers continued to recognise the Khmer Rouge as Cambodia's legitimate government-in-exile for another ten years. A Khmer Rouge nominee continued to sit in the United Nations as Cambodia's legitimate voice. As a result of support by the international powers, civil war continued through the 1980s between government forces and the Khmer Rouge located on either side of the Thai border. In 1985, Hang Samrin was replaced as prime minister by Hun Sen, also a disaffected officer from the Khmer Rouge army.

Despite the domino theory that still gripped the minds of Western politicians, Vietnam had no ambitions to acquire

Cambodia as a colony. Like Thailand, Vietnam merely sought peace on its borders. Cambodia was an expensive operation that Vietnam couldn't really afford. In 1989, the Vietnamese army finally withdrew.

DEMOCRACY, CAMBODIAN-STYLE

Well into the 1990s, Cambodia remained an anarchistic country, with significant areas not under government control. Pol Pot, who could not be arrested or otherwise taken out of circulation, commanded his forces to harass the population in the western provinces. The Khmer Rouge operated black markets trading commodities such as illegally logged timber and gemstones to finance their operations. Sheltered by the Thais, nourished by money from smuggling and US aid, and supplied with arms from China, the Khmer Rouge rebuilt their strength.

After the Vietnamese departed the scene, the Khmer Rouge saw the chance to make a comeback. Pol Pot's army stepped up its war against the civilian population in border areas, with more loss of life and a further influx of refugees into Thailand. Still more landmines were sown by both sides. For a while it looked like the Khmer Rouge might succeed in re-taking the country. They captured and briefly held the important western towns of Pailin, Battambang and Sihanoukville.

But active lobbying by Sihanouk and others prompted the international community to intervene. At a ceremony in Paris in 1991, Cambodia's political factions, excluding the Khmer Rouge, signed the Peace Accords that stipulated a democratic election be held in 1993. The Accords were successful in severing ties between China and the Khmer Rouge, as well as between Vietnam and Hun Sen's Phnom Penh government. The United Nations appointed Sihanouk chairman of the Supreme National Council (NSC) to supervise repatriation of refugees from the Thai border and disarm militant groups.

What then remained was to stage the country's first democratic elections for over two decades. In 1992, the United Nations Transitional Authority in Cambodia (UNTAC) arrived in Cambodia with the mandate to organise the transition to democracy. The UN deployment involved around 20,000 foreigners, mostly troops and police, and 6,000 locals. Costing somewhere around US$ 2–3 billion, UNTAC was the UN's most expensive political programme to that time.

The results from this massive UN presence in Cambodia were mixed. UNTAC's task of disarming militant groups was difficult (as it has been in every country it has been tried). Mankind's love affair with the gun is universal. On the plus side, refugees were repatriated in large numbers and media censorship was freed to some degree. The UN force also lent a hand against the resurgent Khmer Rouge. UNTAC registered voters for the first time, and set up polling booths across the country. To overcome the problem that only about 30 per cent of the electorate could read, voting slips identified parties by their logos.

On election day, the electorate overwhelmingly endorsed the move to democracy with over 90 per cent of voters turning out to cast their votes. Cambodian electors turned the election into a party, with polling stations packed to the bursting point.

The UN declared its expensive attempts to introduce democracy a success. Others were more guarded in their comments. There were allegations of vote rigging, irregularities and mistakes in the electoral roll—in one case over 800 people claimed to live in a particular house. In addition, the lead-up to the election had taken a number of casualties from Khmer Rouge attacks. At least 78 UNTAC employees were killed plus an unknown number of Cambodians. But the outcome the UN feared, that the Khmer Rouge would turn Cambodia's move to democracy into an election-day massacre, did not occur.

Whatever Happened to the Khmer Rouge?

Pol Pot died in 1998 under mysterious circumstances. His followers who continued to fight in the border areas eventually dispersed or surrendered a year later under an amnesty programme offered by the Hun Sen government. Many of the surviving members of the Khmer Rouge leadership who accepted the amnesty terms are now elderly men who hang out near the town of Pailin, in western Cambodia. For years, Pailin has been the centre of the gem smuggling and illegal logging industries. For dedicated communists, members of the vanquished Khmer Rouge leadership group have made excellent capitalists. Per capita, Pailin is probably the most prosperous town in Cambodia. There, Khmer Rouge leaders, with the blood of millions on their hands, live openly in fine houses.

But what of the lesser lights? What has become of the Khmer functionaries spread across the country who, during their formative teens, the Khmer rebellion tried to turn into homicidal maniacs? When the Vietnamese took over in 1979, ex-Khmer Rouge cadres filled many of the administrative posts of the Heng Samrin government. In ideology, the Khmer Rouge and the Vietnam-controlled governments were not all that different. They were both communist. Unlike administrators from the previous Lon Nol government, recruits from the ranks of the Khmer Rouge didn't need to be sent to re-education camps in Vietnam to get their ideological kinks straightened out.

The consequences of injudicious political comment still live in the memories of many. While many will talk of their suffering, few if any would admit to being a Khmer Rouge soldier. It's as if all the Khmer Rouge cadres who had executed millions on Angkar's behalf have vanished from the very face of the Earth. While some have died, others have not. The ex-Khmer Rouge soldiers merged seamlessly into Cambodian society and may still be around. Now in their late 40s or older, they are still likely to be serving the community, perusing your passport, stamping visas and driving cabs.

No Nuremberg-style court cases followed the exposure of the Khmer Rouge genocide. Pol Pot, now dead, was never brought to justice for his crimes. Of the Khmer Rouge leadership group, only one—Ta Mok, a particularly brutal general in the Khmer Rouge army—is in jail, due to stand trial sometime at a UN-sanctioned tribunal to be set up in Cambodia.

The UN has set the budget for the Cambodian war tribunal at US$ 56 million, a quarter of which is to be met by Cambodia, and will probably be funded by foreign donors. The government has announced that it is ready to start proceedings within a few months of receiving the donors' funds.

A Symbol of Prestige

With the advent of UNTAC personnel preparing Cambodia for the 1993 election, Phnom Penh became gripped by a strange new phenomenon. For the first time in its history, the capital was awash with money. A host of rather tacky industries ready to assuage the bodily and material needs of well-paid UN bureaucrats and service personnel sprang up almost overnight.

Property values and rents rocketed. UN officials riding around in white Toyota Land Cruisers became conspicuous against a background of urban poverty. Other NGOs—the Red Cross, World Vision and others—also moved around in their own white Cruisers. At the time, it was- believed Phnom Penh, sported the highest ratio of white Toyota Land Cruisers to other vehicles of any city on the planet.

When UNTAC disbanded, the four-wheel-drives stayed behind to be sold off at very attractive prices. If you happen to see one carrying the UN logo delivering vegetables to the local restaurant, it is unlikely to be the UN going about its business. It's also unlikely the vehicle has been stolen. You are probably looking at a used car in the hands of its legitimate owner. Not many buyers of ex-UN vehicles repainted their vehicles. The UN logo is thought to carry status and privilege.

CONSTITUTIONAL CRISIS

Prior to the 1993 elections, Sihanouk and Hun Sen drew up the constitution for the new democracy. One of its key provisions, that seemed likely to prevent the formation of a stable government at the ensuing election or any time in the future, was the requirement that the governing party should hold a two-third majority of seats in the National Assembly. The origin and reasons for this clause are uncertain, but could have been the invention of the wily Hun Sen, who may have foreseen the result of the election, and intended to hang onto his leadership, win, lose or draw.

The two main parties that contested the 1993 election were the Cambodian Peoples Party (CPP) headed by Hun

Sen and the FUNCINPEC party (Front Uni National pour un Cambodge Indépendent, Neutre, Pacifique, et Coopératif) formed by Sihanouk and headed by one of his sons, Prince Ranariddh. The results of the election were too close for any single party to form government. FUNCINPEC won 45.5 per cent of the votes and 58 seats. CPP won 38.2 per cent and 51 seats. The minority Buddhist Liberal Party won ten seats.

Even though Sihanouk wasn't a member of the party, and didn't get on particularly well with his son Prince Ranariddh, FUNCINPEC had campaigned under Sihanouk's name. FUNCINPEC's majority was interpreted as a vote for Sihanouk. Despite the political trauma of two decades, Sihanouk was still highly regarded in the provinces, where his support base had always been strong. But under the two-thirds majority rule of the constitution, no party could assume government without joining a coalition with another party.

Sihanouk then pushed the unwilling partners into a coalition. Prince Ranariddh agreed to rule jointly with Hun Sen as co-prime ministers. Since the two parties bitterly opposed each other, this arrangement was never going to last. Rivalries came to a head in 1997 when Hun Sen, who controlled the army, the police, the Cambodian bureaucracy and most of the media, overthrew Prince Ranariddh in a coup. Hun Sen assumed sole power as prime minister and promised to formalise his position in an election due the following year. Prince Ranariddh fled to Thailand, along with other members of his party, but returned the next year to contest the elections.

The 1998 election also resulted in a hung Parliament. Hun Sen's CPP won more than half the seats contested, but not enough to govern in its own right. With more prompting from Sihanouk, the CPP and FUNCINPEC formed another coalition. Hun Sen continued to serve as Prime Minister and Prince Ranariddh became President of the National Assembly.

CPP and FUNCINPEC are still the two major parties in Cambodia. The third-ranking party is the creation of Cambodia's tireless 'Mr Clean', Sam Rainsy, who resigned as a minister in the 1993 government alleging corruption of the ruling clique.

Though he has polled well in the last two elections, Sam Rainsy has not garnered enough votes (according to the official vote count) to get into government. His party, the Sam Rainsy Party, is also subjected to active persecution; the ruling CPP censors the party's views and makes regular attempts to have Sam Rainsy discredited and his party disbanded.

Over the years, this three-cornered tussle has produced a political situation reminiscent of post-war Italy. None of the parties can win sufficient seats to rule in its own right. None of the political parties is ideologically acceptable to the others. Throughout a series of minority governments based on fragile alliances, Hun Sen has continued as Prime Minister.

Democracy, Cambodian-style, retains the edge of violence that has characterised the country for many years. Assassination attempts have been made on both Hun Sen and Prince Ranariddh, allegedly by each other. In 1997, in separate incidents, 41 people were killed in Hun Sen's coup, many others were killed during elections and demonstrations, and Sam Rainsy was slightly injured during a grenade attack on a demonstration outside the National Assembly in which 19 people were killed and hundreds injured.

After the 1998 government ran its course, new elections were held in 2003. The European Union inspection team, sent to Cambodia in 2003, noted that the election was neither fair nor open and made allegations of strong-arm tactics in rural towns. But since only 15 to 20 people died on the campaign trail, the EU team reported that democracy had been reasonably served, at least by local standards.

Once more the outcome was deadlocked. Hun Sen's CPP won 73 of the 123 seats contested, with the balance split between the two minority parties. Though CPP won a clear majority, the result still fell short of the two-thirds majority the party needed to rule in its own right. The major parties joined in talks in an attempt to form a government. Progress was halting. After years of feuding and assassination attempts, that the leaders of the three parties could not get along was no surprise.

After 11 months of ineffective government following the stalemate, the leaders managed to bury their differences. Urged by Sihanouk, on 26 June 2004, Hun Sen and Prince Ranariddh announced an agreement had been reached to form a new government.

To ensure powerbrokers from both parties received accolades, an enormous number of ministers, deputy ministers, secretaries and assistance secretaries were created. Whether this ponderous alliance would be more durable than its predecessors remains a matter of speculation.

THE SUCCESSION

At times during his long career, Sihanouk has been able to hold his country together; at times he hasn't. But even Sihanouk's sternest critics cannot deny this indomitable character has, for much of his life, been his country's unifying force. But by 2004, Sihanouk was 81 years old and in poor health.

After the 2003 hung election, Sihanouk convened meetings to encourage the two major parties to stop their bickering and form a government. Shortly afterwards, he announced an intention to abdicate the throne but without naming a successor. Not too many people in the street believed Sihanouk really intended to go. This method of testing the waters—to announce some action to give others the opportunity to talk him out of it—had been Sihanouk's modus operandi over the years. But Sihanouk insisted he was serious this time.

Discussion then centred on the identity of Sihanouk's successor. The last thing Cambodia needed was another constitutional crisis. There were a number of possible candidates but none stood out. Like Cambodia itself, Sihanouk's family had been fairly dysfunctional. Throughout Sihanouk's life, women ranked high in his list of pleasures. Early in his reign, Sihanouk publicly described his state of mind as *chaud lapin*, which his biographer liberally translated from the French as 'randy as a rabbit'. During the course of his life, Sihanouk has borne 14 officially-recognised children from six women. The Khmer Rouge killed five of his children and others died of natural causes. By 2003, at least six of his direct offspring, male and female, could claim lineage to the Cambodian throne.

As it turned out, the succession was resolved surprisingly easily in September 2004. While residing in Beijing and Pyongyang, Sihanouk had issued notices of his intentions to abdicate. On receiving this news, Prince Ranariddh, not the King's favourite son, flew to Beijing to agree to a successor. Since he was leader of FUNCINPEC the Prince was ineligible to double up as monarch. He could therefore fill the role as honest broker.

By October, all parties, including Hun Sen's government, had agreed to Prince Sihamoni, hitherto a relatively obscure member of the Royal Family, as the country's next King. The coronation of King Sihamoni was a low-key affair, held during the Bonn Pchem Ben holidays when at least half of Phnom Penh's population had returned home to the Cambodian countryside to pay homage to their ancestors.

At the time of writing, it appears that the feared constitution crisis following Sihanouk's abdication, had been avoided.

WHO ARE THE CAMBODIANS?

CHAPTER 3

'The experience that will be with me forever
are the smiling faces of the children...'
—Ed Cohen, a volunteer worker in Cambodia

A WAY OF LIFE
Agriculture

For as long as Cambodia has existed, the majority of the population has made its living from agriculture. For 2,000 years, the most important commodity in the Cambodia has been rice. Today, rice remains an essential part of the country's economy and a staple food, contributing to almost every meal.

During the rice planting season, women work in the fields with limbs and heads covered against the sun. Under a wide brimmed hat is worn the traditional Cambodian *karma*—a large checkered head scarf—that also serves as a towel.

Women make up most of the agricultural workforce. Women have always worked at least as hard as men in Cambodia, and there are more of them since they live longer and their casualty rate from Cambodia's various wars has been lower. Bent over in the fields for hours at a time, these tough women hand-plant nursery-grown rice sprout by sprout. After the growing season, they return to the fields to harvest the rice crop with hand-held implements.

Cambodia farmers plant one or two rice crops each year, depending on where they live. The major monsoon crop is planted in late May through July. In areas in which the monsoon's moisture is retained the year round, a dry season crop is also planted in November. There are regional variations

Planting the rice crop.

on this seasonal pattern, for example in areas around Tonle Sap Lake. At the end of the dry season at the great lake, seed is spread on soil that rising waters will later inundate. Later, at the end of the wet season, 'floating rice'—with stems up to 4 m (13 ft) long—is harvested from boats. Floating rice is low yield. Most of the plant's energy goes into making the stem to keep itself afloat. But it's a crop.

Traditionally, rice farming was conducted along feudal lines, with peasants growing most of the crop for the local lord in return for security and protection. Some peasants owned their own small plots, but two-thirds of the rural population did not own sufficient land to support themselves. They supplemented their own production by labouring for absentee landlords from more privileged levels of society. Arrangements stayed that way until communism arrived to revolutionise the agricultural community and infrastructure built over hundreds of years.

Even before the wars in the 1960s, dissent simmered in the countryside against landlords and moneylenders. In a region that was learning about communism for the first time, the idea that all should share the land equally was not a hard sell. But when the communists got their chance to institute a just system of land allocation, the results for peasants were severe. The Khmer Rouge organised agriculture in the manner of the Soviet collective farms of the 1930s, and with similar disastrous results. About half the rice produced by Cambodia during the Khmer Rouge years was shipped to China to pay for arms. Most of the rest was consumed by Khmer Rouge cadres.

After this experience, the Hun Seng government has trodden a middle path between collective effort and individual ownership, with groups and families sharing their resources of animals, labour and farm implements. In the present day, agricultural land is split between public and private ownership.

CO-EXISTENCE AND
THE BUDDHIST RELIGION

Ninety-six percent of Cambodia's population is Buddhist. Like the Hindu religion that preceded it, the origins of Buddhism are Indian. Buddhism arrived in Cambodia with Indian traders who brought with them their retinue of priests, religious icons and beliefs.

Buddhism comes in two main forms—the Mahayana and the Theravada. Cambodia adopted the Theravada variant of Buddhism in the 13th century. After King Jayavarman VII switched from Hinduism to Buddhism, Buddhist religious icons were added to many of the temples that had already been built along Hindu architectural lines.

Since its introduction, Buddhism has survived the country's many wars and invasions. Cambodia's neighbours in the area—Thailand, Laos and Vietnam—were also converted to Buddhism when Indian traderrs arrived. Of Cambodia's many colonisers over the centuries, only the French were of a different religion. But the French came to Cambodia on an economic, not a proselytising, mission and wisely left the Buddhist religion undisturbed.

Buddhist beliefs govern much of the culture, behaviour and attitudes of the Cambodian people. The complexities of Buddhist beliefs are beyond the scope of this book, but the basic idea is of a deeply personal religion of self-improvement and self-actualisation. The key ideas of Theravada Buddhism are social tranquillity and placid acceptance of the trials and tribulations of life.

Some historians link Buddhism to the weakening of the Angkor Empire. In this view, the passive beliefs of Theravada Buddhism are considered inconsistent with breeding a warrior culture. Certainly the timing fits this argument since the widespread adoption of Buddhism in the late 13th century coincided with the start of the empire's decline.

Buddhism has no strong ideology or dogma. In fact, many Buddhists will tell you that Buddhism is not a religion but a state of mind. It advocates peace and harmony as well as tolerance and acceptance of others, including non-believers. Buddhists interact with their faith privately. The religious beliefs of other people are of little concern. Buddhism imposes almost no requirements on the visitor or non-believer other than a reasonable code of behaviour and dress when interacting with monks and entering religious shrines.

Hinduism and Buddhism coexist readily enough. One aspiration common to the two faiths is nirvana, the ultimate sense of being. At the opposite end of the ideological spectrum to materialism, nirvana is attained if, in their pilgrimages through life, Buddhists can achieve complete detachment from the world.

Buddhists believe that living beings are reincarnated after death to return to Earth in some form or other to live many future lives. In this view, advantage enjoyed in the next life must be earned in this life. Feudalism in Cambodia's early history reinforced this fatalistic outlook, where social status was established by birthright and could not be changed much during a person's life. Historically, this view has brought benefits both to the rulers and the ruled. From the viewpoint of the rulers, merit earned in previous has been rewarded in this life. From the viewpoint of the ruled, their burdens were decreed by fate. Social order was preserved at both ends of the social scale.

Until communism arrived, few Cambodians disputed the born-to-rule mentality of the rulers and the born-to-be-ruled mentality of the ruled. Over the course of history, the rulers changed from Cambodian kings and warlords, to Thai and Vietnamese invaders, to the French and back again to Cambodian leaders. But the status of the ruled, as peasants in the fields working for someone or other in return for protection, remained much the same.

When communism arrived in South-east Asia, some of these long held beliefs were held to question. Communism empowered the oppressed. In the 1960s, the Cultural Revolution was underway in China. The colonial regimes of South-east Asia were being overthrown. Buddhism and communism were seen by revolutionaries as being in conflict on a number of levels.

In a sense, the Khmer Rouge revolution was itself a religious style movement under which the community was told that salvation lay in the power of the state. People were asked to make its sacrifices for the good of 'Angkar'— a word that implied some notion of a higher collective community. Buddhism, Hinduism and animism were seen as competing with this fundamental political ideology.

To erase religion from the community, the Khmer Rouge assassinated monks, burned religious texts and defaced religious icons. An estimated two-thirds of the country's temples that existed when the Khmer Rouge came to power were later destroyed. Those that were spared were turned into barracks, forts and prisons to service Angkar's needs. Temples which survived the regime were restored to their original use after the Khmer Rouge regime came to an end, and replacements were built. Buddhism, like other Cambodian institutions, is still recovering from this assault.

The Vietnamese who took over Cambodia had a more lenient view of traditional customs than the Khmer Rouge. The ideologies of Marx and Lenin did not rank high on their revolutionary agenda. Vietnam's communist revolution was inspired more by a burning desire to rid their country of foreign domination, whether French or American, than anything else. The Vietnamese occupying Cambodia were pragmatists. The people wanted change and the new government allowed change to occur. The Vietnamese-backed government gradually reinstituted many of the customs and conventions eradicated by the Khmer Rouge—money, markets, banking, education and religion.

To restore society to its previous values, desecrated temples were replaced and new temples were built. Today, Buddhism is back in force, though not quite to the level that prevailed before the Khmer Rouge. Cambodia now has over three thousand temples and over 50,000 monks. Even in this somewhat cynical age, temple building is a major industry throughout South-east Asia. Thailand and Laos, as well as Cambodia, all host major temple building programmes.

Buddhist temples are tall airy buildings, colourful and richly embellished. Traditionally, temples were built from timber or stone. Today's temples are more likely to be built from concrete. While each temple is different, some architectural features are similar. The centre point of the temple is a statue of Buddha resting on a nave raised to a high point called the *krih*.

As in the past, today's temples serve more than just a religious function. The majority of Cambodians live in villages built around temples, which serve as the cultural and social centre of their community. Temples serve not only as places of peace and tranquillity, but also as centres of learning and sanctuary for the poor and needy.

Nurturing Spirits

Buddhism coexists comfortably enough with the more ancient beliefs of animism passed down from earlier societies. A belief still prevails in Cambodia that the spirits of ancestors remain in their familiar earthly surroundings while in some transitory mode to the next life. To give the spirits a place to live after their land has been appropriated for some earthly purpose, for example to build a house or erect a commercial building, a spirit house is commonly provided for the departed to use.

Believers pay homage to spirits by praying to them and supplying them with offerings such as food, drink, incense and garlands. The spirit house is usually located prominently outside the building, preferably beyond the shadow of the

Keeping the spiritis comfortable.

main house. Like *wats*, spirit houses were once made from timber but are today more likely to be made from concrete. Either way they are usually brightly painted.

Not all spirits are friendly. Some may be downright hostile. Under cover of darkness, unless countermeasures are taken, unfriendly spirits may commit malicious acts, such as sneaking uninvited into houses to bring sickness to children. A scarecrow erected outside the house, raised thresholds at doorways and lucky plants in the garden are all useful devices to ward off uninvited spirits with unfriendly intentions. The counterbalancing effect of friendly spirits around the place also helps. Giving the spirits a comfortable place to live and raising their spirits (so to speak) with garlands and other offerings encourages friendly spirits to prevent entry into the house of evil influences lurking elsewhere in the aether.

The Importance of Making Merit

Buddhism shares with Christianity and many other religions the idea that life on earth is merely a transition state to the next life. Nothing in Buddhism says that life is meant to be enjoyable. Nor is there a promise of a spiritual afterlife. Rather, Buddhism offers the promise of an almost endless cycle of birth and death from which enlightenment or nirvana is the only escape.

Accumulating merit (*tambon* in Khmer) by performing good deeds is a major preoccupation for Buddhists, whether clergy or congregational. While the monks earn merit primarily through their achievements in meditation, lay people earn merit by supporting the monkhood, praying, chanting, worshipping the Buddha and living an ethical life.

Accounting of merit and demerit points in a person's life is termed karma which the dictionary defines as 'the force of existence that determines a person's destiny'. The

idea behind karma is shared by Hindus and indeed most other religions—that every good or bad deed in this life is rewarded or punished in another life (whether on Earth or in an afterlife). Belief in the karma system of justice allows Cambodians to accept whatever earthly travails they are suffering with a greater degree of equanimity than they otherwise might.

Karmic Release

A minor industry flowing from a belief in karma is that people capture birds, imprison them in tiny cages offering to release them on payment of money by passers-by. For believers in karma, paying to have the bird released is meant to earn merit points—though this may have little value in the belief systems of most visitors.

I have paid to have a few birds released in my time, not for the merit points but because I felt sorry for the bird. Later, I found out I was wasting my money. After stretching its wings for a bit, the bird returned to the cage for a meal and a nap. From the point of view of the bird, maybe living in a cage in the close company of other birds is a comforting experience, and not all that different from the nest full of fledglings in which the bird started its life. The bird, it seems, regards the small cage as home sweet home - offering shelter and food—two of the three things living beings are supposed to want out of life.

If we could better remember our past lives, we might understand what these birds are thinking.

Critics of the karma system argue that a downside to this system of belief is that karma stifles ambition. Perhaps so. Karma believers may be less likely than non-believers to aspire to what some see as the better things in this life. But overall, a belief in karma may contribute to a contented and harmonious society.

To the best of my knowledge, Buddhists believe that organisms, human or animal, are mere phases in the cycle of life which can exist as many life forms. From this belief, it follows that deceased human beings, including family members, could conceivably become animals in the lifetime of their surviving relatives.

Throughout my journeys in Buddhist countries, I have observed some intriguing aspects of the relationships between humans and animals. Consideration for animals seems most unevenly applied. Buddhists who might lovingly relocate a cockroach or might avoid stepping on an ant, may have no compunction about eating lobsters or fish boiled alive, or consuming eels that have been skinned alive prior to cooking to improve their flavour.

The Monks

From the point of view of visitors, monks dressed in their simple saffron robes, make excellent photo shots, particularly if they happen to be carrying some modern accessory, such as an umbrella or a mobile phone.

If asked, monks are usually happy to be photographed. But it's worth bearing in mind the Buddhist community treats monks with great respect. Interactions between monks and the community are subject to strict protocol. For example, one of the vows of monkhood is to forego any physical contact with the fairer sex. So if you are a woman, be careful around monks. To give them the personal space they expect, try not to walk too near them. When taking public transport, avoid sitting next to monks so that you will not be thrown into fleeting contact as your bus sinks into a pothole or lurches around a corner.

Chou Ta-kuan, Chinese envoy to Khmer Empire in the Yuan dynasty, provided this description of 13th-century Angkor monks: "They shave their heads, and wear yellow robes, leaving the right shoulder bare. For the lower half of the body, they wear a yellow shirt. They are barefoot." Observers of present-day Cambodian street life may note that this dress code has endured.

Most Cambodian boys enter the monkhood for some part of their lives, perhaps six months, perhaps longer. The minimum age for a monk is 20. However, no minimum age is prescribed for a novice to enter a monastery. Some novices are as young as six years old.

The monkhood offers Cambodians some practical advantages outside religion itself – for example, education. is one benefit in joining the monkhood. For some boys, belonging to a monastery represents their only opportunity to receive any schooling at all. They may also learn some sort of a trade such as fishing or agriculture, which may assist their

Traditional beliefs with a modern touch.

subsequent commercial life. Against that, novices and monks must make sacrifices in other areas. Monks must vow not to kill animals, not to tell lies, not to eat a meal past midday, to avoid contact with the opposite sex, to forgo alcohol and perfume, and to avoid music other than religious chanting.

Monastic existence strips life down to its simplest terms. Monks collect from the faithful congregation a bowl of rice and perhaps some other food. Rice is normally willingly given and must be consumed before eleven in the morning. On receipt of the gift of rice, monks will typically sing a blessing to the donor, thereby earning merit all round. They will then retire to the monastery for the day.

Monks are quite approachable. They may be willing to discuss life in the monkhood and may hold a cross-section of viewpoints like anyone else. A monk I met claimed to have tired of the closed aspect of monastic life, the rules and the lack of purpose, and wanted to leave the monkhood and get a job outside the moment an opportunity presented itself. Whether he did or not, I don't know. He certainly had no obligation to remain in his monastery against his will. A monk can leave the monkhood any time he wants.

An All-Embracing Experience

Compared to some religions, Buddhism is very loosely structured, if structured at all. Instead of a formal service, worshippers each conduct a service of their own choosing. Buddhists pray, light incense and perhaps add gold leaf to Buddha statues and images. The congregation come and go when they feel like it.

It is generally fine to visit temples, participate in the religious experience even if you are not a Buddhist. At your own volition, you can make offerings and buy and light incense sticks. A donation box is provided inside most temples. The money is used for temple upkeep. By contributing, you gain merit with your God, or someone else's.

You can normally take photos inside temples, though it does pay to check. But it is not a good idea to touch anything as you move around religious icons. Scraping the gold leaf off a Buddha image or climbing up on a Buddha statue, as

Setting out for lunch.

tourists have been caught doing on occasions, are serious offences that can land you a stretch in the Phnom Penh 'Hilton' jail.

Buddhism is the majority religion in Cambodia but does not demand exclusivity. Other religions may be practised in the country. For example, if you are on business in Cambodia, chances are you will come into contact with Cambodian Chinese. Most Cambodian Chinese are likely to speak Cambodian, act Cambodian and eat Cambodian in preference to Chinese food. However, Chinese traditions may still retain their appeal. Chinese Cambodians may not only practise Buddhism but may also pray to other deities. Somewhere on the premises of a Cambodian Chinese business you are likely to find a pantheon not only of Buddhist religious icons but Chinese ones as well.

CAMBODIA'S PEOPLE

About 90 per cent of Cambodia's population are Khmer. The Vietnamese make up 5 per cent and the Chinese around 1 per cent. The balance is split between the Cham, a Muslim minority of Vietnamese origin, and the Chunchiet (also known as the Khmer Loeu), a general term for the various indigenous groups who live a subsistence existence in Cambodia's mountainous north-east. Most of the Cambodian population lives in the flat, low-lying country of the Mekong basin.

The Vietnamese

Historically, Cambodia has not been entirely at peace with its ethnic minorities. The Vietnamese, in particular, have been shuffled into Cambodia en masse at various moments of the country's history, only to be forcibly repatriated later. During colonial rule, the French thought the Vietnamese were more industrious and better educated than the Cambodians. French-speaking Vietnamese were brought into the country as minor bureaucrats. Vietnamese labour was later imported to work the rubber plantations near the Vietnamese border.

After the French departed Cambodia in the 1950s, the Vietnamese lost support. Their fortunes revived during the communist revolution in the early 1970s and ebbed again after the Khmer Rouge victory. During 1975–1978, Pol Pot forced about 250,000 Vietnamese living in Cambodia back to Vietnam, a country many of them had never seen. After the Vietnamese army removed the Khmer Rouge in 1979, most of the Vietnamese thrown out by Pol Pot returned. When the Vietnamese army withdrew in 1989, the Vietnamese population in Cambodia largely stayed put. But long-standing grudges resurfaced among the Cambodians, many of whom resented the 1979–1989 occupation by the Vietnamese Army.

Today's immigrant Vietnamese are amongst the least privileged people in Cambodia. Their communities are located at a number of spots across Cambodia. One such community is in Cambodia's poorest province near the Vietnamese border, where Vietnamese rice farmers work their fields in pointed hats that no Cambodian would wear for fear of being thought a Vietnamese. Another Vietnamese community lives around Tonle Sap Lake and relies on fishing. The current government has disadvantaged this community by leasing out fishing rights to concessionaires. Previously, people could fish wherever they pleased. Now they must pay rent.

The Chinese

The fortunes of the Chinese in Cambodia have, likewise, waxed and waned over the years. Like the Vietnamese, the Chinese have been in Cambodia a long while, congregating in their traditional industries of retail, banking and trading. The Chinese merchant class prospered during French rule and its good fortune continued after Cambodia won independence. But after the 1970 coup that put US-backed army general Lon Nol into power, the officer corps of Lon Nol's army moved against the Chinese merchants, who they saw as their rivals in commerce. Later, the Chinese suffered even more under a Khmer Rouge regime that persecuted anyone who wasn't a rural peasant. After the Khmer Rouge were defeated, Chinese fortunes once again improved. In recent times, the Chinese have fared reasonably well under the country's present neo-capitalist policies.

The Chams

The Cham people came from an area that spans the present-day border of Cambodia and Vietnam. They speak a language related to Malay, practice Islam, and wear traditional Islamic dress. At the height of their power, the Chams ruled over most of Vietnam and southern Cambodia. In the 12th century, they conquered and briefly held Angkor.

In the 14th century, the Chams converted from Buddhism to Islam. From then on, both Vietnam and Cambodia have squeezed the Chams from their traditional territory. While the Chams can be found in many parts of Cambodia today, visitors to the country are most likely to encounter them at Kampong Cham, north-east of Phnom Penh. Though the Chams and the Khmers maintain separate cultural identities, societies and beliefs, the two groups presently coexist harmoniously enough.

The Chunchiet

The Chunchiet is the generic term for the many hill tribes who live in the Rattanakiri and Mondulkiri provinces in the far east of Cambodia. Both of these provinces are situated in the Annamite Cordillera mountain range. The Chunchiets practise a combination of subsistence farming and gathering the fruits of the forest in which they live. The Chunchiet have their own languages, and they continue to live their unassuming agricultural lifestyles, as far as they can in a world of rapidly shrinking wilderness areas. Their mountainous territory spans both sides of the Cambodian-Vietnamese border. Ethnically, they have little in common with either the Cambodians or the Vietnamese. Over many years, the Chunchiet have been persecuted by the Cambodians and the Vietnamese as well as various international powers who have, from time to time, conducted wars in their territory

Population Numbers

During the 1960s and 1970s, wars and genocide greatly reduced the population of all ethnic groups, including the Khmers. Statistics are scanty. The number of people killed in Cambodia from US bombing and the civil war in the late 1960s and early 1970s has been variously estimated at between 250,000 to 500,000. Further casualties from 1975 to 1979, when the Khmer Rouge were in power, may have numbered one to two million. According to Yale University's Genocide Program, Pol Pot's regime killed 1.7 million Cambodians or 21 per cent of the population. Some were executed. Others died from overwork, starvation or disease. The famines and general mayhem that followed the defeat of the Khmer Rouge added further casualties between 1979 and 1980.

Since then, Cambodia's population has been rising by a bit over 2 per cent per annum. In 2004, the population was estimated at slightly over 13 million. Life expectancy figures in Cambodia are difficult to calculate due to its recent turbulent history. The fit and the young had a much higher survival rate during the Khmer Rouge genocide than the old and the sick. Life expectancy commonly quoted for Cambodia is around 57 years—one of the lowest rates in Asia.

THE FAMILY

Like most Asian cultures, Cambodians are family orientated, with several generations likely to live under a single roof. The concept of family in Cambodia runs wider than the immediate family of fathers, mothers, sons and daughters. It includes aunts, uncles, cousins and second cousins. Marriage between distant members of the same family is common and even encouraged.

In China during the Cultural Revolution, Mao Tse Tung tried to destroy the family as an institution. But the bonds were too strong and the culture too deep. After Mao passed away, the Chinese family reformed itself. Cambodia has followed the same pattern. Pol Pot's regime viciously split up families, wrenching people from their villages, sending children to collective farms in one part of the country and parents to another. After the Khmer Rouge cadres were sent packing, the very first thing most Cambodians did was seek out their missing relatives. Within six months of the fall of the Khmer Rouge, the family unit reformed as the backbone of Cambodian society.

The family takes care of its own. Most social welfare is provided by the family, and little by the state. Traditionally, women run household finances. The role of the healthy, of either sex, is to provide for the weaker, the infirm and the young. Both women and men go to work. Most of the people working in the fields in the countryside are women.

EDUCATION

Cambodia has one of the lowest standards of adult literacy in Asia. The Khmer Rouge (led by Pol Pot who was himself a teacher) devastated the ranks of the teaching profession when teachers, learned monks and anyone suspected of having an education were put to death in the interests of furthering the ideology.

Today's educational system, gradually re-established after the demise of the Khmer Rouge regime, has barely existed for two decades. As a result, about 10 per cent of Cambodia's primary school teachers have never attended secondary school and of the balance, four out of five have only lower secondary education.

Cambodian schooling is held in all sorts of places under all sorts of conditions, often with very little equipment and educational aids. Students make do with what they have.

Despite the lack of resources and qualifications, teachers enjoy high status in Cambodia. Education tends to be passive with the 'chalk and talk' form of teaching very much the traditional method. Whatever the teachers dictate is accepted as knowledge and wisdom. Traditional Buddhist values of

A Cambodian 'school bus'.

harmony and peaceful coexistence prevail in education as in the wider community.

A Floating School From Recycled Material

Cambodia recycles materials that richer societies might throw away. I once visited a school built on a rusty barge floating in a Phnom Penh canal (*klong*.) Both the school building and its furniture were made from packing cases. Forty or so immaculately, wonderfully-behaved children sat on their packing-case stools at their packing-case desks in their packing-case classroom, getting on with the task of learning the Khmer alphabet.

Certainly among individual Cambodians, there is a strong culture of self-improvement. One message seems to have been accepted by Cambodian youth: the secret to a good education and getting on in the world is knowledge of the English language. English is seen not only as the dominant language of commerce, but also as the language of tourism—the country's most rapidly growing industry.

Students of all ages are dead keen to enrol for an English course. The poor of Cambodia, as well as the rich, pay whatever they can afford to spend a couple of hours a day to get their English lessons. Beggars will often claim the need to pay for their English classes as their reason for cadging a little money off you. They may use some of the money raised for this purpose, though eating cannot be underestimated in their hierarchy of needs.

English lessons are conducted at all levels. Courses are normally packed. Besides established language schools, hundreds of backyard tutors, including English speaking expats, run English classes with, or without, qualified teachers. People who speak a little English run English classes for their friends and the friends of their friends who speak less English than they do. To accommodate normal working hours, courses may be held early in the morning or late into the night.

An interesting side issue to education in Cambodia is the practice of surrounding schools at examination time with temporary fencing manned by police. The declared objective is to prevent cheating by imposing a physical barrier between examination candidates and passers-by—suggesting that the ethics of young Cambodians are not all that highly developed. Neither, apparently, are the ethics of some teachers who, underpaid and perhaps under qualified, have, if the bribe is right, been known to pass exam questions and answers to students ahead of the examination.

ADOPTING CHILDREN

Cambodian culture does not greatly favour adoption. Traditionally, children have been a cherished asset to the community and family ties tend to be close. However, poverty has taken its toll on traditional values. From the abandoned child's point of view, adoption by a visitor may present a unique opportunity to get ahead in life, or simply eat properly.

Some Cambodian agencies have turned adoption into a moneymaking business by selling abducted children. By the time the child gets into the hands of the final adopting parents, total fees for the supply chain of US$ 20,000 have been reported. To combat this practice, adoption rules—both of Cambodian authorities and recipient country—have been tightened in recent times. Authorities in recipient countries such as the United States now require proof that the child has legitimately been put up for adoption.

Adopting or Educating a Cambodian Child

If you're interested in adopting a Cambodian child, you can get information from the Cambodian Adoption Community's website at http://www.cambodiaadoptionconnection.com/adoption_community.htm. An alternative to adopting a child physically is to adopt responsibility for the child's education. One such self-help group is the Australian Aid for Cambodia Fund whose website is: http://www.aacf.ws.

TALKING ABOUT THE PAST

Full freedom of speech hasn't completely arrived in Cambodia. Even though Pol Pot is now dead and gone and his forces have dispersed, the consequences of injudicious political comment still live in the memories of many. You may find Cambodians reluctant to air their views on the present government to you, a stranger, on the grounds that you may be a spy for Hun Sen or the CIA or some other malevolent agency.

Most Cambodians are prepared to talk a little about the Pol Pot days. I have yet to speak with anyone in Cambodia over the age of 20 whose family was spared. People will explain how they lost various brothers, sisters, uncles and aunts, fathers and mothers because these family members were teachers or policemen, wore glasses or had soft hands or whatever the reason was for their execution at the hands of Angkar.

Everyone you meet will be a victim. An acquaintance of mine, who has lived in Cambodia for nine years and is married to a Cambodian woman, has never met anyone who will say of the Khmer Rouge days, "I was a Khmer Rouge soldier. I didn't lose any family members"

Cambodians are rather forgiving about their country's horrific past. No Simon Wiesenthal-figures have emerged in Cambodian society to travel to the ends of the world to bring the Adolf Eichmanns of their world to justice. Most of Cambodia's Adolf Eichmanns are still among them, probably living comfortable lives. Most Cambodians seem prepared to let bygones be bygones. People whose families were decimated by the Khmer Rouge, and that's most of the people you'll meet, have little interest in pursuing old grudges.

AIDS AND PROSTITUTION

Prostitution between consenting adults is legal in Cambodia and fairly widespread. Cambodian men, even those who appear happily married, may use prostitutes as a matter of course. Poverty-stricken families may send their children into prostitution with full parental permission, even encouragement, to become the chief breadwinner of the family during their period of service. Prostitutes who quit may retire to their villages, carrying little shame, having discharged their family obligations.

AIDS has disrupted this economic activity in a big way. The disease is thought to have arrived in Cambodia in the early 1990s when a large force of highly-paid United Nations personnel were despatched to Cambodia to supervise the 1993 democratic election. The UN sourced its workforce from all over the world, and none were tested for AIDS before commencing service in Cambodia. A large number of girlie bars sprang up in Phnom Penh during this time to entertain the UN personnel and relieve them of their money. Since poverty, ignorance and AIDS all feed off each other, the disease spread rapidly in Cambodia where all three factors were present.

With little infrastructure, statistics on the disease are difficult to gather. But it is generally thought that Cambodia has the highest incidence of AIDS in South-east Asia. HIV infection among prostitutes may be highest of all in Cambodia's least attractive town, Poipet, the gambling, smuggling and people-trafficking staging post at the Thai border.

In the early years of the 21st century, a concerted campaign against AIDS by the Joint United Nations Programme on HIV/AIDS (UNAIDS) and the Cambodian government appears to have had made some inroads against the disease. Adult infection rate in 2004 was reported at 2.6 per cent, down from 4 per cent some years before. The Cambodian anti-AIDS campaign is based on the successful campaign in Thailand of widespread community knowledge and promoting condom use.

CHAPTER 4

GETTING TO KNOW THE CAMBODIANS

'If you're shy with your teacher, you'll never be wise.
If you're shy with your wife, you'll never have children.'
—Cambodian proverb

SOCIAL RULES

The rules of interpersonal communication within Cambodia are complex, having evolved from feudal times when everyone in society occupied a recognisable rung on the social totem pole. As a visitor to the country, you will not be expected to know the detailed workings of Cambodia's social rules. But it is good to be aware of some of the basic ideas.

The Pecking Order

Status in Cambodian society is determined by an interaction of factors such as age, occupation and social advantage. The old are respected and children are enjoyed. Superior adult figures—teachers, parents and older people— generally receive respect. So do selected professionals, such as engineers and doctors, and people with money. Sometimes the social levels overlap. It may be difficult to determine the pecking order between older people of lower socio-economic status and younger people of higher socio-economic status.

Skin colour is also important to Cambodians as it is to many Asians; light colouration is considered superior to dark. Cambodians go to great lengths to keep their complexions out of the sun. Skin-whitening products are widely sold to the urban middle class. People in outdoor occupations wear large hats and gloves.

Wearing and Removing Shoes

If you are invited to a function at a private house, on arriving at the front door for your dinner date, the first thing you may notice is a pile of shoes somewhere near the doorway. You are expected to add your shoes to the pile and if you fail to remove your shoes, you may well be asked to do so. Not removing shoes on entering someone's house is considered impolite. Socks are another matter. If you are wearing them, removing socks is optional. If your toenails are in poor shape, it's better to leave your socks on. Any deficiencies in your toenails will be noted. Cambodians are assiduous about maintaining both their fingernails and their toenails in top condition.

What to Wear

One of the remarkable achievements of Cambodians is how neat and tidy they manage to look in a country where such a low level of mod-cons is offered. From one-room packing-case shacks with no electricity and running water emerge people without a hair out of place and with their clothes immaculately pressed. How Cambodians manage to create this display of sartorial elegance in such difficult surroundings is one of life's mysteries.

Despite the hot climate, Cambodians keep their shoulders and legs covered in public. Traditional dress for women is blouses, sarongs or skirts worn close to ankle level. Women are demurely clad often from neck to ankle but nevertheless manage to look shapely. On more formal occasions, women may wear a *sampot*—a one-piece outfit that looks like it has been wrapped around a spindle shaped as a female form. Around the cities, Western women's fashions are also catching on to some degree. Particularly popular for the younger generations are jeans. Men dress much the same as elsewhere, in trousers and collared shirts.

Casual clothing that exposes excessive areas of skin may be considered offensive by villagers, though is acceptable in parts of the country where tourists are common. Shorts, for both male and female, are marginal dress code in most

Covering up against the sun.

places. Cambodians, of either gender, generally cover their legs in public.

When visiting temples, custom dictates that certain parts of the body need to be covered while others must be uncovered. You must remove your hat and shoes upon entering a temple, but cover your bare legs and arms. Shorts and skimpy tops are not the ideal apparel for temple visits. Some temples on the tourist trail raise additional funds by hiring out loose fitting trousers that cover expanses of prohibited skin.

Government officials, people in private business and those on public duty such as car-parking staff often wear uniforms to work. A uniform not only carries status but the free issue of clothes also saves money—a commodity perennially in scarce supply in cash-starved Cambodia. Smart-looking uniforms worn by low level officialdom can increase the difficulty of determining who's who in the Cambodian pecking order, although markings on clothing for those in uniform may offer a clue. The shirts of those in charge of car parks and security operations, for example, may bear the three-bar chevron of sergeant's rank.

Gift-giving

If invited anywhere, showing up with a gift is appropriate but not mandatory. As societies go, Cambodians, apart from the few ultra rich, are not particularly materialistic. Many Cambodians own precious few material possessions within their own lifetimes.

Gifts do not have to be particularly elaborate or expensive. But Cambodians tend to be artistic. They appreciate the effort that goes into presenting a gift attractively packaged. Wrapping paper, with perhaps a flower pinned to the package, conveys the sense that the donor has gone to some trouble with the gift. Something from your own country is particularly appreciated. So is straight-out cash. Money goes a long way in this country, and there are many good causes on which to spend it.

How to Sit and Stand

Sitting in a position that to Cambodians is entirely natural can be excruciatingly uncomfortable for people who have spent much of their lives sitting in chairs. For example, if you are invited to a Cambodian-style lunch or dinner, you may be invited to sit on the floor, on a chair or on a low bench half way between the two. Cambodians can sit comfortably on the floor for hours with their legs arranged lotus style or on their heels or with their legs splayed to the side. If they have no experience with Westerners, they may expect the same of their visitors.

Suffering in Silence

A friend of mine in education once attended the ceremonial opening of a new factory. Eight monks from the local monastery were on hand to bless the building in the approved manner. The hosts and my Western friend were shown their appropriate places at the foot of the monks. While everyone else sat on the floor, to afford them the proper respect, the monks were seated on a low platform laid with deep cushions so that their heads would be higher than anyone else's. The monks then conducted an elaborate ceremony of chanting and ribbon passing that went on for nearly two hours.

For my Western friend, this was one of the most agonising experiences of his life. He desperately wanted to stretch his legs. Extending his legs in front of his body was a definite no-no, as the soles of the feet are considered to be one of the dirtiest parts of the human body. Presenting the soles of the feet to anyone else is considered insulting. Extending the soles of the feet to a monk would be unconscionable.

Eventually someone noticed my friend's discomfort as he wriggled around on the floor trying to find a comfortable position that wouldn't convey some insult. They discreetly moved him to the back of the room, and installed him in a chair so he wouldn't tower over his betters.

On some occasions, it is next to impossible to avoid sitting on the floor for long periods. If you do have to sit on the floor, bending your knees and sitting with your feet pointing to the side is acceptable. This may also get tiring, but may not be as excruciating to some as sitting lotus style. Sitting on your feet, as in a semi-kneeling position, is also acceptable.

In addition, certain ways of sitting in a chair can also convey a sense of disrespect. For example, crossing the legs is not a good idea in most circumstances. Sitting cross-legged, sitting on a raised platform, leaning back in the chair, and squatting with legs outstretched all pose problems of protocol. When it comes to arranging your limbs, follow the practices of the locals if you can. Whatever positions you adopt, try to be careful not to point your feet towards objects of reverence, such as monks or statues of Buddha.

Conversations

Cambodians readily strike up conversations with visitors to their country. Since most Cambodians don't get great opportunities to travel beyond their borders, they exhibit a healthy curiosity about the outside world.

Among the first few topics you may be asked are your country of origin, your job and your number of offspring. Of these, the first question is of the keenest interest to Cambodians. Fairly early in the conversation, most Cambodians you meet are likely to express an interest to travel to whichever country you happen to come from. "I come from Iceland," you might say. If you do, the likely rejoinder would be, "Oh, I've always wanted to go to Iceland. Can you help me travel to Iceland?"

Behind this keen interest to travel to your country may lie an even keener interest to leave their own country. Those Cambodians who see their homeland as a land of limited opportunity would settle for a ticket out to anywhere.

The Untouchable Head

The head is seen as the location of one's being and must be treated with the greatest respect. The head of another person should not be touched. Friendly pats to the top of the heads of adults and children older than about ten are not appreciated. Keep clear of touching the hair and face of another person unless it is someone with whom you are intimate.

Exemptions are made for barbers, doctors and dentists, but even barbers may baulk at trimming luxurious facial hair. Cambodians are smooth-skinned and males tend not to have strong beards. They may regard body hair and facial hair as somewhat barbarian. Barbers will normally give you a haircut; but if you have a full beard, they are not so keen on providing a beard trim. I once had a long discussion with a Cambodian on the link between the amount of body hair of various races and Darwin's Theory of Evolution. The theory was that if mankind had descended from hairy apes, then Cambodians have evolved further from the source than Caucasians and are therefore a more advanced life form.

I am not claiming this is the general prevailing view, but it was an interesting idea.

Keep Your Hands to Yourself

The rules on use of the left hand are similar to those in other countries where toilet paper is not part of the traditional culture. The right hand is used for passing things around and the left hand is kept out of the way.

In some situations, such as handing out business cards, it is more polite to use both hands than one. Never throw anything at anyone in Cambodia. Even an action as seemingly inoffensive as sliding a business card across the table is not ideal practice. Cards should be handed to recipients.

Generally, Cambodians express themselves in body language a great deal less than Westerners. They are not like the French or Italians where the hands conduct a significant part of the conversation. Nor is Cambodia an emotionally exuberant place like the United States, with attendant back-slapping and high-fives. Waving your arms about, placing your hands on your hips and folding your arms across your chest and leaning back in a chair with your arms behind your head are all gestures you won't see much of in Cambodia. Raised voices and boisterous behaviour are also considered impolite. By contrast, smiling, nodding and agreeing are all highly recommended.

Keep Your Soles Out of Sight

The status of human limbs follows roughly the height rule. The head is afforded the highest respect. The soles of the feet, by contrast, are seen as the least desirable body part. No one wants to see the soles of anyone's feet. The bottom of the foot, which is likely to be soiled as well as ugly, should only be shown to your worst enemy. Pointing with the foot at some object close to the ground, such as an item on the bottom shelf of a supermarket, says to the Cambodian, "I can't be bothered to bend down to point this out to you, so I am using the lowest and dirtiest part of my body to do it". Not a good idea if you are trying to win friends and influence Cambodians.

An exception is made for reflexology, a branch of eastern medicine that focuses of the foot's connection to bodily organs, and is widely practised in Cambodia. Reflexologists will spend hours working on people's feet for a modest fee.

Keep Cool

Pressures for social harmony in Cambodia are very strong. The objective is to ensure no one gets upset. To avoid conflict, Cambodians may provide answers they think the questioners will like to hear. They don't like to disappoint by saying "no" and may tell white lies to avoid doing so. You need to ensure your questions are really understood, since Cambodians are likely to answer "yes" to just about anything if they think this is the answer you want to hear. For example, if you ask a taxi driver if he knows your destination, he will almost certainly answer "yes". If he then drives off in the wrong direction, do not hesitate to turn him around. If you don't, you may will most likely drive around aimlessly while he awaits your revised instructions for the journey.

An acquaintance, a foreigner married to a Cambodian woman, once remarked to me that Cambodians were the Italians of South-east Asia in regard to their displays of emotion. However, this is not the observation of most people. Contemporary Cambodian historian David P Chandler notes that not one of the people he interviewed for his biography of Pol Pot, *Brother Number One*, could remember Khmer Rouge's Number One Brother raising his voice in anger. Yet his actions in torturing and killing thousands were those of a permanently angry man.

Cambodians consider raising your voice or expressing anger or even annoyance as poor form. Firmness, self-control and persistence are the order of the day if you want to get something done. Part of keeping cool is not to get too animated in the body language area.

Generally, Cambodians are private people who are embarrassed by public displays of emotion. Cambodians may laugh at aggression not because they are amused, but because they are confused or discomforted. Cambodian keep their emotions to themselves. They tend to be even-tempered and appreciate the same behaviour from their visitors. You will receive few body language cues to indicate the state of mind of a Cambodian. The cool manner of Cambodians gives little warning that you may have pushed the envelope too far.

In Western parlance, Cambodians tend to keep their cool unless most severely provoked, whereby they may suddenly and unpredictably lapse into a bout of anger or by most standards, extreme physical violence.

Armed Adversaries

It is worth remembering that after 1979, the young Khmer Rouge cadres merely moved back and blended into the community. You just might be conducting your argument with an ex-Khmer Rouge teenage soldier who spent his formative years suspending his victims by the thumbs.

In addition, ownership of deadly weapons is far from uncommon. In a country that was in a state of civil war for the best part of 25 years, there is nothing unusual about having a gun or two around. Typical is a story in the newspaper of two friends who argued over the ownership of a motorbike. Both men were carrying pistols, which is nothing out of the ordinary in Cambodia. Plenty of AK-47s are also stored in the community; but they are difficult to carry around, so a pistol is the preferred weapon for every day use. After discussions over the motorbike reached an impasse, the arguing friends both pulled out their pistols and shot each other. One died and the other was permanently paralysed.

In a parallel story of violence, a German acquaintance, who had a forthright and assertive manner and had resided in Cambodia for a number of years, once entered into an argument with a taxi driver about the fare. After an exchange of words, the two parties were unable to establish their respective rights. With little show of emotion, the taxi driver settled the argument with an iron bar he carried in the cab. As a result, the German now wears a rather large hole in the back of his head and sometimes behaves in an even more peculiar manner than he did before receiving his injury.

Forming Relationships

Cambodians are friendly but traditionally reserved about forming relationships with outsiders. Cambodia is one of the few countries in which the NGO Save the Children tries to prevent you from establishing a personal relationship with a disadvantaged child. You can donate to Save the Children or any one of the many NGOs operating in the country, but the Cambodian government will not encourage sponsoring an individual child (though with persistence, it can be done). In the normal course of events, your donation is added to a pool, which is distributed to child welfare more generally.

As a visitor, you may be interesting to Cambodians. They may want to hear your story. If Cambodians are not quite clear on your status vis-à-vis their status, they may avoid eye contact. But on the other hand, if you a non-Asian on tour and the locals are observing you from a distance, they may stare at you in a way some societies might consider downright rude. This isn't intended, of course. Cambodians unfamiliar with the ways of foreigners may merely be observing you as an object of curiosity. In remote rural areas, Cambodians may have seen your type on television once or twice, but you could be one of the few real-life specimens that has wandered into their line of vision. From their point of view, staring at such an interesting object as you is socially quite acceptable.

Save the Children

Many children in Cambodia could do with a helping hand. You can find out how to help disadvantaged Cambodian children by logging onto http://www.bigpond.com/kh/users/rb.cambodia/ or http://seapa.net/external/countries/cambodia.

If Thailand is the land of smiles that are, some sceptics would say, often none too sincere, then Cambodia is the land of unqualified smiles. Cambodians are extraordinarily friendly and helpful to their visitors. Their smiles are broad and spontaneous and appear genuine.

Though they smile easily, Cambodians fall short of exuberant displays of public affection. There is little contact between the opposite sex in public, even between married couples. While members of the same sex sometimes walk around hand in hand or with linked arms, members of the opposite sex do not. Cambodian women are discreet. They generally do not drink or smoke in public (unless they are employed in the hospitality trade). Nor do they frequent bars or go out unchaperoned. Different rules apply to Cambodian men who, if they so desire, feel quite free to drink, smoke and casually use prostitutes.

The youth of Cambodia—poor but smiling.

Quick Tips on Etiquette

- Cambodians are not used to bodily contact, especially in public, thus avoid kissing, hugging or back-slapping when meeting a local. At the same time, be moderate in your actions and speech.
- Avoid touching the heads of adults and older children.
- Use your right hand for most purposes, such as pointing or eating, but use both hands when passing a business card or similar item to a Cambodian.
- Hand things out to people. Avoid throwing or tossing things at Cambodians.
- Sit with your legs to one side or in the lotus position; do not show the soles of your feet to a Cambodian and never to a monk or a Buddhist icon.

- When sitting in a chair, it is disrespectful to cross your legs, stretch them in front of you or to lean back.
- Gifts need not be expensive but should be attractively wrapped.
- Dress conservatively especially in rural villages and at religious shrines.
- Ask permission first before taking pictures of monks, temples and religious objects.

BELIEFS AND PRACTICES
Time and Date Superstition

As in many other languages, Khmer has named its days of the week after heavenly objects visible from Earth, some of which in turn were named for gods of various religions. For example, the sun in Khmer is *aa-dteut*; Sunday is *t'ngai aa-dteut* (*t'ngai* means day); moon is *bpray ah jun* (*bpray ah* means god and *jun* means moon, much the same as in Thai); and the word for Monday is *t'ngai jun*.

Time, in Cambodia, is measured according to the same scale as the rest of the world. Cambodians operate the Buddhist, Islam and Gregorian calendars, depending on the application. For normal business, hotel bookings and airline schedules, use of the Gregorian calendar is universal.

However in day-to-day conversation, Cambodians may not recognise the 12-hour am/pm clock. Using the 24-hour clock reduces the risk of confusion. So, for example, 6:00 pm is best called 18 hours. In Khmer, the word *muang* (hour) is the first word used when telling the time. Then follows the numbers indicating the hour, and another set of numbers indicating minutes (*nee-ar tee*). Thai speakers will note the words for hours and minutes are similar to the equivalent words in Thai.

Some parts of Cambodia also represent the days of the week by different colours: Sunday is red; Monday orange; Tuesday purple; Wednesday green; Thursday the colour of clouds (a bluish white); Friday blue; and Saturday black. Each of these colours carries superstitious significance. You may find that Cambodian women prefer to wear clothes that are the colours for the day.

Colours and Luck

The Cambodians, like the Chinese, associate colours with luck, or lack of it. Monday (orange), a good day for spending money but a poor day for lending it, is an excellent day to go shopping. Hairdressers may close down on Wednesdays in recognition of a Brahman belief that Wednesday (green) is not a good haircutting day. Saturday, the day of black, is the day when restless spirits get out and about in the community and are likely to have a disturbing influence on your plans. Saturday is a poor day to attempt anything too ambitious, but is an excellent day for getting in touch with your ancestors. Generally lucky colours are red, gold, sky blue and emerald green. Red and gold are considered lucky colours for gambling.

Cambodians recognise the powers of *feng shui* in locating and orientating buildings in the most favourable locations and aspects. Superstition is also included in official ceremonies. For example, agricultural economists and meteorologists in Cambodia (following a similar practice in Thailand) make predictions based not on the presence or absence of the El Nino effect, but on the dietary preferences of King Sihamoni's oxen.

During the Royal Ploughing Ceremony conducted at the start of the monsoon season, royal oxen are paraded before the Royal Palace and invited to consider the merits of seven golden trays containing seven different agricultural commodities—rice, corn, sesame seeds, beans, grass, water and wine. In 2004, the oxen selected only the rice, corn and beans but ignored the sesame seeds, only sniffing at the water and turning away from the wine. Predictions that flowed from this display of bovine behaviour were that the rice harvest would be moderate, yields of secondary crops such as corn and beans would be good, the country would receive average rains and no serious floods would occur in the ensuing season. Since the oxen didn't bother with the wine, the seers knew their country was likely to be peaceful for at least another year. If the oxen had tasted the wine, bad times would have lain ahead. Alcohol and oxen just don't mix.

Weddings and Funerals

Cambodian culture is full of ceremony, with the three states of mankind—hatched, matched and despatched—all comprehensively celebrated. Cambodian weddings and funerals, in particular, are extraordinarily elaborate, complicated and extended events. In a more leisurely past, a full Cambodian wedding ceremony would take three days to complete. In today's busy world, weddings have been compressed to a single day, though funerals may still extend over several days.

Weddings start early in the morning at the bridegroom's home, with an exchange of presents and food provided by the bridegroom, symbolising a dowry to the bride's family. The wedding party may then move to the home of the bride (if that happens to be nearby), making its way noisily through the streets with much singing, chanting and general revelry in which passers-by may participate.

Once at the bride's home, various ceremonies ensue: a tea ceremony; a hair-cutting ceremony in which both bride and groom have their hair cut (these days more ceremonial than actual); ritual feet washing of the bride and groom; an exchange of vows; and a 'pairing' ceremony in which the married couple are ceremonially bound together with silken cords. During the long series of wedding celebrations, the bride may make up to eleven changes of clothing during the day and the bridegroom three.

Typically, marriages in Cambodia are arranged. An astrologer may be consulted (though not necessarily by the partners to the marriage) to check on the compatibility of matches. In arranged marriages, couples do not court though they may meet each other before their wedding day. Often, marriage partners are found within extended families. King Sihanouk himself took one cousin and two aunts among his many official and unofficial wives.

If, as a foreigner, you are invited to attend a wedding, you may find yourself cast in the role of a special guest, even if you know the wedding participants only casually. The prevailing view seems to be that outsiders add status and interest to the wedding ceremony.

Funerals are also ceremonial events. Since Cambodians are Theravada Buddhists, the overriding interest at the point of death is what will happen next to the soul of the deceased. In this matter, correct treatment of the corpse is vital. Buddhists believe that without a proper funeral, the souls of the dead will wander in limbo for eternity. Families who have lost touch with loved ones and fear they have died, turn to clairvoyants to find and return their dead so that a proper burial can be conducted and the disturbed spirits set to rest.

As opposed to Western practice, the colour of mourning in Cambodia is white or, more specifically, the colour of clouds—white with a suggestion of grey-blue. This is thought to be the favoured colour of spirits. Black, preferred in the West for funerals, has enjoyed a very poor reputation in Cambodia after it was adopted as the colour of the uniforms of the Khmer Rouge army.

A key consideration influencing prospects for the afterlife is how much merit people accumulate during their sojourn on Earth. The store of merit acquired over a lifetime is not entirely dependent on an individual's own efforts. Buddhism allows the transfer of additional merit from loved ones to the deceased during the period between the moment of death and the moment of cremation. This belief provides additional purpose to the Cambodian funeral. A major objective is to assist the deceased attain the highest state of grace, by adding to the store of merit already accumulated in life.

Like most things Buddhist, this last increment of merit is achieved by appropriate chanting and praying. The corpse may lie in an open coffin for several days, during which as many visitors as are to show up pray for the departed soul

Setting up for the funeral ceremony—100 days after the funeral.

and pay their respects to the bereaved family. Monks are also hired to perform ceremonies to add further merit.

After community goodwill is finally exhausted, the coffin and its contents are usually cremated. Other alternatives are burial or floating the corpse away on an open boat. If the body is cremated, the ashes are interred in a small shrine somewhere in the local *wat*. Disposal of the corpse by whatever means is still not quite the end of the affair. A further ceremony is held 100 days after the funeral at which the funeral party gathers once more for a final expression of goodwill towards the deceased.

Dealing with Beggars

Begging is fairly widespread in the major cities, particularly in the tourist destinations of Phnom Penh and Siem Reap. Swarms of street children hanging out on the river front at Phnom Penh live by whatever means they can. Beggars come in all styles and ages. Some are orphans. Some are abandoned children or women with babies who lack family support. Some are disabled people of all ages, often landmine victims, for whom no social welfare or employment is available. A standard line that street kids use to justify their begging is that they need the money to pay for educational books and courses. This may be true of course. Then again, they may simply want to buy a meal.

These people are a cross-section of Cambodia's disadvantaged, bereft of privilege and opportunity. If you are a reasonably well-off visitor from an average First World country and someone with no legs and one arm crawls up to your restaurant table and seeks your attention, your sympathies are likely to be aroused. If you do give to a beggar, the word spreads through the network quickly. In short order, you may find yourself surrounded by grasping hands and demanding voices.

Attitudes towards begging vary, as do attitudes to charity in general. The issue of whether to give to beggars or not is a matter of personal choice and philosophy. Some people decide that giving to beggars perpetuates begging. In raw economic numbers, some argue begging is a highly-paid occupation. The average annual per capita GDP in Cambodia is about US$ 300. Beggars, a Phnom Penh taxi driver explained to me, can make US$ 3–4 per day. That comes to over US$ 1,000 a year, or four times the average per capita income of the whole country. Some allege beggars are controlled by a mafia that lays claim to most of their earnings. Others are stirred by the knowledge that beggars are likely to have no means of survival other than the alms they receive. To accommodate both these thoughts, some donors give beggars food rather than money.

Some aspects of the beggar culture have their roots in Buddhism. Monks for example, exist by public alms.

Some beggars may dress as Buddhist monks in the hope of getting money from tourists. However, the genuine Buddhist monk who has followed the articles of his faith and eschewed materialism has no call for money at the personal level and carries only a food bowl into the street. One reason the Khmer Rouge gave for coming down hard on the Buddhist clergy was that monks lived off society and did no work.

Cambodians are not particularly sympathetic to beggars, even though giving alms may earn merit for the donor. The Buddhist belief that reincarnation delivers you into the life you deserve may play a part in this attitude. I have seen a policeman at Angkor move a beggar along with a stun gun.

Taking Photographs

Other than at strategically sensitive targets such as military establishments, Cambodia imposes few rules against photo-taking. Most Cambodians do not seem to mind being photographed at all. I have taken photos of people who seem to me to be in the most dire poverty, living in broken down packing-case houses on the edge of fetid swamps, and been rewarded with a beaming smile. Occasionally, people avert their faces, perhaps some memory from the Pol Pot era raising concerns of a time when it didn't pay to attract the slightest attention.

It is in order too, to photograph monks and religious objects, provided you are reasonably polite and discreet about it. You should obtain permission before taking photos of religiously- sensitive objects and icons such as the inside of pagodas.

One exception is the Chunchiet people in Cambodia's north-east corner. The Chunchiet are a reclusive, indigenous people who are gradually losing their habitat and lifestyle as the jungle around them is cleared for the various reasons people who own bulldozers have for clearing jungles. The Chunchiet speak their own languages, don't speak Khmer and have no reason to welcome the presence in their shrinking territory of anyone from the outside world.

They don't like having their photos taken.

ALTERNATIVE LIFESTYLES

Travel writers sometimes skirt around the subject of sexual exploitation. But Cambodia has developed a minor reputation for catering to the least desirable type of tourist.

Poverty breeds desperation for money acquired by whatever means. One of the avenues to money for young unskilled and uneducated Cambodians is the sex industry. Alternatively, unfortunate young boys and girls may be forced into the industry when people sell unwanted children for a few dollars. Children may be put up for sale by their natural parents. Or they may be abducted, then put up for sale. In addition, a considerable number of Vietnamese prostitutes of all age groups work inside Cambodia.

Posted along Sisowath Boulevard which runs along the banks of the Tonle Sap River are illuminated signs that read, 'Sexually exploit a child in this country, go to jail in your own.' Displayed above the text is a picture of a handcuffed prisoner behind bars. Many hotel rooms post similar notices cautioning against the use of hotels for sex with minors.

Various NGOs are active in Cambodia trying to protect the rights of children against exploitation by foreign paedophiles. International organisations cooperate with authorities in the tourist's country of origin to choke off the demand for child sex on the threat of stern penalties back home.

But within Cambodia, authorities may turn a blind eye. Regrettably, Cambodia's sex industry is mostly run by criminal elements with the cooperation of corrupt police. Now and then a visitor gets arrested for molesting a child, but may be released in short order for 'lack of evidence', a term that may mean a satisfactory bribe has been paid.

Working to Wipe Out Exploitation

ECPAT (End Child Prostitution, Abuse and Trafficking) is one of several international organisations in Cambodia working to reduce exploitation and trafficking of women and children. You can look up its website at http://www.ecpat.net to learn more about its work.

Recently, the Cambodian government is at least paying lip service to tightening the rules on sexual exploitation. Cambodia attempts to discourage paedophiles by bringing to their attention the consequences of their crime. The strategy is to cooperate with countries supplying sex-tourists to break up foreign paedophile networks. Newspapers carry almost daily stories of foreigners facing long jail sentences for child sex offences.

Cambodia has also acquired a reputation for the easy availability of drugs. Drugs that would be difficult or impossible to get in most other countries are easy to get here. Heroin can be bought as readily as candy and for a comparable price. Pharmacists (a mixture of qualified and unqualified) will dispense morphine over the counter without a prescription.

Of course foreigners other than paedophiles or drug addicts may chose to live in Cambodia for a variety of reasons. For example, Cambodia adopts some attitudes that may appeal to those with anti-materialist tendencies. The country has adopted Theravada Buddhism which theoretically eschews money and possessions. Others come on goodwill missions to dispense aid. Motivated by the most worthy of intentions, many of Cambodia's visitors are in the country to help the disadvantaged, earning little in return for themselves in the process.

But a small community of refugees from Western values also lives in Cambodia. With its incredibly cheap cost of living, Cambodia is an easy place to hang out for the less-than-well-heeled, underachieving, disillusioned Western male. In Cambodia, less accomplished foreigners can live a life they could not possibly enjoy in their own country. Most of this community of Western dropouts teach English part-time to earn enough to keep themselves alive. They choose to live in Cambodia simply because it's the only country where they can get a professional job in a country that demands absolutely no proof of qualifications.

Cambodia also offers its unofficial immigrants another advantage. Residence in Cambodia can be maintained for long periods, at least on an unofficial basis. Unlike other South-east Asian countries, foreigners can work semi-legally in Cambodia without the formality of a work permit.

So foreign drifters drift into Cambodia for all sorts of reasons. Some drop out of their own society to take up residence in the only place on the planet where they can get a job and make a living wage. Some come to protest the state of the rest of the world. Some come to explore their Buddhist beliefs and find their inner selves. Some come to enjoy the world's cheapest and finest ganja. Some come for the harder drugs. Some come for sex. Some come for a combination of all these reasons.

Some just lose their connections with the outside world and end up staying.

SETTLING IN

CHAPTER 5

'Our first task in approaching another people,
another culture, another religion is to take off our
shoes for the place we are approaching is holy.'
—Author unknown

VISAS AND DOCUMENTATION

The requirement for visas varies with the visitor's country of origin, length of stay and the reason for the visit. Currently only citizens from Malaysia and the Philippines can enter without a tourist visa, and stay for 30 days and 21 days respectively. By end 2005, however, Cambodia—as a member of ASEAN (Association of South-east Asian Nations)—will extend visa exemption to visitors from member countries. A tourist visa costs US$ 20 and business visa US$ 25. Tourist visas are valid for one month, business visas for three months. For a small fee the three-month business visa which, can be indefinitely extended while inside the country.

Where to Apply for a Visa

Visas can be issued upon arrival at Pochentong Airport in Phnom Penh or Siem Reap International Airport, or at certain border checkpoints if you are coming by land. You may also apply at the nearest Cambodian embassy back home, in which case you need to provide your itinerary, two passport photos and a valid passport. You can also download the form in PDF format from the Ministry of Tourism website: http://www.mot.gov.kh/visa.asp.

As visas run from the date of issue rather than the date of arrival, and they cost the same whether you apply upon arrival or in your home country, by applying closer to your arrival date you will get more time for your money.

All visas require a passport-sized photo. Photos may also be required for other purposes such as driving licences and visas to places like Vietnam and Laos. Travellers to Cambodia are advised to bring plenty of passport photos of themselves on the principle that the smaller the country, the larger its appetite for the photos of its visitors.

A departure tax is also levied. At the time of writing, the departure tax is US$ 10 from Siem Reap and US$ 25 from Phnom Penh (possibly the world's highest and increasing annually). Departure tax may or may not be levied at land crossings depending, it seems, on the disposition (and perhaps the personal needs) of immigration officials. Departure taxes must be paid in cash in US dollars.

Visa Extensions

Those who would like to extend their visit to Cambodia may request a visa extension at the Department of Immigration situated just opposite the Pochentong Airport at Phnom Penh. Tourist visas may be extended one time only for a month while business visa holders can choose to extend their stay for three months, six months or one year. Both the tourist visa and three-month business visa are for single entry only. If you know in advance that you are likely to stay in Cambodia for more than 30 days, it is almost certainly worth getting a three-month business visa in the first place at an extra cost of US$ 5. Overstaying your visa incurs a fine of US$ 5 each day you overstay. Most travel agents offer visa extension services for a small fee.

GETTING ON WITH THE BUREAUCRACY

One of the difficulties in Cambodia, whether you are an individual, a company, an NGO, or even a Cambodian, is bureaucracy. The word 'bureaucracy' comes from the French, from whom the Cambodians received much of their training in bureaucratic obfuscation. The French originally set up the Cambodian bureaucracy, staffed by Vietnamese, as an efficient tax collection organisation. The French bureaucracy was more interested in extorting taxes (at which it was efficient) than delivering services (at which it was inefficient). Remnants of this culture have lingered to the present day.

An enduring problem with the Cambodian bureaucracy is that its personnel are chronically underpaid, if they are paid at all. Corruption in the civil service, which has always existed, became endemic during the government of Lon Nol in the early 1970s, when generals stole the pay of their men and created phantom armies which existed only on payroll records but not in reality (and caused the United States, which was financing the Cambodian army, to greatly overestimate the military strength of its Cambodian ally). While the generals grew rich by diverting the pay of these phantom armies into their own pockets and selling arms to their enemies, troopers who went unpaid for months at a time were forced to seek a living by unconventional means.

The culture of the Cambodian civil service has not changed greatly since those times. Cambodian bureaucrats are given a uniform, an office desk, an impressive array of rubber stamps, but very little money. To survive, they improvise. Or they moonlight in other jobs, such as driving taxis at night.

With this as the prevailing culture, Cambodian bureaucrats, by and large, are not there to help you or the state, or to assist in the country's development. They are there to help themselves. Their opportunity for making a bit on the side from their day jobs comes when interacting with the public. To get the wheels of bureaucracy to turn at all, they must be oiled with regular dollops of money. Paying stipends at each step of the process not only adds to the burden of cost, but also ties up goods in a maze of red tape. Sorely needed imports and exports can get lost or go missing for long periods.

Various licences, and even professorships at universities, can be brought at the right price. The monetary amounts are small by Western standards, but from the public's point of view, the procedure of providing bribes for service is ticklish. Bribes have to be provided in a certain way that suggests that they aren't bribes at all. The appropriate level of bribe may be set according to an informal scale of charges not widely known. You may need advice from a knowledgeable Cambodian on the best procedures to be followed for specific services.

SETTING UP HOUSE

Under Cambodian law, ownership of Cambodian land is restricted to Cambodian nationals, either a naturalised person or a company. The maximum ownership a non-Cambodian can hold in Cambodian land is a non-controlling interest of 49 per cent. Buying a house in Cambodia is not practical for an outsider; those staying long-term in Cambodia are advised to rent their accommodation.

At the time of writing, typical rental prices for a 4-bedroom, 3-bathroom air-conditioned house in Phnom Penh with off-street parking for 2 to 3 cars was in the range of US$ 600–800 per month. Rental leases can run either for an indefinite period or a specified period. A minimum lease duration of 12 months is normally stipulated.

Rental terms are usually three months' payment in advance and one month's notice of termination at the end of the lease period. A security deposit may also be requested. Service apartments, condominium style, with security and parking are slightly dearer. Rental accommodation is customarily provided with basic furnishings such as beds, dining and lounge suites, refrigerator and washing machine.

Power and Water Supply

Cambodia is not well connected to utilities. Only about 15 per cent of houses in Cambodia have electricity. In rural areas, car batteries are widely used to power the important things in life, like television sets.

Where available, mains supply is 220 volt AC and 50 hertz. Power outages are not uncommon and many commercial institutions have stand-by generators. Sockets are two parallel round pins 12 mm apart with no earth—similar to the system in Thailand and with the same faults. There is nothing to hold the plugs in the sockets. As a result, plugs fall out without notice or perhaps start arcing inside the socket;

this is usually bad news for those running computers with no battery backup. Though adapters for three-pin plugs are sold in Phnom Penh, it is worth bringing universal adaptors with you to run your appliances.

No town gas is available. The principal source of energy for Cambodians is still firewood. But bottled gas is readily available in most places and works satisfactorily. Supply of bottled gas can be organised through local retailers, or even motorbike drivers.

It pays to check on the availability of water supply, sewerage and telephones, especially in rural areas. Since you can't drink the water, a water cooler in your home is highly recommended. Once a cooler is installed, delivery of large bottles of drinking water that sit atop the cooler can easily be arranged.

What to Bring

Since people's needs differ, what to bring with you for your stay in Cambodia will vary from one individual to the next. Tourists on short-term visit are well advised to pack medical kits, up-to-date health insurance, lightweight clothes and US dollars, as mentioned elsewhere in the book.

Getting clothed in Cambodia presents its own drawbacks and opportunities. Cambodians by and large are slight, slender people. Extra large sizes can be difficult to source. On the other hand, tailor-made clothing is cheap in Cambodia, though the range of fabrics may be limited.

Those staying longer in the country might consider importing more of their needs based on their wants and desires. Cambodia is not a favourite destination for die-hard shoppers. The country does not have drive-in department complexes, hypermarts, do-it-yourself warehouses, or even, at the time of writing, a McDonald's.

Goods you have purchased from the department store in your home country may be available at places such as Phnom Penh's Russian Market and Central Market. But goods for sale in Cambodian markets are largely targeted at Cambodians, who are poor by the standards of the rest of the world. No-brand and cheap brands dominate. If you are brand-conscious, you will probably need to import your favourite possessions into the country.

That said, markets in Cambodia do offer a surprisingly wide selection of goods. But finding any particular item may be a lot more difficult than in a First World Hypermarket. Firstly, there is the language problem of describing exactly what you want. Secondly, each vendor in the market is an independent entrepreneur who is unlikely to specialise in any particular product range. You may find socks and power tools sold at the same outlet. Thirdly, there are no directory guides and no information counters in the markets—you have to just walk around until you find what you want to buy, or fail to find it, as the case may be.

If you are renting a house in Cambodia, most residences are let with basic furnishings that can be supplemented with items from a local market. However, any furnishing with special requirements will have to be brought in.

Two specific items that I was unable to source in Cambodia were a coffee grinder and an electric jug with an automatic switch-off facility—both items essential in my household. So if you happen to need items like these, bring them with you, plus other favourite appliances your lifestyle requires.

Mobile phones and computers are ubiquitous in Cambodia as they are everywhere and can easily be purchased. On the other hand, since phones and laptop computers these days fall into the category of personal accessories automatically packed for any extended trip anywhere, there is no compelling reason to buy them in Cambodia.

Servants

Servants are readily available. Most visitors taking up residence employ a servant or two in some capacity or other, either on a part-time or full-time basis. Almost all resident expats, and most Cambodians in gainful employment, hire at least one part-time maid to clean, wash and iron clothes and maybe run the occasional errand.

Houses of expat standard will almost certainly have a tiny room to serve as quarters for live-in maids. Under this arrangement, a maid or cook will live in your house and, if you have children, double as a nanny. Some people will also employ a gardener, either full- or part-time, though the construction of many houses in Cambodia does tend to render gardeners superfluous. Houses are often right to the edge of properties, with the space between the outer wall of the house and boundary wall reduced to a thin concrete strip.

Cambodians are poorly paid by South-east Asian standards. Since trade unionism is unknown in Cambodia, workers fend for themselves. Those in casual employment with small businesses probably fare the worst. A motorcycle mechanic, for example, working for a small street-front shop might get paid about US$ 20 per month for working what is essentially a seven-day week on call. As a fringe benefit, he might get accommodation on the premises in the form of a hammock strung inside the garage and a plate of rice now and then.

Cambodians expect to get better rates of pay from foreigners. Rates for servants are individually negotiated, like most things in Cambodia. The going rate for full-time

maids and cooks is around US$ 100 per month plus board and keep. Part-time gardeners may run around US$ 20–30 a month. Since Cambodians tend to specialise, you may find yourself dealing with quite a number of servants for specific tasks. A driver is unlikely feel any obligation to work in the garden. A gardener won't want to do any driving.

The interaction between servants and their employers develops with the degree of warmth in the relationship. People vary of course but, as likely as not, once their services have been engaged, servants will be fiercely possessive of you. From your servants' viewpoint, your house is their territory. Once they have become established in your house and perhaps your affections, your servants will not want to relinquish their exclusive rights to running your house to anyone else.

Sometimes servants become part of the extended family—yours and theirs. You may well return home some days to find half their family attending to your chores. And, if additional services are required, your servants are likely to offer the services of a family that appears unlimited both in size and talents. They can be relied on to spirit up brothers and sisters who are plumbers, electricians, drivers, gardeners and cooks at a moment's notice.

This all raises the question of to what extent should your servants be allowed to see you as a friend, and whether you want them to be your friends. Friends are certainly harder to discipline than servants, but they are more rewarding and will do more for you.

Like most Cambodians, servants are unlikely to be trained in any particular skills. Even with the best intentions in the world, mishaps occur. Cambodians are likely to have far less experience with gadgets than you have. Clothes may get torn, stained or dyed in the washer when articles in non-fast red dye are washed with whites. Ornaments may get broken and plates smashed. Shocking things can happen to electrical appliances.

Cambodian labour laws are difficult for workers to apply and social services negligible. Servants may feel vulnerable to instant dismissal for trifling misdemeanours. When accidents occur, a cover up may be attempted. Broken objects tend to go missing without explanation.

You are advised to be tolerant of your servant's lack of skill, should that become evident, if for no better reason than that of a replacement servant is unlikely to be any better. Of course there is no reason to put up with anyone you can't get along with. But once a servant has become established, give them a present now and then and make them feel loved. Remember birthdays and important holidays.

As with all employees, terms of contract—pay, duties, etc.— should be made clear and best spelt out on commencement of service. It also pays to find out what normal employment conditions are. For example whether holidays (paid or unpaid) are normally part of the contract, and whether severance pay is paid at the completion of contracts.

Another question to consider: can servants be trusted? Since your servant could well be living on the breadline supporting a family of six on the measly wages you are paying, temptations may abound in your house. Both parties benefit if temptations for pilfering are kept to a minimum. Leaving money lying around is a prime reason that trust sometimes breaks down between servants and employers —perhaps for no better reason than people often think their piles of spare cash amount to more than they actually do.

HEALTH
Preventative Medicine
Health authorities issue plenty of advice for travellers to Cambodia. This is not a good place to get sick. Medical facilities in Cambodia are well below international standards. Phnom Penh and Siem Reap are equipped with basic facilities to handle emergencies. Elsewhere in the country, medical care is hard to get. The general philosophy on health care is to try your utmost to avoid getting sick in the first place by entering Cambodia as fit as you can be and taking minimal health risks when you are in the country.

Some specific recommendations, particularly at night, are to protect yourself from insects by taking precautions—such as wearing clothing that covers your arms and legs, and to keep your feet clean and dry at all times to prevent fungal infections. Bugs can enter your body through your feet and are hard to eradicate. Keep your shoes on (except in homes and other buildings that require you to take them off!) and avoid swimming in fresh water (sea-water bathing is generally ok).

The only injections you need to satisfy the requirements of Cambodian authorities are for yellow fever, and then only if you are coming from an infected area such as Africa and South America. However, as a precaution, you might want to get shots for the following diseases: hepatitis A; tuberculosis; typhoid; tetanus; and rabies. The US Department of State recommends additional shots for hepatitis B and Japanese encephalitis for those planning to work in rural areas for long periods. Cautious travellers may also want to pack anti-malarial pills, water sterilization pills, vitamins and mineral supplements.

Pharmacies

Pharmacies in Cambodia are divided into two types: licensed and unlicensed. Unlicensed pharmacies are quite likely to offer you the choice of a cocktail of antibiotics to treat whatever ailment you may be suffering, serious or trivial. Drugs are widely available to treat any self-diagnosed complaint without the formality of consulting a doctor. If you need particular drugs to treat your health condition, bring them with you. Availability and quality of drugs in Cambodia cannot be guaranteed.

Medical Insurance and Hospitals

Credit cards are not widely recognised in Cambodia. If you need medical treatment in Cambodia, you will need sufficient cash to pay your medical bills inside the country even if you are carrying medical insurance for making a later claim. Since medical care varies from basic to non-existent, for major sickness or accidents you will need to be treated in another country. Hospitals in Bangkok and Singapore are up to world standards, and hospitals in Vietnam are a lot better than those in Cambodia. Prior to leaving on your trip to Cambodia, travel guides advise people to take out not only medical insurance but medical evacuation insurance.

Dental Clinics

The dental profession was another branch of the Cambodian social services devastated when the Khmer Rouge came to town in 1975. Dental hygiene was not a high priority in Pol Pot's regime, perhaps because Pol Pot himself possessed a fine display of immaculate white teeth, as we can see from his many smiling photographs. Under the Khmer Rouge, the dental school in Phnom Penh was ransacked and closed. Dentists and suspected dentists were executed.

Dental services, like the rest of the medical profession and Cambodian social services in general, are still in the process of rebuilding. In 2000, the FDI World Dental Federation reported that 296 dentists were practising in Cambodia, or about one dentist to every 38,850 citizens (the comparative figures in the United States and United Kingdom are about

1,600 and 3,200 respectively). About 30 dentists a year now graduate from the rebuilt University of Health Science, the only medical school in Cambodia. NGOs in mobile units also provide basic dentistry care and oral hygiene services to Cambodians.

Health Tips for Travellers

- Bring your own medication or those of accompanying family members if you need specific drugs as they may not be obtainable in Cambodia.
- Prepare a first-aid kit that includes: antiseptic cream, anti-histamine, disinfectants, bandages and plasters, talcum powder, insect repellent and sunblock.
- Keep your shoes on as far as is possible (except in homes and other buildings that require you to take them off). Bugs can enter your body through your feet and are hard to eradicate.
- Make sure you have adequate health insurance for yourself and accompanying family members, including children. It is also best your health insurance policy provides for emergency evacuation in case of serious injury or illness. Bring enough cash to pay your medical bills.
- Before leaving, go for a health and dental check and ask your family doctor for advice on precautions and necessary vaccinations.
- For further advice, you should check your respective government's health and security advisory such as the US Department of State travel website (http://www/travel.state/gov); the United Kingdom's Foreign and Commonwealth Office at (http://www.fco.gov.uk) and the Department of Health (http://www.dh.gov.uk/PolicyAndGuidance/HealthAdviceForTravellers); and Australia's Smartraveller website (http://www.smartraveller.gov.au/zw-cgi/view/Advice/Cambodia).

SCHOOLS FOR EXPATRIATE CHILDREN

During the years of Khmer Rouge rule, all schools, Cambodian and international, were closed down. International schools remained closed until the Vietnamese forces withdrew in 1989. Since then, a handful of international schools have opened to service the needs of expatriate children.

The International School of Phnom Penh (ISPP) was the first school to reopen in the new era. It offers schooling for pre-schoolers through to Grade 12 and on to the international baccalaureate programme. Institutions in the United States have accredited ISPP, though not all its courses meet entry-level standards for US colleges. In addition, ISPP offers schooling for special needs children. Another US-based school, the Northbridge International School Cambodia (NISC), located near Phnom Penh's Pochentong Airport, is also accredited to run a US-style curriculum for students from preschool through to Grade 12.

The British International School of Phnom Penh offers the British curriculum and it also runs a Montessori kindergarten for children 2–5 years old. Another school offering the British curriculum is the Siem Reap International School.

SHOPPING

Shopping in Cambodia remains traditional. The country has no hypermarkets and few supermarkets and department stores. The best places for bargains are the traditional, street-market stalls. The best-known markets featuring an astonishing range of mostly cheap goods are the Russian Market and the Central Market, both in Phnom Penh. At these two markets, locally-made brand name clothes and imported CDs and DVDs are available at next-to-nothing prices. The Russian Market in particular offers an extraordinary range of goods from chainsaws to ganja. Second-hand clothes are also sold at markets at very low prices, right down to socks with 'pre-formed' holes in the toes. The culture of sock-wearing

in Cambodia is the culture of most material things: an item is only thrown away if it is completely used up.

Commerce in Cambodia is a mixture of fixed and floating charges. Prices at restaurants and hotels are fixed. So are prices for air, road, rail and bus tickets. At the market though, you are expected to bargain for goods. Bargaining is a game usually conducted in good spirit. The vendor knows what the bottom price is; the buyer doesn't. Since bargaining is conducted between individuals, the customary rules of hierarchical behaviour apply. Politeness rules, particularly during commercial dialogue with an elderly person. You are likely to get a better price if you smile, show consideration and enter into the spirit of the occasion.

A modest selection of new English-language books is available from Phnom Penh bookshops such as the Monument Bookshop, the Bayon Bookshop and the International Book Centre. Various other businesses such as supermarkets and restaurants and hotels stock a small selection of used books, usually popular fiction. Editions of new books sold in Cambodia are sometimes printed locally, thereby violating

Quiet moment at the market.

international copyright laws. Presumably Cambodia isn't a sufficiently large market for publishers to take action.

Most grades of photographic film are widely available in Cambodia and processing standards are generally reasonable.

Locating your Buddha Images

Buddha images are for sale everywhere. While Cambodians will sell you a range of Buddhas to make a dollar for themselves, if you are decorating your house in Cambodia with Buddha images, it is not difficult to inadvertently offend your local friends.

Buddhist icons are not really intended as decorative objects, although many are sold to tourists that way. If they are on display, the general rule is that they should be higher than you are. They should certainly not be at floor level. It is not a good idea to use Buddhas as doorstops. Buddha heads mounted on spikes and widely sold as tourist mementos are also likely to be considered disrespectful by your Buddhist friends. Buddhas with head and body intact and located at a respectful distance from the floor are quite acceptable and show you are in touch with local culture.

Replicas of Hindu gods are also for sale. Hindus appear to be fairly relaxed about displaying their many gods.

Bas-reliefs in Hindu temples, including the Hindu influences of Angkor, generally show a pantheon of gods interacting with each other to illustrate their legends.

The creation stories of Hinduism stem from Ramayana legends which occur as many versions in south-east Asia. The on-going balance between good and evil in the Hindu faith is reflected in the basic trinity of Hindu gods, Brahma, Vishnu and Shiva. Brahma is the creator of the world. Vishnu, the conservationist god, intercedes when the forces of evil get the upper hand in their eternal struggle with the forces of good. Shiva, the progressive god, favours change both as death and destruction as well as improvements to the existing order. Hindu gods suffer the full range of human emotions – anger, desire and compassion. They get married to other gods and have children, who are also gods. Shiva, for example, had two wives, Sati and Pavarti, and two sons, Ganesha and Kartikeya.

MONEY AND BANKING

You need to give more thought in Cambodia than in most countries to the question of generating cash for your day-to-day expenses. Credit cards are not yet widely accepted other than in a few top hotels.

Currently, the few ATMs installed in Cambodia are linked exclusively to the Canadia Bank, a local bank established as a joint venture between expat Cambodians living in Canada and the National Bank of Cambodia. Those touring Cambodia need to bring travellers cheques or cash, or make arrangements with Western Union to have money wired into the country. Western Union has four branches in Cambodia, three in Phnom Penh and one in Siem Reap.

In Cambodia two currencies—the riel and the US dollar—circulate freely. The Thai baht is also widely recognised, particularly in areas near the Thai border. Local currency paper notes in circulation have denominations of 50, 100, 200, 500, 1,000, 5,000, 10,000, 50,000 and 100,000 riels. With an exchange rate of about 4,000 riel to US$ 1 (which was the rate at the time of writing), you will need a large stack of riels to make an impression on your daily expenses.

You can change dollar notes into riels just about anywhere, though doing so has little point. US dollars are the easiest currency to carry around for all but the smallest transactions. In any case, since small change is given in riels even when payment is made in dollars, your holdings of riels will accumulate.

Traveller's cheques can be cashed readily at banks, travel agents, jewellery stores and a wide variety of other institutions. The preferred currency for traveller's cheques is US dollars. Other currencies may not be recognised. Traveller's cheques in US currency are cashed directly into US dollar notes at face value, minus a standard fee of 2 per cent of the cheque's face value, which saves the hassle of calculating how much you lost on the exchange rate when converting into another currency. American Express is the most widely recognised brand of traveller's cheque, followed by Thomas Cook.

Those staying or working in Cambodia are advised by most authorities against opening a bank account with a local bank. Banking regulations do exist in Cambodia but they are generally not enforced. Depositor's accounts are not insured and banks in Cambodia have a history of disappearing from time to time, along with the money of depositors. You are better to make arrangements between your regular out-of-country bank and a substantial in-country bank such as Cambodia Commercial Bank or Western Union.

CRIME

Cambodia has lived much of the past 40 years under the rule of the gun. Cambodians are also very poor. Violence begets violence. So does poverty. Violent crime is not that unusual in Cambodia and can be perpetrated by people you normally might trust, such as taxi drivers, police or military personnel.

While this shouldn't make the visitor unduly apprehensive, government agencies, such as the US Department of State, advise their clients to observe sensible precautions to avoid putting themselves in vulnerable situations. Travelling in groups is thought to be safer than travelling alone. Daylight is safer than night-time. Keeping valuables in a safe place, and carrying the minimum on your person is sensible, if obvious, advice. So also is keeping copies of important documents such as passports and traveller's cheques.

Those who get held up are advised to hand over what they have rather than to resist, then report their loss to the nearest authorities. Crimes against persons in Cambodia tend to be opportunistic rather than pre-planned. Petty crime, such as pick-pocketing, does occur, including hold-ups at knifepoint and gunpoint.

I have to say, my own experience in Cambodia has been just the opposite. I have found Cambodians honest to a fault. On one occasion in a Cambodian street, my money belt fell off without my noticing. It was returned to me by an obliging street kid who could have lived for a year on what he returned me. And I have had more that one shopkeeper run down the street to press into my hand a few cents of change I failed to collect. To be sure, disadvantaged people do pester you in Cambodia. But while people on the street do approach you for handouts, I have found their pestering more good humoured than threatening.

TRANSPORTATION
Getting the Hang of the Road

A certain level of enterprise and fearlessness is needed by visitors who intend to travel by ground transport, in particular for those brave souls who intend to drive themselves around. Anyone, foreigners included, is entitled to apply for a Cambodian driving licence. Riding a motorbike does not require a licence). Though most Cambodian car drivers themselves don't hold driving licences and have never taken a driving test, greater effort is expected from you, the visitor. If you are intending to drive a car in Cambodia, either the police or the car rental company may ask you to produce a Cambodian driving licence or at least an international driving licence.

Before taking to the roads, those who have never been to Cambodia might first want to check out the local driving habits. Since most Cambodians do not take driving tests, one cannot reasonably use the expression 'rules of the road' to describe the daily struggle for the right to road space on Cambodia's roads. 'Conventions of road usage' have evolved from the practice of road users rather than a formalised body of law.

The operating principle on rights to road space is vehicle size. If the oncoming vehicle is smaller than yours, you drive in front of it. If larger, you weave around it. In theory, traffic in Cambodia drives on the right hand side. But I have never visited anywhere on Earth where traffic spends such a high proportion of its time on the wrong side of the road as in Phnom Penh. The overriding objective among the Phnom Penh driving fraternity appears to be to avoid stopping. The principal strategy in achieving this objective is to adopt a system that allows motorists at an intersection to turn in any direction at any time.

Right-hand turns without stopping are simple enough since vehicles driving on the right hand side of the road. Left-hand turns are trickier as vehicles turning left must cross traffic coming in the opposite direction. The general procedure here is to weave a path through lines of oncoming traffic in the street from which you are executing the turn, get to the extreme left hand side of the road, make your turn, then

Downtown Phnom Penh—drive any side you like.

weave your way back to the right as and when gaps in the oncoming traffic permit.

Since about three-quarters of Cambodian traffic travels on two wheels, such intricate travel patterns are possible but, from a visitor's perspective, no less daunting. Adding to the hazards of interweaving traffic and the poorly surfaced roads are the frequency with which Phnom Penh's street lights fail, and a persistent tendency of local traffic to travel without lights at night.

Under these circumstances, the frequency of accidents comes as no great surprise to anyone. The one upside of the road conditions is that traffic is prevented from travelling all that quickly. Phnom Penh traffic moves at a leisurely pace, which is just as well, since Phnom Penh driving conventions are clearly incompatible with speed.

Peddling Around Town on a Cyclo

Hiring a cyclo or pedlo in downtown Phnom Penh is not a bad way of getting into the swing of things on the road. The cyclo is a modified bicycle, usually of 1950s vintage, that has been altered to include a passenger seat and a third wheel. The driver sits in a seat beside and slightly in front of the passenger. Spare parts for the cyclo appear to have run out some time ago. The machines commonly lack the most ordinary accessories—like pedals and brakes. Cyclo drivers compensate for deficiencies of their equipment with fearlessness and energy.

Limited to a notional power of about one-quarter horse-power, cyclos are one of the slower vehicles on the road. So far as other vehicles are concerned, with the pecking order of Cambodian road usage determined by speed, power and vehicle size, cyclos rank behind cars, motorbikes and trucks, but ahead of pedestrians and ox-carts.

From a passenger's viewpoint, low speed seems like a disadvantage in making your presence felt as a major road user. Undaunted, cyclos weave their way through lines of oncoming traffic, imposing their rights to space on the road in the manner of vehicles ten times their weight and speed. Though this can be stressful for passengers unused to Cambodian roads, a quick survey of your chauffeur may offer a modicum of comfort.

You are likely to find that your cyclo driver is a thin wiry man in his 50s with whipcord lower leg development—legs that clearly have done millions of pedal revolutions over their career. Here is an expert who has peddled these urban roads for 30 years and lived to tell the tale. Surely he should survive one more journey, even if he is travelling in the wrong direction on the wrong side of the road and squeezed in between two lanes of oncoming traffic!

Riding a Bicycle

People in South-east Asia are not widely into cycling as a form of recreation, though working bikes, often laden with

Biking the goods home.

all manner of materials and maybe small animals and birds, are plentiful on Cambodian roads. In terms of local culture, cycling is for those who cannot afford a motorbike, which in turn is for those who cannot afford a car.

Cycling fits in somewhere in the social order between walking and riding an ox-cart, and is afforded commensurate respect and precious few road rights. Broadly speaking, cyclists are expected to give way to other road users with the exception of pedestrians.

The Ubiquitous Moto

The next step up from a cyclo is a moto—South-east Asia's ubiquitous vehicle. The word moto is an abbreviation of motorbike and is used in Cambodia to describe any motorised two-wheel vehicle. Thousands of small motorbikes, mostly driven by men in baseball caps, roam the streets, prepared to take you any place you might need to go.

The moto has the advantages of availability and flexibility. Someone once tried to start a bus service in Phnom Penh but the idea didn't take off. Passengers weren't prepared to walk to a bus stop, wait for the bus and get dropped off somewhere other than at their front door. In Phnom Penh, no one waits

The moto—Cambodia's all-purpose vehicle.

more than 30 seconds for a choice of motos, and they take you anywhere! No bus service can compete with that.

Motos are the principal form of personnel transport in Phnom Penh and regional towns. Far more motos ply the streets of Phnom Penh than there are passengers to use them. Stand on any street corner in Phnom Penh and a dozen motos will materialise before you to offer their services. One reason for this large fleet of motos is that a moto provides part-time employment. Since no licence is needed to operate a passenger-carrying motorbike in Cambodia, anyone with access to a moto can set themselves up in business in short notice. Many of the moto drivers around Phnom Penh are students earning income in their off-study hours.

For those whose paramount need is to get from Point A to Point B as quickly as possible, the moto's ability to dodge other traffic will usually deliver you to your destination faster than other means of travel. A downside is that moto riding is moderately hazardous. In any given day of moto travel, you will have a number of near misses, and on a bad day you will have a collision, usually just a scrape against someone with little harm done.

As a passenger you have little protection, either in the physical sense or the legal sense. Few drivers wear crash helmets and the chances of a crash helmet being available for the use of a passenger are slim. It almost goes without saying that, from the point of view of the moto passenger, no luxuries such as insurance are offered. If you have an accident of any sort in Cambodia, you are very much on your own. All guidebooks on Cambodia advise their clients to take out the maximum in travel and health insurance before entering the country.

The moto knows no passenger limits. The most people I have ever seen on a single moto is seven, four in line, two babies on the handlebars and one small child clinging to the back. Positively identifying which individual was driving the moto was impossible, though it probably wasn't either of the babies.

Cambodians have far more advanced two-wheeled-passenger skills than the average visitor, and can carry an extraordinary range of cargo while perched on the moto's pillion seat, or elsewhere on the bike. A group of three Cambodians will think nothing of flagging down a single moto and clambering aboard. Girls perch demurely, two at a time, on the back of the bike, riding side-saddle while clutching their packages with nary a finger on the moto.

As well as taking the family out for a Sunday drive, motos are Cambodia's general purpose vehicle, modified to perform almost any task. Cargo-carrying motos transport anything and everything. They deliver rice to the rice mill, live chickens and ducks to the market. They tow lumber, carry thatch and transport food stalls to and from point of use. They get hitched to trailers, acquire additional wheels and carry any manner of accessories from chicken coops to the tray of a flat-bed truck.

Though a family of Cambodians will fearlessly clamber onto a moto, the uninitiated will most likely find their first ride as pillion passenger on a moto a little daunting, even when travelling solo.

For a start, you don't want to be carrying too many possessions when you hail a moto. You need at least one hand free to hang onto the grab handle (usually located at the rear of your seat), a very necessary accessory every time the bike hits a pothole or glances off another bike. Aware of your likely lack of skill as a passenger, some drivers may oblige you by carrying your spare parcels on the space between him and the handlebars.

According to some reports, an additional risk to accepting a ride on a moto is that passengers may be dragged off the backs of motos by thieves acting in collusion with the moto driver. Such incidents, though most uncommon, have led not only to loss of possessions but also, in some cases, to serious injury or even death when a passenger suffered a fatal head injury after hitting the ground.

Taxis

Cambodia has plenty of taxis competing for your custom. Taxis hang out at the usual places—airports, expensive hotels— or just cruise the streets. Taxis in Cambodia don't have meters, so negotiating the fare is part of the contract. Local practice is for the customer to estimate the worth of the journey upon arrival at the destination and to hand over the precise amount estimated. This saves the hassle of extracting change from the taxi driver. If the taxi driver doesn't agree with the customer's assessment, he lets the customer know. Visitors used to taxis with meters may find this procedure difficult. The alternative is to inform the taxi driver of your destination and ask for an estimate in advance.

Towns in Cambodia are small, trips are short and fares within urban areas are a maximum of a few dollars. The taxi driver's first asking price is likely to be around twice the going rate. From there on, you can bargain if you feel you have the energy, in the sapping tropical heat, to argue over a few dollars, or more likely, a few cents.

One further point that should also be noted is that taxi drivers, even while driving with passengers onboard, follow the tradition of acknowledging the presence of religious monuments and personnel by bowing in their direction, with both hands brought to the forehead. Seeing the taxi-driver's hands leave the wheel and his eyes leave the road to pay respect to a passing temple may trouble the visitor. Probably the least stressful thing you can do while riding in a taxi in Cambodia is to look out the side window and let the driver get on with what he does best.

To Drive or to be Driven

Opportunities for motoring in Cambodia are limited. The road system, as has already been noted, presents a challenging driving environment. Hiring a self-drive car is one of the most flexible options for getting around, though this does carry some risks. Cambodia's roads are tough on cars and no roadside assistance is likely to be available in the event of a breakdown. In addition, part of the car hire contract may require that you leave your passport as security with the car hire company, increasing problems you might face from accident, breakdown or theft of the car. In addition, proving who you are as you drive around sans passport, especially if you are traversing the country, can also complicate your journey.

Those on long-term assignments may consider buying a car or leasing one on a long-term leasing deal. Cars are moderately expensive by the standards of most countries. Lease repayments are likely to set you back around US$ 250–350 a month. A permanent driver, if required, is likely to cost a further US$ 150 per month.

Those thinking of buying a second-hand car need first to convince themselves that the car they want to buy hasn't been stolen. Cambodian law states that cars are meant to carry licence plates; but many don't. According to Cambodia's Ministry of Transport, a computerised database of car ownership will be up and running by 2006, when all cars are scheduled to be equipped with licence plates. Until then, ownership of cars is difficult to establish.

Black or White, Closed Eye or Open Eye

Relative to other countries, the most expensive commodity in Cambodia is probably petrol. Cambodia has regular petrol stations, but it has many more roadside stands where petrol can be bought in fractions of a litre out of a Coke or whisky bottle (Johnny Walker Black Label is a popular brand of petrol in Cambodia). Two types of petrol on sale are regular 'white' or 'open eye' petrol selling at regular fully-taxed price, and 'black' or 'closed eye' petrol, thought to be stolen from

Filing up, Cambodia-style.

pipelines in Thailand and selling at about 80 per cent of the regular price.

Oil-company service stations sell open eye petrol. Roadside stands sell the closed eyed variety, in 375 ml, 500 ml and 750 ml containers. Since 80 per cent of vehicles are motos, people may buy petrol one bottle at a time, generally just before they are about to run dry. Petrol gauges in Cambodia spend much of their time lodged on 'empty'. One litre of petrol is considered an average purchase.

Having an Accident

No one seeks a car accident, but the nature of accidents is that they happen. In the event of an accident, the chances are that the authorities will try to make a dollar out of everyone's misfortune based on the ability of the parties to the accident to pay. Under Cambodian law, no one is meant to move anything until the police arrive at the scene. When the police do show up, their procedures are unpredictable. They may also take the vehicles involved into custody until they complete their investigations, and this will complicate your life. If the accident is minor and no one is seriously injured, it is better to make your arrangements with the other party to the accident before the police get involved. If the accident

Transport Tips for Cities

- Driving in Cambodia is not advisable unless you have nerves of steel and feel up to navigating the roads of Cambodia's cities.
- An international or Cambodian driving licence is required if you wish to hire a car.
- Spend a few days observing the traffic before proceeding to drive on your own. Watch how the locals negotiate the turns and overtake other vehicles.
- Watch out for the potholes!
- Public transport in ascension by speed: cyclo/pedlo; bicycle; moto; larger motorbike; taxi and hired car.
- Bicycles can be hired very cheaply, but the quality can vary considerably. Those coming to Cambodia from Thailand can choose to buy or hire a bike from Thailand prior to entering Cambodia.

is major and people are injured, then there is little alternative than to allow events to take their course.

GETTING ACROSS COUNTRY AND BEYOND
Catching the Plane

The safest way around Cambodia is by air. Cambodia has two international airports: Pochentong or Phnom Penh International Airport about 8 km (5 miles) west of Phnom Penh, and Siem Reap-Angkor International Airport. Flights to either of these two airports connect to most of the major South-east Asian cities such as Bangkok, Kuala Lumpur, Singapore and Ho Chi Minh City. Daily flights from Vientiane in Laos are also available. The cities serving both Cambodia's international airports are readily accessible by taxis, at fares of about US$ 5 or below. Cambodia also has seven domestic airports: Rattankiri, Mondulkiri, Stung Treng,

- Carry no more that one item when riding a moto so you have a hand available to hang onto the grab handle.
- You may hire a motorbike in Cambodia, but you may have to leave your passport with the hire firm as security. Unless the firm offers you insurance, should the motorbike be stolen, you may have to reimburse the owner the price of a new bike.
- If you decide to buy a motorbike, check first that it has a road tax sticker.
- Cambodian taxis do not have meters. You either negotiate the fare at the start of the journey, or pay what you think the journey was worth at your destination.
- You may buy or lease a car for long-term use. You may choose to drive the car yourself or hire a driver. Compared to most other countries, the price of cars in Cambodia is high.

Battambang, Koh Kong, Previhear and Kratie. At the time of writing, an eighth airport at Sihanoukville was available only for charter flights.

Domestic airlines in Cambodia have started up and closed down with some regularity in recent times. Anything that's written about them can date fast. An airline casualty in August 2004 was First Cambodia Airlines which discontinued flights indefinitely after heavy financial losses. Siem Reap Airways, a Bangkok Airways subsidiary, offers flights to most internal destinations at about US$ 60 per ticket. Two other domestic airlines, President Airlines and Phnom Penh Airways, were also in operation. An intention to launch a new international airline has also been announced. At the time of writing, the scheduled launch date for this enterprise, a joint venture including Air France and Phuket Air of Thailand, was 'unspecified'.

Boating Across Cambodia

River travel is practicable if you happen to travel north-south, the direction most of Cambodia's rivers flow. East-west travel by boat is more difficult.

The major navigable rivers running through the centre of the country are the Tonle Sap River, which runs down the western flank of the central alluvial plain, and the Mekong, which runs down the eastern flank. Phnom Penh is built at the confluence of the Mekong and the Tonle Sap River. Downstream, not far from Phnom Penh, the Mekong splits into two branches, the Mekong and the Bassac, both of which are navigable.

The Siem Reap to Phnom Penh boat trip is the most popular boat journey in Cambodia. A choice of boats is available for the trip, with ticket prices increasing with boat-speed. A speedboat ride costs around US$ 25 and the slow boat US$ 10–15. The speedboat is a substantial craft about 21 m (70 ft) long and powered by a couple of large diesel inboard engines. Prices for locals, like most things in Cambodia, are considerably less than tourist rates. The separate price scales do annoy some visitors, but you shouldn't allow this to spoil your day. Compared to most places, prices are still cheap in this poor country where the cost of a boat ticket may be two weeks' wages for a local.

The boat journey runs the length of Tonle Sap Lake where conditions may get choppy. The smaller boats may have negligible spray protection. Both passengers and luggage of budget class boats may need to enter into the spirit of the occasion since either may be splattered with water from time to time. Speedboats, by contrast, offer totally enclosed, air-conditioned cabins and sport closed channel television to entertain you while they whisk you to your destination.

The journey to Siem Reap from Phnom Penh by speedboat is about three hours. Going by boat is altogether easier and more comfortable than using Route 6, the overland alternative. That said, for most of the way across Tonle Sap Lake, there is little to see except patches of water hyacinth and distant shores, whereas Route 6 runs through some interesting scenery, including the laterite bridge at Kampong Kdei, dating from the Angkor era and still in use, a tribute to the engineering skills of the bridge builders of that time.

One drawback of boating during the busy season is that operators may overbook, selling more tickets than there are seats. In these circumstances they will still take you, but may expect you to perch on the roof of the boat, from which vantage point the view of the proceedings is excellent and relatively dry, but the handholds are precarious.

Boats on the Mekong route take you as far as Kratie to see the area's main attraction, the Irrawaddy freshwater dolphins. Availability of boats depends on the level of the river. In the wet season, from June to November, water level is high and the boats run. If plenty of rain falls in the wet season, the boats may run as late as February. But by the end of the dry season (April to May), boats can become stranded at low points in the river.

Crossing the Country by Land

Though air is the easiest way to get around between population centres in Cambodia, you do see more of the place if you travel by land transport. If you are thinking of travelling by road by whatever means, unless you are training for the Paris-Dakar Rally, the first thing to do when planning your trip is to check the latest road conditions.

During the wet season, Cambodia's flat low alluvial plain areas are subject to seasonal flooding. Major towns, including Phnom Penh, flood readily. Road conditions vary with the weather, the season and how recently a maintenance crew passed that way. Many of the major roads are now surfaced, though often with sections of unmade road somewhere along the way.

From a road transport point of view on secondary roads, Cambodia's seasons can be regarded as the season of dust (the dry season) and the season of mud (the wet season). Of the two, the season of mud is probably more comfortable for the passenger; but harder on the transportation equipment and more prone to delays and stranding. During the monsoon season, secondary roads may become impassable even to four-wheel drives. Even roads shown on the map as major motorways can be closed at times.

Touring on Two Wheels

Cycling in Cambodia, like most forms of surface locomotion in the country, is more hazardous than in most other places. Cambodians are likely to regard cycling tourists as a curiosity, affirming a widely held belief that tourists from the non-Asian world are strange beasts. Here are a group of people who have spent thousands of dollars to visit a small poor country, toiling away in the hot sun, something most Cambodians wouldn't dream of doing unless they happen to be a labourer in a rice field. And they are not even paid for their efforts! Why wouldn't these foreigners hire a car or at least get around on a motorbike? And when they get somewhere, they proceed to photograph rundown rural villages without water, electricity or sewerage. What is the fascination? And why would these foreigners in expensive cycling gear travel miles to buy handwoven, rudely-made fabrics?

That said, cycling is a great way to see the countryside for those who aren't in a hurry. In some ways it's more comfortable to negotiate potholes at low speed with big wheels than at higher speed with smaller wheels. If cycling is your interest, you can bring your wheels with you or hire a set when you get there. Hiring bikes, like most things in Cambodia, is a hit-and-miss affair. The quality of the offerings varies considerably. Prices are low; US$ 2–3 per day is a reasonable budget. Ideally, for most journeys you make, a sturdy mountain or hybrid bike designed for tough conditions is recommended. On the other hand, you may be offered a 50-year-old fixed-wheel machine with no gears, no brakes and a pedal missing. The other option for those considering a bicycle holiday in Cambodia is to hire or buy their bike in Thailand, assuming they are coming from that direction.

When cycling cross-country, one thing that is widely available throughout Cambodia, like the rest of South-east Asia, is food and drink. It's very difficult to travel more than a few kilometres down through roads without encountering a roadside stall that offers a wide range of basic food commodities—fruit, rice dishes, nuts, soft drink and beer along with a wide selection of cooked food, from noodles and sticky rice dishes upwards.

Buzzing Around on a Motorbike

While motos, as in motor-scooters, are Cambodia's most popular form of people moving, larger motorbikes are quite a bit less common. For the skilled bike rider, a motorbike of 250cc and upwards is a pretty good way to travel across country, particularly in the dry season. The roads are a lot easier to traverse on two wheels than four. However, the risks of hiring a bike are greater in Cambodia than most places. Whatever you choose to drive, the country's unique conventions of road usage increase the hazards of driving yourself.

For those who want to rent a motorbike rather than bring their own, there is also the question of whether the transaction is legal. The law on this subject is uncertain. After many accidents, leasing bikes to foreigners is certainly discouraged, though what the law has to say may not make much difference to the motorbike rental shop. In all likelihood, they'll rent you a bike anyway. If so, you will probably be asked to sign an agreement that the bike be returned in good condition and lodge your passport as security.

The greatest risk to fulfilling your end of the bargain on this contract is that the bike will be stolen. According to some (unconfirmed) accounts, some rental shops have an arrangement with street kids to steal their own bikes back from their hirers to make themselves an extra dollar! Other problems are accident and breakdown. Some dealers may offer insurance against accident, breakdown and theft. If so, this cover is worth getting. But if worst comes to the worst and you are unable to return the bike, you are left with the task of negotiating the return of your passport. Failing that, you may have to reimburse the owner the cost for a new bike.

The alternative for bike riders is to buy a bike. There are plenty of old bikes for sale in Cambodia. If you do decide to buy a bike, do first check it has a road tax sticker.

Coaches, Minibuses, Taxis and Trucks

Other assorted land vehicles you may wish to consider range from shared taxis, buses, minibuses, lorries and pick-ups, in that order of ticket price. A normal maximum passenger load for a taxi is seven, including the driver. If you want to travel in greater comfort and leave at a time of your choosing, you have the option of buying up all the seats in the taxi and having the taxi all to yourself.

Coaches are a cheap way to get between major centres. The level of comfort varies with the routes, but is generally reasonable. Buses are usually air-conditioned, at least to some extent, and generally run to a schedule. Regular coach services are cheap; typical ticket prices are US$ 3 from Phnom Penh to Sihanoukville and US$ 14 from Phnom Penh to Bangkok. Buses can be booked in hotels, guesthouses and street-kiosks. Tickets are issued with seat numbers to avoid overbooking. In addition, you are usually relieved of the responsibility and effort of finding the bus terminus. A minibus or the coach itself will pick you up from wherever you bought your coach tickets from. This system works well.

The alternative to a coach is the minibus, for which there is often no timetable for departures or arrivals. Vehicles will leave when they have assembled a full load of passengers. Minibus services have decreased greatly in recent years and there is really no compelling reason to take one. Coaches are an order of magnitude more comfortable than minibuses.

Downmarket of the minibus is the lorry and below that is the pick-up. Ubiquitous around Asia, lorries are fitted with a pair of benches on both sides running down the length of the vehicle. A lorry will only get going when it's full or overflowing. For the pick-up, you just pile in the back and sit wherever there is a space.

Lorry and pick-up travel in Cambodia is for the hardy, the life-weary and the exceptionally poverty-stricken. If you are travelling in the dry season, you are not only going to get covered in red dust, you will also breathe plenty of it too. Dust in Cambodia may come replete with pathogens and bacteria that will not improve your health.

The most nerve-wrecking aspect of travelling by land may be the journey itself. Cambodian roads being what they are, scrutinising the talents and techniques of Cambodian road users is not the most stress-free way to pass the time. You may be wise to spend the time travelling immersed in a good book!

A Near Miss

I had one near miss while travelling by bus in Cambodia. En route to Battambang our bus was following another bus. The elements of the incident were poor maintenance and good driving. The bus in front braked suddenly to avoid a dog but its brake lights weren't working. Our driver reacted pretty quickly and slammed on his brakes, but the rate of deceleration was poor. The bus in front had far better brakes than we did. For a moment, it looked like we would concertina the bus in front, but our driver with great skill and relentless use of the horn managed to thread our vehicle between the bus in front and an oncoming ox-cart.

Touring by Car

The easiest way to travel around Cambodia may be by organised tour, complete with air-conditioned cars or vans, guides and possibly accommodation en route.

However, some people may consider this too restrictive. For the more adventurous, the most flexible way of getting around under your own steam is a hire-car. Like hiring a motorbike, this comes with the disadvantages that you may have to leave your passport as security with the car hire company and no assistance is likely to be available in the event of accident and breakdown.

An alternative to a self-drive hired car is to hire a car and driver. This is little more than a long-distance taxi ride. Taxi drivers hang out at tourist spots offering to take you anywhere you want for the right price. Since driving skill and vehicle condition vary widely in Cambodia, if you are contemplating hiring a car and driver, a short road test of driver skills and equipment is recommended before embarking on a longer journey. Ask your driver to take you some place downtown on a trial basis. If you feel his skills measure up, you can suggest a longer journey the next day. Most drivers will jump at the chance to get a full day's travel. They may even suggest a trip round the country for a fixed price.

For those planning their own itineraries, travel agents, tourist offices or large hotels provide car hire information and help you plan your trip. Road and tourist authorities advise against travelling at night. Potholes are harder to see and so is the traffic, since many vehicles travel at night without lights—usually caused by nothing more serious than a blown globe that hasn't been replaced. Cambodian attitudes to maintenance might be described as casual. Other hazards, particularly at night, are cattle straying onto roads and banditry. Since Cambodia is not a big country, you can easily break your journey into short steps and travel only during daylight hours.

Hopping on a Train

The Cambodian railway system was built by the French. The last major rail project in Cambodia was the Phnom Penh to Battambang line, completed in 1932. Little construction and maintenance have been undertaken since. As a result, Cambodian Rail holds the title as the worst railway in South-east Asia. Trains creak along and journeys take a long time. On most routes, the condition of the track is so poor that trains travel at a maximum speed of 30 km an hour (19 miles an hour), with the average speed much lower, depending on the state of the track, the rolling stock and perhaps the weather. Trains quite often get cancelled when the state of the track gets too bad.

Not only is the service slow, it is notoriously uncomfortable. Seating is spartan. You are advised to bring your own cushion, or not to travel by train at all if you have a bad back. On the other hand, the rail track passes through some spectacular landscapes. At the speed of travel, and with the frequent stoppages, there are some wonderful photo opportunities for those within range of a window.

For rail lovers, the Cambodian rail system may be worth the trouble for the sake of the trains and the stations. In the 1950s and 1960s, during the heyday of Sihanouk's leadership, the prince would travel around his father's kingdom in a luxury train that, in 2000, was restored to its former glory by steam engine enthusiasts. Regrettably, this grand old engine has rarely been sighted since being launched into limited service a few years ago.

Cambodia has plans to upgrade its rail infrastructure, including a link to the proposed ASEAN railway to run from Singapore through several South-east Asian countries to Kunming, China. The country is presently seeking foreign aid funds of between US$ 100–300 million for the proposal. The scheme includes a 48-km (30-mile) line connecting Poipet to Sisophon, and an upgrade of the existing 338-km (211-mile) line between Sisophon and Phnom Penh. The Malaysian government has already pledged US$ 8 million worth of used equipment to the Poipet-Sisophon project.

THE CULINARY FARE

CHAPTER 6

'Fish is prepared and served in a variety
of ways: fresh and raw; steamed or boiled...
utilising heads, tails and the in-between;
dried and salted, and pickled in brine.'
—Carol Selva Rajah in *Seafood Sensation*

RICE IS LIFE

Rice is Cambodia's most important agricultural product and the country's staple food. A large shallow bowl of polished white rice will be provided as the base for almost all meals. Brown rice, in contrast, is much harder to come by. Other major ingredients in the Cambodian diet are fish and 'morning glory'—a leafy plant grown in ponds and tasting a bit like spinach. Meat is used sparingly, usually chopped into tiny pieces and stirred into the mix.

Flavour additives include the full range of spices, sauces and garnishes like coriander, lemon grass, ginger, spring onions, garlic, basil leaves, chives, grated mango, chilli and fish sauce. The results are like a mild variation of Thai food, though with not quite the range of flavours, dishes and ingredients. In addition, the French culinary influence is still evident. French restaurants in Cambodia offer the full Gallic fare. From streetside stalls, French-style bread and long loaves along with cheese are on sale in most places.

The Cambodian version of sticky rice, called *grolan*, is sold as bamboo tubes stuffed with a mixture of rice, sugar, black beans and coconuts. *Grolan* is a complete food source, and sells for almost nothing. If you run short of money in Cambodia, survival is still possible on an all-*grolan* diet. As an alternative, Thai style sticky rice wrapped in a banana leaf makes a nutritious high-energy meal, also for a few cents a serve.

Bananas a speciality: Central
Market at Phnom Penh.

The most common method of cooking Cambodian-style is stir-frying in a large wok over a gas or charcoal flame. A wide variety of stews and curries are also part of the diet. Charcoal-grilled chicken and fish are offered at roadside stalls all over the country. Sit down or takeaway meals can be customised anyway you want from combinations of vegetables, meat, fish and seafood. Chicken and pork are the two most common meats, though most things that once ate, lived and breathed may be added to the pot.

Among the exotic food items for sale at Cambodian markets are small birds, frogs' legs, eels, grasshoppers and spiders. The spider range is headed by large tarantulas served deep-fried. Those unfamiliar with this delicacy are advised to nibble cautiously, starting from the outside and working inwards. Legs can be broken off and the skinny threads of meat inside pulled out in the manner of crab's legs. But a taste for the bitter soft body at the centre may take some generations to acquire.

The range of soft drinks on offer is typical of most places. To serve their drinks cold, small roadside cafes lacking electricity stack their drinks in iceboxes. Now and again, large blocks of ice are delivered and sawn up into manageable chunks for loading into the freezer and into the drinks themselves.

EATING OUT

The cheapest food in Cambodia, and some of the best food, is sold from street stalls that line the country's roads. Simple, delicious and nutritious meals are available all over the country at ridiculously low prices. Like its neighbouring countries, eating out is a tradition in Cambodia. The majority of the Cambodian population eat at street stalls or roadside restaurants as a matter of course.

Noodle and rice dishes are staples. Each day, if you get up early enough, you will see the noodle stands being set up. In the simplest case, proprietors will arrive at their designated spot carrying their cooking utensils, cutlery, crockery and ingredients contained in baskets suspended from each end of bamboo poles slung across their shoulders. Roadside restaurants are a bit more elaborate; those at the top end of the market provide tables and chairs for the comfort of their customers. Roadside vendors and streetside restaurants offer excellent value.

Ordering is slightly complicated if you don't know the language. Pointing, smiling, head shaking or nodding at the appropriate moments can get you a long way. Restaurants, even in markets, may have bilingual menus and the second language is likely to be the ubiquitous English.

In more formal restaurants with table service, the accepted method of attracting a waiter is to gesture with the hand held palm down, extending the fingers and drawing them into the palm in the manner of gripping a monkey bar. The gesture is repeated a few times until eye contact is established. In theory at least, the waiter will then come to your table.

When you are invited out, the senior person normally volunteers to pay the bill. Going Dutch Western-style, as in splitting the bill between diners, is considered stingy. The Cambodian government introduced a 10 per cent VAT (value added tax) on goods and services in 1999. On top of this, a service charge of around 10 per cent may be levied in some establishments. Tipping is not universally practised; though waiters are likely to be so poorly paid that a tip will be greatly appreciated. And there's a fairly good chance tips collected will go to the waiter rather than the establishment. At least that's what the law provides. Article 134 of the 1997 Labour Law stipulates that '...tips must be collected by the employer and distributed in full to the personnel in contact with the clientele'.

Cutlery protocol is typical for South-east Asia. Most meals are eaten with a spoon and fork. Chopsticks may be supplied for some dishes such as noodles. A bowl of toothpicks is provided at most tables. Discreet tooth-picking at table is normal behaviour. Accepted protocol for picking teeth at the table is to wield the toothpick in the right hand while obscuring its activities from the view of other diners with the left hand. After use, the toothpick is left on the dinner plate.

French legacy—fresh roadside baguettes.

Food and Indigestion

If you are from the West, you will probably eat healthier in Cambodia than in your country of origin. The nutritional content of traditional Asian food is higher than most Western foods. There is less fat and sugar, and the preservative content is low as most meals are prepared with fresh ingredients. Meals, simple or complicated, are delicious.

Nevertheless it pays to be cautious. While accounts of 'Bombay belly' or 'Bangkok belly' may be exaggerated, no one wants a 'Cambodia catastrophe' and most people who have been in Asia a long time can cite a personal experience or two with food poisoning. Some hardy bacteria that have no place in your digestive tract make their living in this region.

The most dangerous food additive in Cambodia is water. By the time it reaches Cambodia, the citizens, animals, insects and bacteria of five upstream countries have used the waters of the Mekong River for many purposes. Cambodia offers no guarantees that residue from this frequent usage will be removed by their water treatment plant. You should never drink water out of a tap, or even wash your teeth with it.

Water needs to be boiled for at least five minutes to kill off the hardiest of troublesome organisms that it might contain. The US Department of State, always super-cautious about the welfare of its clients, recommends boiling for ten minutes.

People from the West are accustomed to using tap water for all sorts of purposes so it's easy to slip up. The key to avoiding tap water is to keep bottled water on hand, whatever you are doing. For example, it's wise to have a bottle of water on your bedside table for those thirsty times in the middle of the night when you might otherwise stumble to the bathroom to refresh yourself from the tap.

When buying bottled water in Cambodia, check the cap on the bottle before use. Cambodia is a poor country in which the recycling psychology finds all sorts of ingenious ways to express itself. Street kids who pick up discarded bottles can earn a handy piece of small change if they can refill the bottle with tap water and sell it to you as a new product. Be careful too with ice. The act of freezing does not kill bacteria. By adding ice, you run the risk of contaminating your bottled water or canned soft drink with the very organisms you are trying to avoid by not drinking tap water.

Food may be cooked in a single pot that isn't likely to be cleaned very often. Since Cambodian food mixes its flavours, this is not a problem for most dishes and diners. However, vegetarians may not be completely sure that food is free of animal products. The ubiquitous shrimp appears in many vegetable dishes.

To the chagrin of some from the West, common dishes don't normally come with a serving spoon. Diners will use their own spoons to help themselves to food from common dishes. During the course of dinner, diners may dip their spoons into common dishes a number of times. The degree to which infections are spread as a result is not known. Nor are survival chances of bacteria introduced by someone's spoon into a bowl of Cambodian curry.

As well as paying the greatest respect to the water supply, staying healthy in Cambodia may take a little more effort than in more sanitised parts of the world. Health authorities advocate washing hands with soap before eating.

Cambodians themselves tend to be fastidious about personal cleanliness when dining out, even to the extent of wiping all their cutlery and glassware before use with tissues provided at the table.

Government authorities and some guidebooks warn against eating street food. However, the worst Bangkok belly incidents in my experience have come from food in upmarket restaurants where you can't see what's going on in the kitchen. There are two advantages in eating off the street if you are concerned about food poisoning. One is that you can stand next to the food vendors while they are cooking your meal. Most dishes are either boiled in large vats or fried at high temperature. Viewing the ingredients sizzling in the pot may reassure you that no living organism is going to survive the cooking process. Secondly, you can verify the ingredients are fresh since you will see them chopped up prior to entering the pan. Ingredients, fresh or otherwise, are laid out before your eyes.

'The Turkey Did Him In!'

The most severe stomach infection incident I know of, that took place in South-east Asia, was that of an acquaintance who was served a turkey sandwich in a five-star hotel that has occasionally been voted one of Asia's top three hotels. Shortly after his meal, the victim of the turkey sandwich episode was in hospital with a severe intestinal infection that took some days to overcome. He subsequently informed the hotel who admitted liability, paid all his hospital bills and as compensation offered an extended period of five-star accommodation for absolutely nothing. The condition was he wouldn't divulge the story to the media. (For this reason the hotel cannot be named here).

Some off-the-street dishes do carry extra risks. One is fried chicken. Since you don't normally see the chicken killed and plucked, you might well be getting something that has been re-heated a few times. Bacteria enjoy taking up residence in the skins of chickens. Salads may also be suspect since the ingredients may have been washed in stream water at the back of the shop. Local dairy products are also to be avoided. Fruit is best bought in nature's

Cambodian mobile fast food restaurant.

container, with peel still intact rather than peeled by someone else.

Of course if you want to stay Western, Cambodia offers a selection of Western restaurants. French menus are a speciality of the region. Western fast-food chains are less well represented. Those who yearn for the reassuring sight of the golden arches are likely to be disappointed. The global-standard culinary delights of familiar names like McDonald's, Dunkin' Donuts or Burger King have yet to arrive in Cambodia. However, finger-lickin'-good substitutes, such as KFC (Khmer Fried Chicken) are available in some places.

DINING IN A CAMBODIAN'S HOME
Much of Cambodian life revolves around the family. This is where the strongest relationships are formed. But

Cambodians are a sociable people who may seek your casual acquaintanceship by inviting you to dinner at their home. An invitation to visit a Cambodian's home is not all that common but not unknown.

Family dinners may be very polite, almost formal affairs where the different social positions are much in evidence. Cambodia is a highly-structured society where everyone is either superior or inferior to everyone else. Once inside the dining room, you will most likely be ushered into an inter-generational family group around a single, very large round table. You will probably be the focus of attention. If there is no common language, someone will probably volunteer to translate. Children in particular tend to be impeccably behaved, at least by Western standards. Flattery, compliments and gratitude are abundant. As a visitor you will get honorary superior status, at least for the duration of the meal.

At first you will most likely be offered a cup of hot tea as the traditional gesture of welcome. When the more serious eating gets under way, diners typically share a number of dishes among themselves. Dishes tend to come in a random order and at no particular time. A large number of courses, a mixture of fish, meat, vegetables, will be served in communal dishes. Eating utensils could be chopsticks, though a fork and spoon are also commonly provided. It pays to get into the habit of using cutlery the Cambodian way. Since, for most dishes, nothing needs to be cut, no knives will normally be supplied. Forks and spoons for main courses are used in the same way as for desserts in the West. Cambodians use the fork held in the left hand to load food onto the spoon held in the right hand. This method is actually a lot easier than the Western practice of balancing food on the convex side of the fork en route to the mouth.

Like most Eastern cultures, the left hand is kept away from proceedings at the dining table. It is inappropriate for anyone to hold the fork in the right hand and push spillage onto it with fingers of the left hand. The left hand has a very specific purpose on the dinner table: to hold cutlery and nothing more. Under no circumstances should it actually touch the food.

DRINKING AND OTHER ENTERTAINMENTS

Socialising between the sexes in traditional Cambodian culture is strictly regulated. Cambodian women leading the traditional life are meant to avoid drinking alcohol or entering bars. Only recently has it been proper for single girls to frequent restaurants.

However, as one of the poorest countries on the planet, Cambodia would like to obtain the tourist dollar without damaging itself too much in the process. Alcohol, entertainment, sex and tourism pose the same cultural conflicts that other countries face.

Beer girls, bar girls and 'taxi' girls frequenting bars offer a range of services from marketing beer, to hostess services to prostitution. Girls usually come from very poor backgrounds and may even be sponsored, or in some cases sold, by their families to find work in the bright city lights. Besides, Cambodians will tell you that most of the good-time girls in their country are Vietnamese.

Beer, bottled or canned, is the most common alcoholic drink in Cambodia. The most common brand of beer is Angkor brand, which is brewed locally and exported widely. A similar sounding brand, also widely available, is Anchor beer. Sales of brand-name spirits are restricted to major centres. Imported wines are available in upmarket restaurants and five-star hotels.

If you want to try some local hooch, Cambodians can supply you sugar-cane beer, brewed and served in a bamboo tube. Rice wine is also widespread. Made from the same ingredients and by the same methods, rice wine tastes much like saké. But watch out! After fermentation, rice wine may be fortified so the final product has an alcohol content of higher than 20 per cent.

SIGHTS AND SOUNDS OF CAMBODIA

CHAPTER 7

'A closed mind is like a closed book; just a block of wood.'
—Chinese proverb

CAMBODIAN FESTIVITIES

Festival days are a combination of political and religious occasions. They derive from the mixture of cultural backgrounds; Chinese and Buddhism are two major influences. Three different New Year's Days are recognised: the Gregorian on the first of January; the Chinese in January or February; and the Cambodian or Buddhist in mid-April.

The Gregorian New Year's Day is the least recognised of the three. Chinese New Year has quite an impact on the commercial side of life, with many businesses closed for a day or two and fireworks going off night and day. Bonn Chaul Chhnam or the Cambodian New Year is a major event on the annual calendar. Pagodas and Buddhist statues are decorated with flowers. Presents are exchanged. People who are away from home travel back to be with their families.

As part of the Cambodian New Year tradition, participants throw non-injurious objects, such as water, at each other in a light-hearted manner. For a while, water ceremonies in Cambodia looked like they would degenerate to the level of Songkran ceremonies in Thailand (also held to commemorate the Buddhist New Year), with groups of marauding youths in the back of lorries with barrels of water and industrial water pumps hosing down passers-by, cars, dogs and anything else that moves. The police have curbed this practice in Cambodia and the festivities have returned to the gentle expression of joy they were meant to be.

Entertaining tourists at Angkot Wat.

Apart from the more widely recognised festival days such as New Year's Day, Cambodians also celebrate festivals that are uniquely Cambodian. Bonn Pchem Ben, a day in the lunar calendar (sometime in September/October in the Gregorian Calendar), is Ancestor Day. During Bonn Pchum Ben, families are meant to visit at least seven different pagodas to pay their respects to their forebears. Cambodians don't need much of an excuse to stage a party. Bonn Pchum Ben celebrations include buffalo races through villages in the country with young riders precariously perched on the backs of the charging beasts, wrestling matches and boat races that usually degenerate into water fights.

Calendar of Festivals and Holidays

1 January	New Year's Day
7 January	Victory Day over the Khmer Rouge
January/February	Chinese New Year
8 March	International Women's Day
13–16 April	Cambodian New Year
1 May	Labour Day
May	Royal Ploughing Day
	Buddha's Birthday
1 June	International Children's Day
18 June	Queen's Birthday
24 September	Constitution and Coronation Day
September/October	Ancestor Day
23 October	Anniversary of 1991 Paris Peace Accord
October/November	Retreat of the Water's Day
9 November	Independence Day (from the French)
10 December	United Nations Human Rights Day

In addition, traditional Cambodian festivals spanning a number of days are held at the beginning and end of the monsoon season. On Bonn Chroat Preah Nongkoal or Royal Ploughing Day, which celebrates the start of the ploughing season in May, two oxen draw a plough to dig a furrow in front of the National Museum in Phnom Penh, after which the King's soothsayers predict the weather and harvests for the ensuing year. (*Refer to* 'Beliefs and Practices' *in* Chapter 4: Getting to Know the Cambodians *on page 87–89*).

Sometime at the start of the dry season in November, the Tonle Sap River reverses its flow. Water which had flowed from the Mekong into Tonle Sap Lake starts flowing out again, refreshing the irrigation systems in the lower Mekong delta with a vast volume of stored water. Cambodians find this natural phenomenon reason enough to celebrate. When the flow in Tonle Sap Lake is judged to have changed direction, Bonn Om Tuk or Retreat of the Waters' Day is declared. For days, live music plays from temporary stages on the river banks around Phnom Penh, dragon boats race each other down the river and people consume a great deal of beer.

Recent additions to the schedule of public holidays include occasions that celebrate historical events rather than religious festivals, such as Independence Day from the French (1953), Victory Day to celebrate the demise of the Khmer Rouge (1979) and the anniversary of the 1991 Paris Peace Accord.

TOURIST ACCOMMODATION

We can only give you the most general advice on accommodation. *Lonely Planet* and similar publications do the job much better. In 2003, tourism provided about 30 per cent of Cambodia's foreign exchange. Major sources of visitors to Cambodia were Japan, the United States and South Korea, as well as Europe and Australia. The prime tourist spots in Cambodia are where the country's two international airports are situated: Phnom Penh and Siem Reap. Within Phnom Penh and Siem Reap, a range of accommodation is available from five-stars downwards, priced commensurately. Only the top hotels offer international pre-booking services. The other location offering a five-star option is Sihanoukville, where an ocean frontage five-star resort had just been opened at the time of writing, and another was under construction. Sihanoukville's airport has recently been upgraded to receive chartered flights and is scheduled to receive international and regional flights in the not too distant future. The five-star, 180-room Sokha Hotel, complete with private beach, opened in 2004. Sihanoukville's first golf course, also beachfront, opened in 2005.

Away from the five-star league, guesthouses and budget hotels are fairly widely available and at terrific value. You can get clean, comfortable accommodation with private bathrooms for between US$ 5–10.

Some guidebooks advise budget-class travellers to pack a sleeping sheet or bag, pointing out that sleeping on suspect bedding poses a health risk from bedbugs that can make quite a mess of both your holiday and your skin. My experience is that accommodation, even at the low end of the market, has improved greatly. Cleanliness and quality of accommodation is no worse than that of equivalent lodging in, say, London and at a fraction of the price. Guesthouses, even at the US$ 5 level, will almost always include a private shower, handbasin and toilet. Most larger towns in Cambodia have adopted Western toilets, though Eastern toilets are still in vogue in the smaller centres and at rest breaks along major bus routes. Those travelling budget-class are advised to pack toilet paper for their journey.

No Weapons Permitted Here

Curiosities of some Cambodian hotels, like bullet holes in walls, are reminders of Cambodia's fraught recent history. Like hotels elsewhere in the world, Cambodian hotels display their instructions to guests on the back of the door, where they lie, mostly unread, in a puddle of darkness. During the Vietnamese war, Sihanoukville was a staging point for the supply of equipment to the Viet Cong. Even as late as the 1990s, the town had served as a Khmer Rouge base. The area is still awash with guns the authorities are keen to collect. Boldly displayed from a picture hook in the middle of the wall in a particular Sihanoukville hotel where I stayed were some additional instructions to the customer:

'Please hand in all guns and explosives at the reception desk.'

AROUND TOWN IN PHNOM PENH

Built on the Mekong alluvial plain, Phnom Penh is quite flat. In Khmer the word *phnom* in Phnom Penh means hill. The city's highest point at 27 m (89 ft) above the surrounding land is the hill on which Phnom Penh's best-known temple is built. The temple is called Wat Phnom, meaning 'temple on the hill'. According to popular accounts, possibly apocryphal, Wat Phnom was financed in 1372 by a wealthy Khmer woman called Daun (Grandmother) Penh. The combination of the site for the temple and its financier provide Cambodia's capital its name. Literally, the name of the capital, Phnom Penh means 'Penh's Hill'.

The location of Phnom Penh, close to the geographic middle of the country, might be described as central. Much of Phnom Penh was a 19th-century French creation, with a few major Cambodian-style buildings added for good measure.

Once thought to be the prettiest metropolis in South-east Asia, Phnom Penh is now a city of faded elegance, a curious mixture of grand and ghetto architecture. Magnificent tree-lined boulevards styled on the Champs Elysée in Paris sweep through the city to the Tonle Sap River. Stylish Mediterranean style buildings flank Sisowath Boulevard, Phnom Penh's riverside promenade. From comfy cane chairs under wide verandas built in a more graceful period you can watch the sun rise over the river, the street life passing by and the river traffic beyond it.

The city also offers a few spectacularly graceful buildings in Cambodian style. The Royal Palace in Phnom Penh, erected by the French to a Cambodian design, is a leading example. The Royal Palace complex houses a number of buildings in a mixture of styles, including the rather out-of-place Napoleon Pavilion, prefabricated in Egypt (where it was used by Napoleon III's wife, Empress Eugenie, at the 1869 opening of the Suez Canal) and shipped piecemeal to be reassembled in Phnom Penh.

The Royal Palace is best known for its Silver Pagoda, so named for the 5,000 silver tiles that make up the floor of the building. Cambodian traditional architectural features include open-style interlocking roofs for ventilation and elaborate gable decorations of elaborate whorls and whirls, somewhat reminiscent of the Khmer alphabet. Spires have faces on each side, similar to the four-faced statues at the Bayon temple in Angkor. Some of the Royal Palace buildings are off-limits to the public. The rest can be toured during daylight hours for a modest fee of around US$ 3.

Against these selected examples of architectural splendour, much of the city cries out for repair: streets are full of potholes, mortar falls out of building walls, building facades need restoring or a good clean and paint. In the back streets, shacks and permanent housing compete for frontage onto red dirt roads in an untidy jumble of unfinished and poorly maintained masonry. Residential and commercial areas are intermingled, with no apparent zoning. Cambodian tertiary industry spills out of its premises and merges into the street. From their street-front shops in residential areas, motor repair shops litter the footpaths with motor parts, steel sections, tools and welding machines. Cambodian small business entrepreneurs take whatever space they can find for themselves. Rent-free footpaths make for far cheaper operations than a factory building.

For a while, street names of Phnom Penh kept changing, as each conqueror that swept into town renamed the major streets to honour the heroes of the ascendant nation. When the French antagonised the citizens of Phnom Penh by renaming streets after French heroes, they significantly advanced the cause for Cambodian independence. After independence, the Cambodians once again tore down street signs and renamed the streets after their own local heroes.

Arterial roads in Phnom Penh are now named after ex-King Sihanouk's favourite people. First among these was himself. Sihanouk Boulevard, Phnom Penh's Champs Elyseé, is the city's most splendid streetscape. Other arterial roads include Mao Tse Tung Boulevard, Nehru Boulevard and Tito Boulevard. Former French President de Gaulle, who Sihanouk greatly admired, supplies the only French name on the current Phnom Penh street map—Charles de Gaulle Boulevard.

Lesser roads in Phnom Penh are hero-neutral since they are nameless. Instead of bearing names, the streets are numbered. Streets running east–west have even numbers and those running north–south have odd numbers. The even-number sequence starts in the north of the city and runs in ascending order towards the south. With remarkable foresight, to avoid going into negative numbers as the city grew, city planners started numbering even-numbered streets at 60. The odd-number sequence starts at the river and increases in order towards the west.

Once you know where you are on the grid, you can, theoretically at least, find your way to another location fairly easily without a street map. For the sake of tourists everywhere, all cities in the world should adopt the Phnom Penh street-numbering system! Though it has to be said the system isn't quite perfect. Not all the adjacent streets have adjacent numbers and some streets that run only a block aren't numbered at all.

SIEM REAP

Siem Reap, set in the heartland of the ancient Angkor Empire, is Cambodia's second city. In Khmer, *Siem Reap* means 'Siam Defeated'. The name commemorates a successful victory over the Thai invaders about a thousand years ago. Since this memorable victory, few similar military successes have been enjoyed against the neighbours.

Siem Reap, as the starting point for Angkor adventurers, is probably the most Westernised, tourist-friendly town in Cambodia. It offers the full suite of tourist facilities, with an abundance of tour operators, hotels, guest houses, restaurants and entertainment centres.

The major streets of Siem Reap are wide shady boulevards fronted by buildings with a French colonial feel. The more mundane parts of town have their share of unsurfaced, potholed streets you find in most Cambodian towns. The land around Siem Reap is graced by lush vegetation and towering trees. That hundreds of Angkor temples are sprinkled among a tropical forest of stately hardwoods adds greatly to the attractiveness of the region.

In Siem Reap, like most places in Cambodia, taxis, cyclos and the ubiquitous motos cruise the streets looking for custom. One of Siem Reap's oddities is that most cars in the area are right-hand drive in a left-hand drive country. Explanations vary on this point. One is that cars are brought in second-hand from Japan, a country that drives on

the left side of the road. Another is that they are stolen from Thailand, which also drives on the left side of the road, and smuggled across the border with immigration authorities of both sides paid to turn a blind eye. The second explanation sounds more likely than the first. Since cars in Cambodia do not carry number plates and no national car-ownership database is kept, such a scam seems highly feasible.

ANGKOR

Angkor's temples and other structures are amazingly well preserved. Thousands of tourists pass through the temples every day. While pathways are worn smooth from the passage of millions of feet and centuries of rain, some of the bas-reliefs seem so starkly new they might have been carved into their sandstone walls as recently as yesterday. In fact, thanks to the on-going restoration programme they may have been! Angkor's monuments feature an abundance of 'Do Not Touch' signs which tourists ignore, or not depending on their disposition. When multiplied by thousands of such contacts, the sweat from laying a finger on the stonework contributes to the deterioration of the site. The natural conflict between restoration and inadvertent degradation from natural and human causes is ongoing.

For tourists who arrived at Cambodia by way of either Thailand or Vietnam, by the time they reach Angkor their tastes may be jaded by the weight of temple exposure. But the Angkor temples will dazzle even the most temple-weary with their splendours, their intricate workmanship and their sheer magnitude. Angkor Wat, rated by some as one of the seven man-made wonders of the world, stands testament to an age-old advanced civilisation with building skills unequalled anywhere.

Angkor is Cambodia's national treasure and its major source of foreign exchange. No other asset is as important to its beleaguered economy. Several million dollars, most of it financed from overseas donations, have been spent over the 1990s in cleaning and restoration works. In 1992, Angkor

The word 'Apsara' crops up continually in Cambodian arts. It originates from Hindu cosmology and refers to the celestial dancers who, according to legend, were employed to entertain the gods. Apsara characters can be seen on many of the bas-reliefs around Angkor.

was declared a UNESCO World Heritage site. Major restoration projects are still in progress at the site under the aegis of APSARA (Authority for Protection and Management of Angkor and the Region of Siem Reap), an NGO specifically tasked with the duty of protecting and maintaining Angkor's artefacts. Various other NGOs are involved in other more specific restoration projects.

Angkor Wat and Angkor Thom

Angkor Wat, the centrepiece of the Cambodian flag, is the country's biggest tourist attraction. For students of temple layout, Angkor Wat has some unusual design features. Built originally as a Hindu temple dedicated to Vishnu and other Indian deities, the temple's outer galleries are arranged in an anti-clockwise fashion—a reverse of the usual arrangement for Hindu temples and the entry to the temple faces west, not east, which is opposite to common conventions of temple building. Various theories have been advanced to link the unconventional orientation of building features with astronomical objects.

The other striking relic in the Siem Reap area from the Angkorean period is the walled city of Angkor Thom, which at various times served as the administrative centre of the empire. Angkor Thom is surrounded by substantial moats, thought to have once been inhabited by crocodiles to discourage would-be invaders. Water from distant catchments was, and still is, trapped by a massive dam that feeds the moats around the city walls through enormous hand-dug channels which are still in good order today. The labour force that built Angkor Wat and Angkor Thom must have numbered in the thousands. The standard of artisanship that produced the wall adornments and statuary of these massive structures was extraordinary. In scale and skill, these structures are comparable to the pyramids of Egypt and the Great Wall of China.

Guarding the territory at Angkor Thom

In the hot humid atmosphere of Cambodia, cut timber does not last long. The timber features of Angkor's buildings—doors and roofs for example—have long since succumbed to decay. But the stone temples, city walls, bridges and statuary remain in generally good condition, a testament to the engineering skills of the empire.

After the Thais captured Angkor in the 15th century, the Cambodians retreated south. Angkor lay abandoned until the Europeans 'rediscovered' it in the 19th century. By this

'Ta Phrom' Temple—locale for the smash hit movie *Tomb Raider*.

time, the jungle had infiltrated many of Angkor's temples with enormous trees that can still be seen today. Nature's resurgence against the creations of man fascinated the Europeans almost as much as the structures themselves. Reports of Angkor's amazing features, both man-made and natural, circulated in Europe and beyond. The area has attracted international interest ever since.

The Khmer Rouge were probably the most destructive force to occupy the site in a thousand years. Khmer Rouge cadres, who had burnt down thousands of Buddhist temples across Cambodia, made their religious statements at Angkor by throwing the bodies of the revolution's victims into Angkor's ornamental lakes, and by decapitating generations of Angkor's stone Buddhas. However, Khmer Rouge forces were perpetually short of bullets for their guns and explosives for the demolition projects they may have liked to undertake. Despite their mayhem, Angkor's treasures survived the turbulent Khmer Rouge regime in surprisingly good condition.

The creations of Angkor are spread across an area of approximately 300 sq km (116 sq miles). Such a dispersed and extensive site is difficult to guard. Despite attempts at security, artefacts pilfered from temples and spirited out of the country under the noses of government officials (and, in all likelihood with their full cooperation and connivance) command a high price. Pilfering on a smaller scale for immediate sale to visitors is also rife. If you feel inclined to buy a piece of Angkor as a keepsake of your visit, try to avoid the genuine article. In the interests of preservation, ensure you buy a fake!

Pillaging at Angkor has been more than incidental. Ostensibly peaceful institutions such as the Guimet Museum in Paris carried off more of the area's bas-reliefs than the Khmer Rouge destroyed in their three years of power. Following the tradition of the Elgin Marbles, taken from Greece in the 19th century and held in the British Museum ever since, Western museums have claimed the moral high ground for plundering the national treasures of weaker countries. They argue that artefacts removed from their rightful place are kept in good condition in their museums for the general good of mankind. (These rules do not seem to apply to property more generally. Criminals who steal cars have far less success mounting such an argument in a court of law.)

Cambodians would like to see their national treasures returned and restored to their rightful places. The country feels capable of looking after its own assets as well as anyone. Accordingly, I take the opportunity here of addressing a memo to museum curators in Europe reading this book who have Angkor treasures under their care:

In August 2004, Angkor has been removed from the United Nation's list of endangered landmarks. The UN's scientific and cultural organisation, UNESCO, states it is confident the preservation of Angkor has now been assured. This being the case, please return the 'borrowed' property in your possession to its rightful owners. The historical icons of Cambodia belong in Cambodia.

SIHANOUKVILLE

Sihanoukville, known also as Kampong Som, was renamed for King Sihanouk in 1960. It had long enjoyed a quiet identity as a seaside village, reaping abundant harvests of fish and seafood from the Gulf of Thailand. Remodelling the area started with a deep-water port built in 1956. This is still the country's only port for large ships.

In the early 1960s, Sihanoukville became a strategic area in Indo-China's seemingly endless wars. To speed the distribution of goods landing at the country's only port, the United States funded the Friendship Highway between Sihanoukville and Phnom Penh. Later, this convenient piece of infrastructure became a supply line for both sides of the war. In daylight hours, US arms were moved through Sihanoukville port and up the Friendship Highway to Lon Nol's forces in Phnom Penh. At night, the same facilities were used to distribute arms from sympathetic communist countries to Viet Cong sanctuaries inside Cambodia.

For many years after the mid-1960s, Sihanoukville was a centre of various war efforts, including those of the Khmer Rouge. Now that peace reigns in Cambodia, development at Sihanoukville is on the move. Interests connected to the prime minister have built a luxury hotel complex on the seafront. Not to be outdone, Sihanouk built a palace on a small hill offering a fine view of the sea. The town also sports two casinos; their clientele are predominately well-heeled Thais and Chinese.

Sihanoukville is built on a peninsula with sandy beaches on each side and interspersed with rocky headlands. Nature has provided the ingredients for a tropical beach paradise; so far, man hasn't quite matched this standard. Fortunately, man-made ugliness and natural beauty have been segregated to some degree—the centre of Sihanoukville is located some distance from the beach. From a beachgoer's viewpoint, much of the natural beauty of the area remains intact. Except around the port area, the sands are white, fine and clean. Coconut palms on the seafront cast pools of shade. The water is warm, calm and pollution-free. Out to sea, nearby islands dot the horizon.

Not many Europeans have yet found their way to Sihanoukville. Phnom Penh to Sihanoukville was once an arduous eight-hour bus ride, or a 12-hour crawl by train. But since the road to Phnom Penh was fixed, the trip between Sihanoukville and Phnom Penh is now a mere three hours of smooth riding. At the time of writing, Sihanoukville was an uncrowded seaside resort, with expanses of mostly unspoiled beach. When the airport is finally opened to international flights, tourism into Sihanoukville may well take a great leap forward.

In its present state of development, the ambience at Sihanoukville is fairly relaxed. For those who like to spend their vacations doing nothing more strenuous than lying on the beach, you can obtain many goods and services without stirring from your deckchair. At your request, hawkers patrolling the beach will supply your favourite beverages, a five-course meal, sunglasses, sunscreen or a live snake. They can also organise a massage, a haircut, reflexology, fortune telling, a date for the evening and a visa to Vietnam.

POIPET

Cambodia is a focus of gambling in South-east Asia. To service the needs of gamblers from Thailand—a country in which gambling is illegal—a number of casinos have been built near the Thai border, at Poipet, the closest Cambodian town to Bangkok. Poipet is a hard-edged, ugly, dusty, untidy town of unmade roads, where smiles are dispensed grudgingly and dark fortunes are made from smuggling, gambling and trafficking people across the Thai border. Despite its lack of charm, Poipet is a great success commercially. Gambling is popular with the Thais. Thousands of Thais head across the border each weekend to leave their surplus cash in the Poipet casinos.

Following the success of Poipet, similar facilities have also been constructed, both at Sihanoukville and Koh Kong in the south-west, for Thais who wish to take the southern route to their favourite casinos. Another casino is under construction near Anlong Veng, 2 km (1.2 miles) inside Cambodia's northern border with Thailand, the site of Pol Pot's last stand against the Phnom Penh government. With a casino or two at every border crossing with Thailand, Cambodia has laid siege to Thailand's gambling dollar.

THE KILLING FIELDS

Two suggested destinations you are likely to encounter on any tourist brochure for Cambodia are the Genocide Museum at Tuol Sleng and the Killing Fields at Choeung Ek. Tuol Sleng is a suburb in Phnom Penh. There, the Khmer Rouge turned a secondary school into a centre for political interrogation. Choeung Ek is an orchard 20 km (12 miles) south-west of the capital, where Pol Pot had his real and suspected political opponents executed after interrogation at Tuol Sleng.

Tuol Sleng was the most well-known of all the Khmer Rouge interrogation centres. Its captives were tortured then executed after 'confessions' were extracted. The value of these confessions extracted under torture is illustrated by the fate of foreigners who fell into Khmer Rouge hands. In 1978, the Khmer Rouge captured an Englishman, John Dewhirst, who had been cruising the Gulf of Thailand in a yacht. He was taken to Tuol Sleng for interrogation as a suspected foreign spy. Under torture, Dewhirst said what he thought his interrogators wanted to hear. He confessed to having been recruited by the CIA at the age of 12 through a friend of his father while still in England. He agreed his father was also a CIA agent, whose cover was the headmaster of a local school where he indoctrinated his youthful charges with imperialist ideology. He confirmed his interrogators' suspicions that his father's friend was a high-ranking CIA operative in England.

When the interrogators had extracted an account that reflected their own view of the world, Dewhirst was executed, along with his companions who had come up with similar stories under similar circumstances. Records of interviews with Dewhirst and his companions were found after the Khmer Rouge hurriedly abandoned Tuol Sleng in early 1979, as the invading Vietnamese army swept through the city.

Tuol Sleng's clients were executed and buried at Choeung Ek. The much photographed 8,000 punctured skulls enclosed in their glass sarcophagus at Choeung Ek bear silent witness to Pol Pot's method of despatching his victims. The Khmer Rouge, perpetually short of ammunition for their armies, saved their bullets for purposes more important than

Khmer Rouge victims—the skulls at Choeung Ek.

murdering children and intellectuals. They despatched most of their victims with a hammer to the back of the head.

Taxi drivers, hotel desks and tour agencies will brightly advise you to visit both Tuol Sleng and Choeng Ek, which have been preserved in their original condition. The torture chambers and the Killing Fields of the Khmer Rouge remain Cambodia's biggest tourist attractions after Angkor.

Why is Cambodia so keen to display the evidence of this gruesome recent history to its tourists? This is a question I have asked a number of Cambodians. The answers vary from a simple need to generate tourist revenue to some deeper compulsion to retain a record of the past.

Of course Cambodians are not the only people to turn genocide museums and torture chambers into exhibits. Jews have recreated gas chambers and other similar sites of torture to keep the Holocaust in the public's mind, decades after the event. Hiroshima preserved its bombed-out dome so that the world would not forget the first atom bomb dropped in anger. London has retained relics from the blitz of the 1940s. Until the value of real estate overwhelmed other considerations, the Americans had proposed preserving their own Ground Zero to commemorate the tragedy of 11 September 2001. But these are political reminders of what one race did to another, not what a single race did to itself.

A possible reason for preserving the relics of the Khmer Rouge regime is political. The Khmer Rouge were defeated in 1979, but not totally destroyed. For the Vietnamese-backed Phnom Penh government in the 1980s, it was important to remind anyone in the world who was still prepared to listen that the Khmer Rouge were still around, and preserve the evidence of how they ruled the country. It may also be that Cambodia needed to endure a period of introspection and self-examination to recover from the wounds the Khmer Rouge inflicted. Perhaps, over 30 years later, the country still needs to assuage its grief and guilt as a collective cathartic exercise.

Any Cambodian over 40 years of age is likely to have some memory of Khmer Rouge rule. When I visited Choeung Ek in 1999, a middle-aged man approached me and offered to show me around. I accepted his invitation and was taken on a tour. Pretty quickly I got the impression that my guide was a deeply troubled man with a graphic memory of events at the Killing Fields. As the tour progressed, he provided me with detailed accounts of how many bodies were buried under a particular mound and how the brains of babies had been dashed out against a particular tree.

I sensed my guide had been there at the time. Since the death rate among Choeung Ek victims was 100 per cent and my guide was still alive, I realised that if he was recounting a personal experience, his role at the site must have been as a guard. At the time of the Khmer Rouge, my guide would, maybe, have been 10–12 years old. The Khmer Rouge inducted children as young as seven into their armies. Perhaps my guide was spending the days of his middle age unloading to whatever tourists came his way or, in a roundabout way, confessing, seeking daily peace of mind through atonement.

Whatever their reasons, Cambodians seem pleased to show their visitors their interrogation centres and killing fields and tourists certainly visit them in considerable numbers.

UNUSUAL HAZARDS

No one goes to Cambodia to get their arms and legs blown off. But since this book is not only about the delights that await visitors to Cambodia but also its dangers, it should be noted here that adventurous souls who like to stray from beaten paths should take care.

Hostilities may have ceased years ago, but the detritus of decades of military activity remain—landmines and bombs that none of the participants in history's wars have bothered to tidy up after their battles came to an end. Some of the most visited tourist places, such as Siem Reap and Battambang, are high-risk areas.

The rule in Cambodia—it can hardly be overemphasised— is to stay on the beaten track. In particular, avoid forested areas. Even dry rice paddies may contain concealed hazards. Approaches to bridges on secondary roads are particularly dangerous.

Landmines are the size of an apple and are buried just beneath the surface. They are activated by the weight of a footfall and explode when the pressure is released, as the foot is lifted to take the next step. They are designed to blow a leg off, but not to kill. The objective is to demoralise the civilian population by maiming them, thereby creating general misery and a burden on the community.

Since having a leg blown off is, at the very least, demoralising, the strategy is generally successful, although the intent to leave the victim alive perhaps needs some tweaking. Statistics show that about one-quarter of landmine casualties die from shock or loss of blood before they can get treatment. Prospects for the survivors are poor, particularly for females who lose all chances at marriage.

Visitors to Cambodia should also be wary. Landmines are equally effective against tourists. Even a minefield that has been cleared can reseed itself. Deeply buried landmines have a tendency to float to the surface after heavy rains, reactivating the minefield.

Landmines are particularly prevalent in the west and north of the country, near the Thai border that was the last refuge of the Khmer Rouge. After the Vietnamese army took over Cambodia in 1979, the United States, Thailand and China pursued their hostilities towards the Vietnamese by promoting instability in Cambodia. Still in thrall of the domino theory, that the Vietnamese would spread communism throughout the region, the international powers kept the Khmer Rouge in business as their agent provocateur. The Thais supplied the Khmer Rouge their sanctuary, the United States their money and the Chinese their arms. Thus refreshed and re-equipped by an odd alliance, the Khmer Rouge conducted a guerrilla war against the newly-installed Cambodian government, planting thousands of Chinese-manufactured landmines in the process. The Vietnamese army stationed in Cambodia answered in kind, planting their own, Russian-supplied landmines. No one knows how many landmines have been sown, though estimates of 10 million are widely quoted. Nor do they know where the landmines are, since no records were kept.

None of the international powers involved in supplying and financing the use of landmines—China, Russia, and the United States—has signed the Ottawa Convention banning anti-personnel landmines. None has returned to Cambodia to clear the country of the dangerous litter, although the United States claims to send limited aid money specifically earmarked for landmine clearance. As a result, the landmine problem is ongoing,

Cambodia has the highest per capita rate of amputees of any country in the world. Cambodians, tourists, and oxen have all been victims. The total casualty count from landmines since the 1980s is around 40,000. In the 1990s, these lingering mines claimed victims at the rate of 80 per week. In the first eight months of 2004, the casualty rate from UXOs (unexploded ordinance) was still averaging nearly three a day.

Welcome to the Landmine Museum

'Welcome to the Landmine Museum', reads a sign stuck at the side of a dusty rough road, just north of Siem Reap. The Landmine Museum, open to the public during daylight hours, is the creation of Aki Ra, a man who has spent most of his life involved with landmines.

A Life Strewn with Landmines

By the standards of 1970s in Cambodia, Aki Ra had an unexceptional upbringing. His handout reads, "When I was 5 years old, my parents were killed by the Khmer Rouge. I was then forced to leave my village and work in the fields. Later the Vietnamese army arrived. As a conscript with the Vietnamese Army, I used to lay mines in the same fields I had been working. Later, when I was a young man I cleared the mines for the government."

Today, Aki Ra works at clearing the mines in his own time, as a private individual under the sponsorship of no one. He runs his landmine museum to generate some cash and increase public awareness of the problem. And he is assisted by a number of amputees who show people around the museum. On display are various landmines and UXOs from US bombing operations over Cambodia in the early 1970s.

A Valuable Asset; A Dangerous Device

Dealing with UXOs is another area in which Cambodians exhibit their recycling instincts. Half-casings from unexploded 500-pound bombs make excellent flowerpots. However, recycling, when taken to extremes, has its dangers. During construction of a golf course at Sihanoukville, a cache of grenades was found between the fourth and fifth holes. Word of this treasure spread, tempting recyclers who came over the golf-course boundary fence under cover of night. An unexploded grenade offers plenty of recycling value. Explosives can be reclaimed for the country's unregulated and highly destructive fishing industry and copper can be extracted from the grenade casing. But risks of recycling explosives are high and, in due course, two additional fatalities were added to Cambodia's UXO body count.

The most commonly used technique for clearing mines is still the 'creep and probe' method. Mechanical methods of detecting and clearing landmines, such as by heavily reinforced bulldozers, are expensive and have been less successful. Landmine clearers work within their prescribed area with metal detectors, carefully excavating around the buried object, whether it be a landmine or a discarded coke can. Creeping and probing is certainly a dangerous way to make a living, even if you get paid for it. At present, apart from Aki Ra's courageous efforts, various NGOs, mostly European, are doing their best to clear the mines. Landmine-clearing remains a hazardous, painstaking and expensive operation that costs up to US$ 1,000 per mine cleared, many times the cost of the mines themselves.

Reporting Suspected Landmines

The best approach to avoiding damage from landmines is to stay out of known hazardous areas. However, landmines are ubiquitous. If you happen to observe what looks like a landmine or another form of UXO, security clearance authorities recommend treating the object with great caution and request people encountering suspected landmines to report their existence and location to the Cambodia Mine Action Centre at tel: (023) 368-841 or (023) 981-083/ 084.

THE ARTS AND MEDIA
Cambodian Dance

Classical Cambodian dance traces its roots to Indian origins. Images of Cambodian traditional dance, performed by Apsaras, Cambodia's mythical celestial beings, are depicted in bas-relief on many of Angkor's temple walls. King Jayavarman II, founder of the Angkor Empire, is credited with introducing Cambodian classical dance in the 7th century. Apsara dancing reached its peak during the reign of King Jayavarman VII in the 12th century. He was estimated to have around 4,000 Apsara dancers in his royal court.

When the Angkor Empire finally fell to the invading Siamese a couple of centuries later, according to some reports, the Siamese expatriated Angkor's entire Apsara troupe to Siam. Cambodians claim this appropriation of talent as the origin of Thai traditional dance. Thais would probably disagree. But to the inexpert eye, Apsara dance and Thai traditional dance certainly seem to share many common elements.

Apsara dance combines the grace and restraint that underlies Cambodian culture. Dancers maintain controlled

Apsara dancers in bas-relief at Angkor.

emotions and fixed expressions, and exhibit deference and avoid conflict. They move in unison, but do not touch each other. Common dance elements are turned wrists, arched fingers and feet raised and bent backwards. Movements are gradual as one position moves to merge with the next. Accompanying music is provided by a band of traditional instruments featuring xylophones, drums, horns, gongs, guitars and flutes.

Art, dance and theatre, in fact any show of enjoyment of life, were all activities the Khmer Rouge took exception to during their regime. The impact of their ideological disapproval lives on in Cambodian dance. The Khmer Rouge executed nearly all the professional dancers in the country. Only 17 of 200 trained dancers attached to the Royal Palace in the 1970s were thought to have survived the massacre. One of the survivors was Pol Pot's sister-in-law, Chea Samy, who spent most of her life at the Royal Court where a number of Pol Pot's family members also worked in various capacities.

In 1994, the Royal University of Fine Arts in Phnom Penh re-established the royal dance troupe disbanded by the Khmer Rouge. A Cambodian arts troupe formed by students of the Royal School of Fine Arts and going under the name Sovanna Phum (Magic Village), stages one show a week of traditional dance and Cambodian music. The dancers for this show wear the traditional *sampot*, made from a single piece of cloth looped around the legs to look like a pair of trousers, secured with a fine silver chain passed around the waist.

Back-lit shadow puppet plays (Nang Sbaek Thom) also have a long tradition in Cambodian culture. Narrators concealed below an illuminated screen tell stories dating from thousands of years ago. Plays are accompanied by music from traditional instruments. Stories are of Cambodia's creation myths, the life of Buddha, conquests, love affairs, tragedies and comedies. Puppet shows are also a channel for contemporary political views, with ironic comments on modern life woven into the script. In its regular shows, Sovanna Phum combines shadow puppetry with its dance routines.

Literature

Apart from its creation myths, Cambodia lacks a strong literary culture. Like the Khmer Rouge who came later, a major strategy of the French colonialists during their time in power was controlling the population through maintaining their ignorance. Dissemination of knowledge was not encouraged. Absence of paper may have contributed to the lack of literary output in the early days. So may have lack of a printing press, the first of which the French introduced in the late 19th century, exclusively for their own use. Cambodia's earliest novels written in Khmer were *Sophat* and *Waters of Tonle Sap*, both published in the late 1930s.

When they came to power, the Khmer Rouge sought not merely to maintain community ignorance, but also to destroy the community's store of knowledge. They ransacked the nation's libraries, burnt books and murdered authors, librarians and anyone with a pair of reading glasses. Curiously, despite their contempt for literature, the Khmer Rouge were assiduous record keepers, maintaining the most accurate accounts of their doings at Tuol Sleng and other interrogation centres. Names, serial numbers and 'confessions' of Tuol Sleng's victims were recorded and preserved as an enduring witness to the troubles of the time.

Used by the Khmer Rouge as a stable, the building housing the National Library, near Wat Phnom, survived the regime substantially intact. In recent years, with generous donations from overseas learning institutes, the National Library has been restored and extended. Its collection of books in Khmer, French and English has been greatly expanded.

Movies

One of the key contemporary figures in the Cambodian art scene has been the irrepressible King Norodom Sihanouk, a man of boundless energy and interests. Starting in the late 1940s, Sihanouk took to writing film scripts, directing movies and writing musical scores. In 2004, at the age of 81, he was still at it, offering his films to the Cannes Film Festival.

Film-making came naturally to Sihanouk whose entire life had a theatrical flair. In politics, Sihanouk's theatre was Cambodia, the country was his story, and he was its principal character. At receptions for foreign dignitaries, instead of reading speeches, Sihanouk would sometimes sing romantic ballads composed by himself and delivered in the high falsetto that was his natural speaking voice.

Sihanouk took time out from the movies in the 1950s and early 1960s to concentrate on affairs of state. But by the mid-1960s, as the Cambodian economy collapsed after Sihanouk renounced US aid, and with war clouds gathering, Sihanouk once again became absorbed by the movie industry.

The Movies and Music He Made

An account of Sihanouk's movie activities, including downloadable music scores he composed can be found at his own website, http://www.norodomsihanouk.org/.

Sihanouk's critics claim that movies were his escape from reality. With Indo-China sliding into war, Cambodia's prime minister turned himself into a one-man film industry, scripting, directing, producing and starring in eight full-length movies which the Cambodian press, controlled by Sihanouk, acclaimed as masterpieces and the foreign critics trashed. Major roles were not performed by professional actors but by Sihanouk's acquaintances. His casts included generals from his army, princes from his family, members of the Royal Ballet, and himself. Sihanouk's first movie, *Apsara*, was a love story set in a Cambodia depicted as a fairyland where aristocrats travelled from one party to another in Cadillacs and Rolls Royce cars. Perhaps this was the country Sihanouk would have liked Cambodia to be. But at the time he was making his movies, Cambodia was being bombed to bits and sliding into a civil war that, amongst others, claimed Sihanouk as a victim.

Films were later made *about* the Khmer Rouge era, but the only film known to have been made *during* that period was a Yugoslav documentary sponsored by Pol Pot, depicting

Cambodia as a Shangri-La of communist triumph. This film became best known for the comment a film crew member made that the only person he saw smile throughout his entire time shooting the film in Cambodia was Pol Pot himself.

Since the Khmer Rouge have been removed from office, the Cambodian film industry has been slow to revive. In the first years of the 21st century, half a dozen cinemas opened in Phnom Penh. However, there was no return to Sihanouk's frenetic movie making in the 1960s.

Newspapers

The Foreign Correspondents Club of Cambodia, on Sisowath Quay in Phnom Penh and overlooking the Tonle Sap River, has long been a favoured hang-out for foreign journalists. Even for non-journalists, the place is well worth a visit to share a drink and a meal and air your views on the world.

Nagara Vatta, Cambodia's first newspaper, appeared in 1936. The editorial stand of *Nagara Vatta* was pro-Cambodian without being anti-French. Vietnamese domination of the civil service, Chinese domination of commerce and the lack of opportunities for Cambodians were its principal themes. Its readership was the small society of Cambodian intellectuals plus a handful of progressive colonialists promoting Cambodian intellectualism. By 1937, circulation of the paper was running at about 5,000.

The present Hun Sen government has declared the media in Cambodia to be free. Sceptics have their doubts. International observers found that the Cambodian People's Party (CPP) received around 90 per cent of airtime during the 2002 election, with the rest split between the two main opposition parties. Other candidates and smaller parties were almost completely ignored. The 2002 national election committee also banned the smaller of the two main opposition parties, the Sam Rainsy Party (SRP), from using recordings of debates on corruption in the National Assembly. Informational literature produced by NGOs has occasionally been banned in Cambodia, on the grounds that they advanced viewpoints that were considered 'too liberal'.

Over the years, journalism has been a hazardous profession in Cambodia, with the occasional journalist opposing government policy turning up dead. Two prominent newspaper identities murdered in the 1990s were Nuon Chan, editor of the weekly *Samleng Yuvachen Khmer* (Voice of the Khmer Youth), and Thun Bun Ly, editor of the newspaper *Oddomkete Khmae* (Khmer Ideal). The murderers of these two individuals were not apprehended, even though the identities of the culprits were widely suspected. By contrast, in 2001, five journalists supporting anti-government views were jailed after being charged with 'terrorist activities and membership of an armed group'. The most common charge the government makes against the free press is that of jeopardising 'national security'.

Television and Radio

Though the general infrastructure is poor, one utility widespread in Cambodia is television. Even villages without electricity are likely to have a communal battery-powered black-and-white TV set, around which the community will gather to be entertained. Content is similar to that elsewhere in the world. Programmes aired contain a high percentage of sitcoms from Thailand dubbed into Khmer, game shows and kick-boxing. Behind the storyline, the overwhelming message from much of this form of entertainment is that the outside world has higher material standards than the village.

SPORTS

Cambodia's traditional sports include cockfighting and kick-boxing, neither of which attracts a wide international following. The Retreat of the Waters Festival at the end of the monsoon season features boat racing along the Tonle Sap River, with teams from various regions in Cambodia competing against each other in traditional boats. Also popular in Cambodia, as in most South-east Asian countries, is the backyard sport of *sepak takraw* (or kick ball) in which two teams of four or five fit young men achieve impossible feats of elevation and athleticism kicking a rattan ball at each other across a high net. Other sports in which the general public can participate, and needing minimum equipment, such as football, basketball and volleyball, are also becoming popular.

Expats visiting the kingdom will find the usual range of sports facilities attached to their employment or to their accommodations. Hotels and large firms offer the usual facilities with swimming pools and gyms. Phnom Penh does have a football ground, somewhat optimistically called the 'Olympic Stadium'. For the wealthy, the premier sport is golf. Since the wealthy in Cambodia (apart from tourists) are few, the need for golf courses is limited. There are two golf courses in Phnom Penh, one under construction in Sihanoukville and none anywhere else in the country.

With day-to-day survival still a major preoccupation, sport does not grip the public imagination in Cambodia quite to the same degree it does in other countries. Besides, a country that cannot afford to fix the many holes in its road system has not yet found much in the way of surplus funds to devote to sports infrastructure.

'Khmer speakers construe and perceive the
world differently from English speakers because
their concrete and abstract worlds are different.'
—Stephen Moore, *Phnom Penh Post*

CAMBODIA'S LANGUAGES

The national language of Cambodia is Khmer, spoken by about 95 per cent of the population. One of the world's oldest languages still in common use, Khmer is the most widely spoken member of the Mon-Khmer group of languages spoken across the South-east Asian peninsula. Its origins lie in the ancient Indian language of Brahmi, with later influences from Sanskrit and Pali.

In the early days, Khmer was spoken, but not written. The earliest surviving Khmer-language inscriptions, carved on stone, have been dated from around AD 600. Prior to that, the earliest written language in Cambodia was probably a form of Sanskrit which the educated class adopted as the language of poetry and religion. When first written, the Khmer language used a Sanskrit-based alphabet. Modern Khmer script is still based on this ancient alphabet, though various letters have been added, and various others modified to produce the current alphabet of 33 consonants and 23 vowels.

Cambodians have struggled successfully over the years to maintain their unique language, and continue to do so in the modern age. Written Khmer is widely used and has been adopted by modern technology. The standard 101 keyboard can accommodate the 56 letter Khmer alphabet with plenty of room for numbers and special keys. Leading software companies like Microsoft, Adobe and

Mozilla have developed products that enable the use of Khmer script in word-processing, Internet and other applications.

During the mid-1940s, the French promoted the Romanisation of the Khmer alphabet. This move was seen by Cambodian intellectuals as an attack on their culture. The proposal was quietly shelved by the French during World War II, on instructions from the occupying Japanese Army. Khmer kept its unique alphabet, though like many

A few elephants remain in the wild.

other languages, it adopted words from other tongues. Chinese, Thai, Vietnamese, Malay, French and English have all contributed to the Khmer vocabulary.

For nearly a century up to independence in 1953, Cambodia's second language was French. Today, a little over 50 years since independence, French influence has greatly declined. After independence, French signage in Cambodia was removed or painted over. Spoken French declined during the time of the Khmer Rouge when French-speaking Cambodians from the educated classes were executed.

Currently, the second language of Cambodians varies with the region. To the west, Thai is widely spoken. To the east, the second language is Vietnamese. Increasing numbers of Cambodian across the country speak some English, particularly in large towns and tourist centres, e.g. in Siem Reap, where it is possible to get around speaking only English. Although it has little tradition in the region, English is perceived as the key to getting on in life. English is widely recognised by Cambodians as the language of commerce and computers. Although some English is spoken in most places, in more remote areas, it pays to learn a few basic phrases in Khmer and carry a Khmer phrase book with a phonetic version in your first language.

Learning Khmer

For many, the task of learning Khmer may not seem worth the effort. Khmer is never going to be one of the world's major languages, and learning any language is an arduous undertaking. On the other hand, since few visitors to the country bother to learn a single word of Khmer, Cambodians will be impressed and flattered if you can master a dozen words of their language and perhaps a phrase or two.

If you intend to work in Cambodia, and in the process win friends and influence people, attending a Khmer-language school should at least be considered. Cambodians put great store in the preservation of Khmer in a world where the number of spoken languages diminishes each year. Long term visitors to Cambodia will considered polite if they try to learn some Khmer, and impolite if they don't.

For Westerners, Khmer has one advantage not shared by many Asian languages. It is non-tonal. In addition, compared to European languages, Khmer grammar is simple. There are no articles. Nouns have no gender. Verbs have no tenses. To indicate a future action, you add the word *neung*, meaning 'will', in front of the verb. To indicate the past, you add the word *hai-ee*, which is roughly equivalent to 'already'. If you want to explain where an action will be or was undertaken, you use a time indicator with the present tense, e.g. "I go to China last week/next week." Like French, adjectives follow the noun they qualify. (You ask for a 'drink cold', rather than a 'cold drink'.) Speakers of other Asian languages may notice contributions to the Khmer vocabulary from Thai, Laotian and Vietnamese, and this may make Khmer easier to learn.

On the other hand, Khmer is difficult to read. Khmer letters are combinations of loops and whorls, each of which, though masterpieces of calligraphy, are not easy to distinguish to the Western eye. In addition, no spaces are provided between words. Since determining the beginnings and ends of words is difficult, a dictionary is hard to use. Another difficulty is that Khmer contains combinations of consonants that do not exist in English and are difficult to get your tongue around. The slightest mispronunciation on your part can leave your listener utterly baffled. That said, Khmer is phonetic and regular. If you learn the alphabet, it is theoretically possible to pronounce whatever you read, even if you have never seen the word before.

If you are new to the country, have never spoken Khmer and wish to practice your language skills, a handy technique is to start your conversation with the commonest possible Khmer phrase. This will cue your Khmer partner to the conversation that the noise you are about to utter is your attempt to speak the local language. Otherwise, your Khmer-speaking conversational partner may think you are trying to speak German, Icelandic, or some such barbarian tongue, and your attempts at conversation may founder at the start. For this purpose, one suggestion is to start all conversations with some introductory phrase such as *Chum Reep Soo a*, meaning 'Hello'. After a while, should this become boring, other suggestions for conversational openers are contained in the Glossary on page 247–251. For those who want to get deeper still into the language, specific suggestions regarding the availability of language schools are included in the Resource Guide on page 252-261.

Pronunciation Guide

No standard rules exist to transliterate Khmer into English. If you buy a phrase book, the pronunciation guide is likely to differ somewhat from the suggestions beneath. Most of the Khmer letters sound the same as their English counterparts when transliterated, but there are some which do not exist in the English language. Below are those you need to look out for:

Unique Consonants

bp	difficult to get it, a sound halfway between *b* and *p*
dt	halfway between *d* and *t*
gk	halfway between *g* and *k*
ng	same as in English, but unlike in English, it may occur at the beginning of words
ny	both letters pronounced, as in *canyon*

Vowels

a	as in *fact*		**o**	as in *spot*
aa	as in *far*		**oa**	as in *cloak*
ai	as in *my*		**oo**	as in *toot*
ay	as in *day*		**or**	as in *sport*
e	as in *get*		**ow**	as in *howl*
ee	as in *bee*		**oy**	as in *boy*
eu	as in *urrh!* (as in disgust)		**u**	as in *but*
i	as in *bit*		**uu**	as in *book*

Taxi Cambodian

For those staying awhile and likely to ride around in hired transport, a language that might be termed 'Taxi Cambodian' is worth learning. Less than 50 'Taxi Cambodian' words will get you a long way. Since you are riding in a taxi or on the back of a moto attempting to give directions, your conversation has a context, and your driver will probably understand your directions even if your mangled Khmer departs a long way from accepted phonetics. The main words are *bot ch'wayng* (turn left), *bot s'dum* (turn right), *dtou trong* (go straight ahead) and *chop tee nee* (stop here). A fuller list is in the Glossary section. Most Cambodian taxi drivers can't read a street map and the only Cambodian city likely to have one is Phnom Penh. If you know your way around or can figure it out from a street map, these simple phrases and a few more may help you around.

MAKING CONVERSATION
Terms of Address

Social status determines language of address. Obsequiousness and superiority are displayed not only by actions but also by vocabulary. Depending on the relative status of those conversing, different forms of address should be used.

The general rules on address are that people of your own age or younger are called by their names. Except for special titles, people older than you are addressed as *borng*. Elderly women are addressed as *yeay* and elderly men as *ta*. Government officials and people of similar rank are called by the respectful titles lok *srey* (Mrs) and *lok* (Mr). You call your brother or sister *bong*, but a younger brother *bpohn brohs* and sister *bpohn srei*. For younger people to whom you are not related, you will address the male as *kmouy brohs* and the female as *kmouy srei*. Properly addressing monks requires special words or even a special language, since to afford them their full measure of respect, monks should be addressed in the ancient language of Pali.

If you happen to be a white foreigner, in Khmer you are a *barang*. The origin of this word is uncertain. One suggestion for the source of the word is from the Thai *farang*—meaning any Caucasian. This word is thought to have come from the Thai pronunciation of the word 'France'. As the Khmer alphabet does not have an *f*, the Cambodians replaced it with the equivalent *b*. Thus if this word had strayed across the border from Thailand, *farang* became *barang* in Khmer.

Striking a deal for tourist guidebooks at Angkor Wat.

Another possibility is that both *farang* and *barang* are corruptions of the Chinese word for France, *Fa Guo*.

Whatever the origins of the word, as a *barang* you are, at the very least, a curiosity. As a visitor you will not be expected to master the rules of grammar regarding correct pronoun usage. In addressing your conversational partner, you can get by quite adequately using a person's name. It is worth noting that the Cambodian practice for various forms of address does not transfer with complete accuracy into other languages. If you are walking down the street and some Cambodian calls out to you it will probably be "Sir!" if you are a man and "Madam!" if you are a woman. These terms don't carry quite the overtones of respect that might be assumed from their transliteration into English. They are probably pitched somewhere in tone between "Excuse me!" and "Hey, you!" and they may often accompany a request to donate or buy something (a) you don't want and (b) has already been offered to you many times that day.

NON-VERBAL CUES
Meeting and Greeting

If someone regards you as a superior, on your first meeting you may get little eye contact and not much indication verbally that you have been understood. If your message has not been received or understood you are unlikely to be asked to clarify it. This can make communication difficult, particularly if there is a language barrier. If you have doubts that important instructions are going to be carried out, it's best to summon the assistance of a Cambodian intermediary if one is available.

Many of Buddhism's customs are incorporated into everyday life, in particular the *sompeyar*, the Buddhist gesture of respect. Tradition holds that people acknowledge the presence of religious monuments and personnel by making the appropriate gesture. Cambodians *sompeyar* not only temples and monks, but also each other.

The *sompeyar* is the Cambodian equivalent of Thailand's *wai*. It is performed as an act of greeting or reverence, by placing the palms together with fingers pointing upwards somewhere in front of the body and bowing to a degree that is determined by the relative status of the two parties involved. While the essential elements of the *sompeyar* are simple, the variations subtly recognise the relative status of those delivering the *sompeyar* and those receiving it. In any encounter, the social inferior takes on a physically inferior position to the social superior.

The basic principle of the *sompeyar* is the 'height rule'. The *sompeyar* is delivered at different heights and with different degrees of bowing depending on the relative status of the two parties in communication. The higher the hands are raised, the greater the status of the person receiving the *sompeyar*.

The hands are placed near the forehead when paying homage to the Lord Buddha. Towards monks, the hands are placed in front of the face. When submissive to someone of higher status, the tips of fingers are at nose level. The most neutral position is with the tips of the fingers just below the chin. Dominant is with the hands at chest level. The angle at which the hands are held is also important. A *sompeyar* delivered with fingers pointing upwards is respectful. With fingers pointing outward, it is more dominant.

Sompeyars between the same individuals can vary according to the circumstances. A mother will deliver her *sompeyar* to her six-year-old son with her hands in front of her body, and the son will reciprocate with hands in front of the face. If the six-year-old son suddenly enters the monastery as a novice, the rules of communication are radically revised. When he is clad as a monk, the mother's *sompeyar* will be rendered to her young son with hands high on the forehead, head bowed and eyes downcast.

Visitors to Cambodia unfamiliar with the intricacies of the *sompeyar* are probably better off avoiding the practice altogether and sticking to their traditional meet-and-greet gestures. If, as a visitor, you receive a *sompeyar*, you can reciprocate, although it is not an obligation. If you do, sooner or later on delivering your *sompeyar*, you will almost certainly mess it up.

Niceties aside however, I have on occasion found the *sompeyar* to be contagious. You may well have decided not to *sompeyar* in response to a greeting, but when people are *sompeyaring* around you, your brain may go its own way and decide to *sompeyar* back as a sort of involuntary reaction. (At this point your Cambodian colleague may take you aside for a quick lesson in correct technique).

Cambodians are quite familiar with Western ways of address. It is quite acceptable for foreigners of either sex to shake hands with Cambodians of either sex. If a Cambodian offers his hand, it is well to remember this is an Eastern style handshake. The Cambodian handshake tends to be soft by Western standards. Demonstrating macho superiority by delivering a bone-crunching, finger-snapping handshake will not be appreciated in Cambodia.

In whatever gestures of physical contact you decide to adopt, remember that Cambodians are modest. Close body contact activities—kissing and hugging—should be avoided in public. On the other hand, despite the prohibitions on touching, Cambodians have a much narrower sense of personal space than the average Westerner. While not actually making physical contact, Cambodians with whom you are sharing a conversation may seem to get awfully close to you at times.

DOING BUSINESS

CHAPTER 9

'When you speak in anger, your words do not go far;
when you speak sweetly, you reach your goals.'
—Cambodian proverb

THE ECONOMY

South-east Asia has been the world's fastest growing economic area over the past few decades. The years after World War II saw the extraordinary rise of Japan, followed by the Asian Tiger economies of Singapore, Hong Kong, South Korea, Taiwan, Thailand and Malaysia.

While this great regional economic advance was under way, Cambodia found itself left out of the Asian Tiger phenomenon that gripped most of the region. Cambodia was still preoccupied by its wars and their aftermath. The effects from decades of war and other disruptions still linger in the present-day economy.

Cambodia is not over-blessed with mineral resources. The country has minimal energy sources—little coal, no oil and no gas; though offshore geological structures along the country's coastline offer some promise of commercially-viable undersea deposits of hydrocarbons within Cambodian territory. Apart from the rapidly growing tourist industry, much of Cambodia's economy still stems from traditional agricultural products such as rice, palm sugar, rubber, logging and fishing.

Lingering problems from Cambodia's turbulent history have significantly inhibited the development of a modern economy. On assuming his role as Brother Number One, Pol Pot proclaimed a long-term ambition to build a prosperous industrial economy. But his greater compulsion to wipe out the educated class who might pose a threat to his leadership put paid to that idea. Traditional industries were shut down. A generation of skilled workers was eliminated. Schools were closed and libraries burnt. Knowledge was destroyed. Present-day Cambodia still suffers from a skills shortage as a consequence of these policies of targeted genocide.

After the Vietnamese took over from Pol Pot, Cambodia's efforts to join the global economy met another roadblock. To punish Vietnam for winning the war in Asia, the United States imposed a trade boycott on Hanoi that lasted 18 years. The United States also boycotted Cambodia, a move that created more misery for the long-suffering country.

After the Vietnamese withdrew from Cambodia in 1989 and the US boycott was lifted, the country's trading position improved. Though Cambodia has made solid gains since its shaky situation in the 1980s, it still lags behind its competitors in the region by a considerable margin. Cambodia's GDP per capita is one of the lowest in Asia, and only a little higher than the most disadvantaged African countries.

Broad economic statistics collected by institutions such as the World Bank suggest the country has at least turned the corner. Annual GDP growth has been about 5 per cent in recent years. Exports have been increasing. Cambodia's total export earnings have grown from US$ 100 million in 1990 to US$ 1.77 billion in 2002. But, at the time of writing, the growth in exports has still not been sufficient to generate a trade surplus.

The South-east Asian Tiger economies all started their industrialisation in a similar manner: they invested in the textile and footwear industries based on low labour cost. Cambodia has, to an extent, followed this model. Pay rates for workers in the textile industry in Cambodia are about US$ 50–70 for a seven-day work week with 12-hour shifts. Around US$ 20 is deducted from that for food and lodging.

But, even with its low labour costs, Cambodia has difficulty competing with countries like Bangladesh and China for investment in textiles. Low labour cost, while important, is not the only factor that determines where international textile companies locate their factories.

Keeping a weather eye at the roadside market.

A reliable supply of cheap inputs, good industrial and commercial infrastructure, a cooperative tax regime, low tariffs, an efficient bureaucracy and proximity to major markets all play a part in investment decisions.

Against this background Cambodia has, in recent years, done fairly well with its textile industry. From almost zero ten years before, textile exports in 2002 reached US$ 1.35 billion. The principal export markets are now North America, Europe and Singapore. Of great assistance in developing its export markets has been Cambodia's success in winning Normal Trade Relations (NOR) with the United States in early 1998.

This measure reduced tariffs into the US on Cambodian made textiles from 40 per cent to 3 per cent.

The World Trade Organisation's (WTO) garment quota allocation system, introduced to encourage industry the industries in smaller countries, has also enhanced Cambodia's garment industry by restricting the market for more competitive economies such as China. However under World Trading Organisation (WTO) rules, garment quota ended in 2005. As a result, Cambodia's garment industry has come under increasing pressure from competing countries.

Traditional craft industries of basket weaving and metalworking have also been reinstated since the days of the Khmer Rouge. The sericulture industry (the breeding of silkworms and production of silk), closed down by Pol Pot, has not yet fully recovered. Sericulture remains a cottage industry. It struggles to compete on price with silk produced through more capital intensive techniques in places like India and Thailand.

Silver-smithing is another traditional industry in Cambodia. As the country has limited deposits of alluvial silver and gold, raw materials for this industry are supplied across the border from Laos.

Despite some economic improvements in recent years, the country still relies heavily on foreign aid. Overall, Cambodia continues to struggle to balance its books. In 2004, an estimated 75 per cent of the Cambodian government's budget was funded by overseas aid of one sort or another. Apart from its tourist industry, the country has been unable to develop its economy much beyond cottage industry pursuits such as textiles. Multinational companies have yet to set up in Cambodia in a major way.

CAMBODIA AS A BUSINESS DESTINATION

Currently, among the pluses of investing in Cambodia from the investor's point of view are: a cheap labour force, few labour regulations, fairly low infrastructure costs for services like rentals, utilities and the like, a low corporate income tax rate (9 per cent), and reasonable proximity to markets of adjacent larger countries, such as Thailand and Vietnam.

One specific attraction for some businesses may be an absence of labour unions. The notion of labour rights has not been part of the country's traditional culture. Cambodians— males and females—tend to accept sweatshop conditions that might dismay higher paid workers in First World countries. In fact, employees in Cambodian sweatshops may well consider themselves lucky to hold down regular paying jobs, given that the alternatives to working in a factory may be not working at all, hustling, begging, or scratching out a living in agriculture.

Factors on the minus side of the ledger for the local economy include: a poorly-developed infrastructure with limited port facilities, roads in poor condition, negligible rail links, limited air links, inadequate communication infrastructure, a poorly-skilled labour force, a small domestic market, a barely-developed financial centre, perceptions of serious corruption, and a bureaucracy dedicated to making life difficult for all who deal with it, including business.

Cambodia has no strong culture of legally binding contracts. Foreign-owned businesses and NGOs operating in Cambodia bring their contracting culture with them. But for contracts entered into inside the country, Cambodia has the same ambivalent attitude to written and verbal contracts that is common throughout Asia. A contract may be regarded merely as a vague expression of intent, or it may be more. Generally speaking, contracts with Cambodian organisations will be less binding than in most First World countries. The weight of the contract terms is more likely to be set by the nature and culture of the contracting parties than the written word. Fine points of law are unlikely to be debated. On the other hand routine contracts may look familiar to Cambodia's visitors. A lease contract for a renting a house in Cambodia will, for example, be much the same as a similar contract anywhere.

The government is attempting not only to change the country's legal culture, but to upgrade its legal infrastructure. As a result of an almost perpetual state of warfare for most of its time since independence, Cambodia has barely had a court system in place to hear contract disputes. Since resolving contractual disputes is difficult for this reason, continued goodwill between contracting parties is all important. Party A might want to bring a lawsuit against party B. But, likely as not, no court may be available to hear the case. Establishing the legal system is one of Cambodia's most vital tasks in creating a modern state.

Cambodia has become a great deal more sensitive to the international economic environment in recent years. Over the last decade, after its long period of economic and more general isolation, Cambodia has been reconnecting with the rest of the world. Cambodia has been a full member of ASEAN (Association of South-east Asian Nations) since 1999, on the condition that by 2010 it will implement the ASEAN's required tariff-reduction programmes. Cambodia has also joined the wider world trading community, in 2004 becoming the 148th member of the WTO (World Trade Organisation).

Old rivalries between Cambodia and its ASEAN neighbours surface now and again. In January 2003, Cambodian newspapers reported that a 24-year-old Thai actress, Suvanant Kongying, on a mission to promote a well-known brand of cosmetics, had claimed that Cambodia had 'stolen' Angkor from Thailand, and that she (Ms Kongying) wanted it back.

This somewhat outrageous comment from someone with no official standing was sufficient to inspire rioters to take to the streets of Phnom Penh to vent their anti-Thai feelings. The Thai Embassy and a number of Thai-owned hotels and businesses were torched in the resulting mayhem, causing millions of dollars of damage. Counterpart demonstrations were held in Bangkok, with Thai demonstrators besieging the Cambodian Embassy there. Ms Kongying later claimed she had been wrongly quoted. One of the theories floated was that Ms Kongying's remarks were the result of a smear campaign by a rival cosmetics company, trying spike her product launch.

To heal this breach of international relations, prime ministers of bother countries became involved. A payment of US$ 8 million was made by private business interests in Thailand for damages to the Thai Embassy in Phnom Penh.

IMPROVEMENTS ON THE WAY?

Three frequently cited explanations for Cambodia's failure to stage an economic miracle along the lines of Thailand, China and even Vietnam, are political instability, corruption and bureaucracy. Throughout its 30-odd years in power, the present Cambodian government has been perceived as a hotbed of corruption and crony capitalism, as were the previous governments of Lon Nol and Sihanouk. Critics of the government point out that Cambodia still has essentially the same people in power now as it did in 1979 when the Vietnamese army freed the country from the Khmer Rouge. During the 1980s, government policy was run from Hanoi. Two decades later, critics claim, little has changed.

Small-scale corruption is evident wherever you travel in Cambodia. A common sight is a policeman holding up a line of traffic to demand a small payment to allow the traffic to proceed. On a larger scale, logging is probably the most corrupt industry in Cambodia, as it is in other countries. Temptations abound. Stands of mature teak and other species can convert to US$ 10,000 of saw-logs per tree once they reach the market. Logging of the western forest in the Cardamom Mountains was probably the greatest source of finance for Khmer Rouge guerrilla operations in the 1980s. Timber taken from the forest was shipped out through Thailand, a country in which illegal logging operations also prospered.

Continuous restoration and maintenance work is undertaken of the Angkor structures. This work is largely performed and financed by Western NGOs. But if you want to visit the site, you are obliged to purchase a visitor's pass (US$ 20 per day or US$ 40 for three days). The pass is issued in the name of Sokha Hotel Co Ltd, a private firm that has taken over ticketing sales under a controversial arrangement with the government. According to news reports, Sokha Hotel's parent company, Sokimex, pays the government a flat fee of US$ 1 million a year to run Angkor's ticket system. Anything above that, Sokimex keeps. In 2000, Sokimex and Apsara, the authority overseeing the reconstruction work in Angkor, negotiated a new deal that gave Apsara half of the first US$ 3 million earned, and 70 per cent of all subsequent income. How much cash Sokimex actually returns as upkeep of the site is unknown. Arrangements within the government are too opaque for an outside audit. From most accounts, the company does little more at Angkor other than provide personnel to run its ticketing operations.

The government occasionally pays lip service to stamping out corruption. Little happens for no better reason, according to minority parties and politicians, than that the government itself is corrupt. As a business person, you may be compelled to enter deals favourable to particular cronies of the government. For example, if you want to run a restaurant in Phnom Penh, you will be forced to hire a private security guard from a particular security firm thought to have links with the prime minister.

In 2001, a report by the NGO Global Witness detailed arrangements for an illegal logging operation between generals of the Cambodian army and business. An editor of the opposition newspaper *Samleng Yuvachun Khmer* (Voice of the Khmer Youth) was fined 18,000 euros for publishing an exposé of the deal. This was not the sort of publicity the Cambodian government liked to hear.

The best-known world watchdog on the relative levels of corruption between nations is Transparency International, an organisation whose declared objective is to stamp out corruption worldwide. Among its observations, Transparency International notes that, in the world generally, corruption is one of the biggest barriers to economic development. From time to time, the organisation releases its 'Transparency Index', listing its assessment of perceived corruption in various countries. The 2004 Transparency Index ranked Finland the least corrupt country in the world, and Bangladesh and Haiti the most corrupt. One hundred and thirty three countries were included in the list. Cambodia was not among them for the reason that its data was too scanty and difficult to collect. Where Cambodia would have stood in the Transparency Index cannot be determined. The apocryphal evidence suggests it would be down towards the Bangladesh-Haiti end of the scale.

In addition to eliminating corruption and fixing its bureaucracy, the government has much to do to provide for an improved regulatory environment for business in Cambodia. One such measure is to establish a stock exchange —presently non-existent in Cambodia. Under the aegis of Cambodia's reserve bank, the National Bank of Cambodia (NBC), the programme to launch the Cambodian stock exchange is under way. A target date between 2008 and 2010 has been set for this program.

The NBC notes that prior to opening a stock exchange, the country must first implement a number of reforms and regulations in the financial sector. Chief among them is adopting standard business accounting practices that in many other countries are taken for granted. These programs are also under way.

In addition, the banking sector urgently needs an upgrade. As the NBC observes, the 'spread' of interest rates between borrowing and lending rates is extremely high in Cambodia, a banking practice that inhibits development of the Cambodia business sector. In addition, payment systems between creditors and debtors are poorly developed. Difficulty of conducting normal commercial transactions, such as paying bills by direct debit or even cheques, is an important factor that adds to the cost of doing business in Cambodia.

GETTING A JOB IN CAMBODIA

Though the majority of foreigners in Cambodia come as tourists, visitors in other categories arrive to take up paying jobs or do good deeds. Most of Cambodia's non-tourist visitors work for NGOs (Non-Government Organisations).

Outside NGOs and casual teaching vacancies, Cambodia offers few job opportunities for foreign workers, since few multinational corporations have established a presence in the country and few foreign employment opportunities exist with local firms.

Pay rates vary from Western-scale wages and conditions for people hired outside the country to local wages, or even nothing for voluntary service. For local hires who travel to Cambodia without having made arrangements in advance, the terms of employment by Western standards are likely to be onerous. No sick pay, accommodation or other fringe benefits is likely to be provided. Paid holidays are unusual.

For drifters from the outside world who come looking for work, the chances of a well-paid job are slim but a poorly-paid one is quite easy to get. Many foreigners residing in Cambodia work as English-language teachers. A constant supply of teaching jobs is advertised in Cambodia's English-language newspapers.

One advantage Cambodia has over other South-east Asian countries in the matter of getting employment is that rules on work permits are very rarely enforced. If you wish to work in Cambodia, or even think you might want to work in the country, you are better off entering the country under a three-month business visa (described on page 99–100) than under a tourist visa.

THE NGOS

Today's Cambodia relies on aid that comes from a number of sources. A significant portion of foreign aid enters Cambodia through official government channels, particularly direct financial aid. The country also relies on the continuing presence of its NGOs to provide community services that in other countries are the responsibility of government. About 250 NGOs are currently active in Cambodia where they work on a not-for-profit basis.

NGOs deliver a wide range of services essential to Cambodia's economy and community, such as education, medical services, child welfare, food supply, opposition to sexual exploitation. NGOs are active in all sectors of the community, establishing schools, health care services, counselling services, sheltered workshops and small industries such as seafood aquaculture. Private individuals are also at work in Cambodia doing volunteer work of various kinds. Typically, NGOs are financed by overseas donations and staffed by volunteers plus Cambodians on modest salaries. Their running costs are generally low.

NGOs probably achieve greater returns per dollar invested than most other forms of charity. Of the various types of assistance that can be provided, aid for services such as medical attention are the easiest to give. Patients turn up at mobile clinics and have their ailments fixed, to the general satisfaction of all. The most difficult form of aid in which to achieve success is monetary aid.

NGOs have their critics. Some aid programmes are criticised for coming with strings attached, such as conditions that require aid recipients to purchase the products of their donors. Other aid appears to be blind to local needs. Institutions like the World Bank have been criticised for schemes that require large injections of capital, such as dam-building, when recipients really require projects such as training and education.

The best type of aid, most NGOs realise, is that which breeds self-sufficiency. The maxim 'you can feed someone for a day if you give them a fish, and for life if you teach them to fish' underlies the principles on which many NGOs operate.

Despite their good intentions, the role of NGOs in Cambodia is a fraught subject. Perhaps based on no more

Bullock cart driver and his smile.

than the presence on the streets of Phnom Penh of white four-wheel-drives bearing NGO logos, suspicion lingers that administrative costs of larger NGOs are higher than they ought to be.

Aid programmes are also criticised for perpetuating dependency. In his book, *The Lords of Poverty: The Power, Prestige and Corruption of the International Aid Business*, author Graham Hancock contends that aid agencies are not long-term solutions to the problems of poor countries. Hancock writes mostly about countries in Africa. There, as Hancock points out, many people driven by desperate circumstances, have given up trying to help themselves. But Cambodia is not Africa. Though the country is poor, it has not given up. If you ask Cambodians what the key to a better life is, most will reply 'education'. While Cambodia takes its handouts from other people and countries, it maintains its quest for self-sufficiency and its own identity. Cambodians have lived on hope for a long time and continue to do so.

The role of providing aid to the community can be surprisingly taxing on both the donor and the recipient. It may take steely resolve to make a success out of an NGO career. Empathy with the local culture is essential. Shattered hopes and dreams of well-intentioned NGO workers who make an early and disillusioned exit from Cambodia are commonplace. Things move gradually in Cambodia, compared to the culture in the West where progress must be made in a tearing hurry. Advice given, but not necessarily sought, often involves a clash of cultures. Stories abound of well-meaning disappointed ideologues from the First World whose ideas appear to be received but are not adopted. The role of care-givers is not only to teach, but also to learn. Advice given may infer a mistaken assumption of superior knowledge that doesn't really exist.

For example, Cambodia practises essentially subsistence, organic agriculture, whereas the accepted practice in the West is to obtain massive yields from the soil with liberal application of fertilisers, pesticides and herbicides. In Cambodia, the ox pulls the plough. In the West, the tractor

On the road: a Cambodian farmer and his oxen team.

pulls the plough. Which does the job better? Which is better suited to a Third World country?

NGOs from different cultures may disagree amongst themselves on the methods most appropriate to their client state. Though scope for increasing the efficiency of farming no doubt exists, not all NGOs would want to see Cambodia turn itself into a monocultural, fully-mechanised agricultural collective—the corporate farming idea of the western world—that could put most of Cambodia's population out of work. A German conservation-minded NGO believes a conversion to organic farming to supply lucrative markets in the First World is a far better option. The Cambodian proverb: 'Don't take the straight path or the winding one; take the path your ancestors have taken' summarises this Cambodian viewpoint well enough. Since fertilisers, pesticides, herbicides and tractor fuel are all products of an industry that relies on what is currently the world's fastest dwindling major resource—hydrocarbons—Cambodians might reasonably contend that their methods of agriculture are more sustainable in the long run.

Cambodia has come a long way from the ruined country the Khmer Rouge regime left behind in 1979. Nevertheless, the goal of self-sufficiency remains elusive. Whatever the downside, the fact remains that if NGO activity in Cambodia were to lapse overnight, many in the country might die of starvation or neglect. NGOs have become embedded in this country. The dependency has been created. It exists and cannot easily be reversed. In the long term, the objective should be, and is, to create a country that can take care of itself. But for the time being, the country relies upon the financial and other assistance it receives from NGOs as well as the more formal aid it receives through foreign-government aid programmes.

Mosquito Nets for Homes

Services provided by NGOs may not require all that much money if a simple need can be met. For example malaria is a big problem in Cambodia's more rural areas. Apart from the health consequences to the sufferers themselves, the costs of treating malaria are high. The malaria virus is carried by mosquitoes. Since 98 per cent of Cambodian homes are unscreened against insects, malaria spreads easily. On the basis that prevention is better than cure, the NGO, American Assistance for Cambodia, will purchase and deliver mosquito nets to malaria affected areas for around US$ 5 each. According to the NGO, this modest fee is likely to save the lives of three people over the life of the mosquito net. The American Assistance mosquito net distribution programme is hardly the stuff of rocket science. But for all that, it is a highly-effective low-cost way to meet an important need. Those who want to assist this program can find out more from American Assistance for Cambodia, P.O. Box 2716, GPO, New York, NY 10116.

BLESSING THE WORKPLACE

In Cambodia, like most of Asia, business culture and etiquette is subtle. Cambodians are generous in making allowances for foreigners. However, complying with local customs, at least to some extent, will serve the interests of guests to the country and their businesses, as well as pleasing the locals.

For example, if you are launching a new project in Cambodia you will be well advised to have it officially blessed. Buddhist monks are happy to perform the appropriate ceremony for you at the cost of a modest donation towards their temple.

The important first step is to establish is a suitable date of the ceremony. An intermediary will need to consult the monastery's abbot to ascertain the most propitious days on the calendar.

The ceremony may take around two hours. Because monks are forbidden from eating after noon, projects are blessed in the morning. Chanting and singing is accompanied by ribbon tying and posting of good luck charms at strategic points in the building. Organisers must transport the monks to and from the ceremony and provide hospitality. After the ceremony, a traditional feast of light meats, vegetables and fruits follows. Monks will customarily bring their food bowls to whatever blessing ceremonies they attend.

Throughout the ceremony, protocol rules. Cambodians are familiar with the rules for handing food to monks, since their community provides this service daily. For the business blessing, the head of the client organisation has the honour of serving the food first, with the abbot being the first served. If, as a non-Cambodian, you happen to be the head person, you may be serving the monks directly. So prior to the event, get some advice on serving protocol.

Women should take special care as women are not merely prohibited from touching a monk, they are also prohibited from touching any extension to the monk, including the food bowl the monk is holding. Women have two options for delivering food to a monk: they can drop the food into the monk's extended bowl, taking care to make no contact with the bowl or the monk; or they can hand the food over to a man to give to the monk.

Once the ceremony is complete and the monks have returned to the monastery, a certain amount of spiritual upkeep may still be required from time to time over the life of the project. As a sensitive employer, it pays to investigate whether a spirit house should be provided to accommodate spirits inconvenienced by structures erected to serve the project's needs. Normally, a spirit house would be located outside the premises in a position beyond the building's shadow, though spirit houses and altars inside businesses are also common enough. Local advice should also be sought on this subject. The spirit house itself requires a certain amount of maintenance, since spirits need frequent offerings of food, garlands and incense. Usually, the local staff will take care of this day-to-day task.

WORKING WITH LOCAL STAFF

Suggestions for interacting with Cambodians in the workplace are an extension of those for getting along with Cambodians more generally. (*Refer to* 'Social Rules' *in* Chapter 4: Getting to Know the Cambodians *from page 75–86.*)

Like the wider Cambodian society, the hierarchy of the workplace is influenced by Buddhist beliefs regarding birthright. A culture of social harmony and collective cooperation stems from the twin sources of Buddhist beliefs and the traditional agrarian society. A driving force governing the relationships of many Cambodians with other people is the Buddhist 'middle path' of peace and harmony. In the workplace, the desire to avoid conflict with colleagues, customers and suppliers alike, may supplant more Western-style objectives of achieving project goals and fulfilling corporate obligations.

Hierarchical structures tend to be rigid. Formal assemblies of staff are highly structured affairs. Meetings tend to be addressed by the boss, rather than the easy interchange of views sometimes seen in Western corporate culture. Cambodian underlings are less likely to suggest new ideas and much more likely to endorse whatever they think the boss wants to do, whether they agree with it or not. This imposes a greater obligation on bosses to come up with the most appropriate solution to problems, and to find out what is going on, not only in the organisation but also in the mind of employees.

Closely aligned to the Buddhist middle path, is the issue of 'face', a sentiment in the West somewhat akin to 'self-respect'. Embarrassing employees in front of their colleagues is mortally offensive, much more so than in the West. No one should be taken to task in front of their peer group. Criticism of an employee's performance is best tendered privately, sensitively and indirectly, accompanied by suggestions for improvement.

Whereas in the West reprimands are customarily delivered at the time an employee's lack of performance is first noticed, employers in Cambodia are better off waiting for an emotionally calm environment where the problem can be analysed at a private meeting between employee and employer, even if this is sometime after the event.

If you hail from the First World, you are likely to find competition between staff for kudos and promotion less intense in Cambodia than in your home country. The workplace is generally more laid-back and less ambitious for personal advancement. Office workers in Cambodia are likely to work cooperatively with colleagues rather than compete with them for promotions. To a greater extent than in the West, the workplace is a venue in which social relationships are forged.

Foreign employers may expend more effort in developing workplace relationships than they might in the home offices. Fostering a caring culture in the workplace is beneficial to all. It is a good idea to comment on your employees' life outside work—their wives, children and interests. Gifts to staff to mark special occasions are also widely acceptable, even expected. As an employer, you should never be seen as mean in granting small favours. Bosses are expected to create social occasions now and again to entertain their staff. Whatever bills due from such events should be picked up by the boss without question. Any generosity extended to your staff, both of spirit and in the material sense, will be well rewarded.

A calm demeanour is also very important. Some light and polite conversation is expected in most circumstances before coming to the point. Exhibiting anger, raising one's voice and bad language are all seen as a lost of control of oneself and very bad form, causing loss of face all round. Outward appearance also matters.

Your standard of dress is a symbol of rank. Since Cambodians with minuscule resources achieve miraculous results in the dress and hygiene area, you will gain more respect and cooperation if you are well turned out and dressed neatly. Those visiting Cambodia on business should err on the side of formality and dress conservatively. Men on business are advised to wear a tie and at least carry a coat. A business suit is appropriate dress for women.

Foreign employers may experience frustrations in making things happen in Cambodia. By and large, Cambodians are not pushy. Some say they bring to the workplace an attitude towards time that is not far removed from their rural culture. Sowing and harvesting are activities imposed by external forces such as weather rather than running to a man-made schedule. Even urban Cambodians tend to be laid-back. They allow things to happen, as distinct from making them happen. They are accustomed to forming slow-moving queues at post offices and banks. The government and the bureaucracy, in particular, take their time. Cambodians are patient. In many of their transactions, they need to be.

Some Cambodians have a similar relaxed attitude to appointments. Cambodians have a sense of hierarchy, and you may not be at the top. Things may crop up that demand they reschedule your meetings at the last moment. However, this is one area where those working in Cambodia may best be advised to diverge from local practice. As employer, if timekeeping and schedules are important to your operation, you have the opportunity to set the example to your staff in your own punctuality and adherence to schedules.

GETTING THE MESSAGE ACROSS

Entire library sections of books have been written about techniques of communication within organisations. Without a doubt, ineffective communication is a principal reason that organisations run into problems, regardless of where they are located in the world. As a working rule, most textbooks on the subject tell us that organisations with transparent, clear communications operate more efficiently and harmoniously than those where established communications are absent or impaired.

In the real world however, clear and transparent communications often run up against that overwhelmingly strong force called human nature. For a variety of reasons, human beings in organisations like to keep secrets from each other. Typical reasons are competition among employees for promotions and other advantages, and various versions of the established, well-documented human tendency to 'kill the messenger'. Bearers of bad news rarely fare well in any society, and Cambodia, where bad news is barely considered polite, is no exception. It is much easier, at the moment of telling, to share with our bosses the news they would like to hear, even if doing so creates bigger problems later.

For those operating critical path schedules, the casual attitudes of Cambodians towards time can be a source of irritation. For example, you would be unwise to assume that your Cambodian staff will inform you that a particular project is running past its deadline. Cambodians may be most reluctant to pass on bad news that may jeopardise their harmonious work environment. If Cambodians have some bad news that ought to known, they generally won't lie about it, but neither are they likely to volunteer it.

If news of the delay does surface, Cambodians are far more likely to explain or accept the delay rather than figure out ways in which lost time can be made up. Delays in government approvals, essential paperwork and getting goods in and out of the country are par for the course. Foreigners running projects in Cambodia may need to spend plenty of time and effort updating their schedules and working around delays.

An additional complication to communication is language. Foreign organisations working in Cambodia must inevitably use the language of one of the parties involved in the transaction. The respective language skills of those involved determines what this language may be. For instance, if English is used, the Cambodian party would be communicating in their second (or third) language.

Circumstances that suit written or oral communications have been widely written about in management textbooks by First World authors. Oral communication is seen as warm, personal and spontaneous, while written communication is considered more precise but distant. Cambodian culture is certainly predisposed to oral communication. Rarely is a written agenda prepared for meetings between Cambodians, and just as rarely are minutes taken.

Oral communications in a second language within a passive culture can be easily misunderstood. For example, if your Cambodian employee does not understand your oral instructions, he is unlikely to press for a clarification. Such an enquiry would involve loss of face for both parties. It would

suggest the employer has failed to communicate clearly, and that the employee has insufficient skill to understand what might be perfectly clear instructions to others.

On the other hand, if you provide written directives that are also not understood, your Cambodian employee can take your instructions away to a private place and mull over them with the aid of a dictionary. Or he can discuss them with a colleague for another interpretation. If all else fails, he may even approach you for an interpretation. For oral communications, he probably wouldn't.

Here are four golden rules of oral communication in a second (or even first) language: (i) Speak slowly; (ii) speak clearly; (iii) use short sentences; and (iv) avoid idioms.

Easy... to... say...

'But slipping into unintended and extraneous circumlocution can all too readily be facilitated, particularly when issuing communications of a highly technical nature.'

Such stilted language is best avoided.

So are expressions like 'let's get the show on the road' or 'a dog and pony show'. Expressions like these aren't easily translated from a Khmer/English dictionary.

Though Cambodians are inclined to oral communications, as a foreign employer you don't need to feel too hidebound by Cambodian culture. A greater degree of written communication is probably justified in Cambodia as compared to home base, since oral communications, in whatever language and however well delivered, have a much higher likelihood of being misunderstood. No one will be offended if you, as the resident foreigner, increase the output of the written word. Doing so will almost certainly serve the interests of your organisation in the long run.

WORKING FOR A LOCAL BOSS

If your role in the organisation requires you to work for a Cambodian boss, you will probably find your employer values the strengths your own culture brings to the organisation. While working within the general ideology of cooperation and teamwork that stems from ancient cultural roots like Buddhism and rural life, you should not be afraid to apply the skills you have brought into the country. These are probably the reasons you were appointed in the first place.

As an employee of a Cambodian organisation, you are not expected to overdo 'going Cambodian' to accommodate the cultural norms of your host society. Foreign workers can take a great deal more liberties than the Cambodians themselves. Within reasonable boundaries, you can afford to be more assertive and opinionated than the typical Cambodian employee. As an expatriate employee, your employer and your colleagues are likely to assume you have superior knowledge and expertise in your area of operation.

You can also impress your Cambodian colleagues and betters with your versatility. In accordance with their general sense of preordained hierarchy, Cambodians tend to work within their specialties to a far greater extent than much of the rest of the world. Foreigners are likely to be admired for their wider range of skills (should they have any).

Do's and Don'ts for the Workplace

Do's

- Try to make your employees feel loved. Take time out to find out about their lives and interests outside the office environment. Try to engage them occasionally in small talk with subjects such as their families.
- Try to remember that Cambodians enjoy a great sense of ceremony. You will be well thought of if you mark the birthdays of your staff with a small gift.
- Share things, such as food, brought into the workplace.
- Try to figure out what resources your staff might need to get their work done more efficiently. Staff may be reluctant to point such things out to you.
- Entertain staff as a group now and again. Taking staff out for an outing at your expense is expected and enhances relationships.

In addition, your Cambodian boss may feel your presence enhances his status among his peers. As such, you may find yourself taken to meetings of important people and discussing subjects that seem to have little relevance to your role in the organisation. After a while you may realise that in this sort of activity, you are filling a mascot role. In certain occupations, having a foreign expert on the payroll is taken as a token of success of the organisation.

GENDER BIAS

A report by an NGO consultative group in 2001 found that women made up 53 per cent of the Cambodian workforce. High concentrations of females in the workplace were found in the garment industry (90 per cent) and in general manufacturing (67 per cent) and agriculture. Multinational garment companies, set up to take advantage of cheap labour rates, employ mainly women as manual workers and men in supervisory roles. The NGO consultative group found that

Don'ts

- Don't assume, unless you have very good reason to do so, that directions you have issued have been understood. Cambodians are more comfortable assuming they know what they are supposed to do rather than ask the questions that would make them absolutely sure.
- Don't be reticent about displaying your talents and skills. Cambodians are impressed by the wide range of talents foreigners possess.
- Don't criticise members of your staff in front of their colleagues
- Above all, don't lose your cool. Loss of temper, indicating loss of control, is the most effective way to lose face in Cambodia.

on average, female workers in manufacturing were paid 30 per cent less than their male counterparts. Women are also more prominent among street vendors and in retail.

In 2000, Cambodia passed legislation prohibiting discrimination against women in the workplace. But this legislation is difficult to enforce. As in most countries, the glass ceiling in Cambodia is still pretty well intact. In many occupations, seniority in the workplace is the man's domain. Sexism too, is alive and well. Attractive young women typically hold down receptionist roles in Cambodian organisations, with the upwardly mobile positions more likely to be occupied by men.

In 2003, the Cambodian parliament had 12 female members (9 per cent of the total seats against an average for democracies around the world about double that). On the other hand, Cambodian women may hold the top job in occupations like teaching and media, and foreign women heading foreign organisations like NGOs will be accepted at face value.

FAST FACTS

CHAPTER 10

'The humble people of Cambodia are the most wonderful in the world. Their great misfortune is that they always have terrible leaders who made them suffer. I am not sure that I was much better myself, but perhaps I was the least bad.'
—Prince Sihanouk in New York in 1979

THE COUNTRY
Official Name
Kingdom of Cambodia

Cambodia has been renamed six times since independence, which is perhaps a reflection on the country's recent turbulent history. Cambodia, the most common name used, derives from the French Cambodge. On some maps, the country is also called Kampuchea, which is close to the country's Khmer name that stemmed from creation myths described on page 19. After independence from the French in 1953, the new nation was called the Kingdom of Cambodia. In 1970, the US-backed Lon Nol government changed the name to the Khmer Republic. The Khmer Rouge amended the name to Democratic Kampuchea. From 1979–1989, the country was known as the People's Republic of Kampuchea. Under the aegis of the United Nations between 1989–1993, it became the State of Cambodia. Since 1993 to the present, the country returned to the Kingdom of Cambodia, its original name after independence.

Capital
Phnom Penh

Flag
Like the name of the nation itself, the Cambodian flag has changed a number of times since independence in 1953.

As governments came and went, all but one of Cambodia's national flags from 1953 depicted various versions of the Angkor Wat theme. The exception was the period of UN administration when a new flag was created in UN colours showing the country in white against on a pale blue field. After six different flags in 40 years, the nation eventually returned to its symbolic beginnings. The present flag is almost identical to the flag that Cambodian independents triumphantly hoisted when the French departed in 1953. It carries a foreground motif of Angkor Wat on a background field of one central red and two blue horizontal stripes.

National Anthem
Nokoreach ('Royal Kingdom')

Time
Greenwich Mean Time plus 7 hours (GMT + 0700)

Telephone Country Code
855

Land
The fertile Tonle Sap-Mekong delta in the centre of the country is ringed by low mountains ranges: the Elephant Mountains in the east; the Cardamom Range in the south-west; the Dangrek Mountains in the north; and the Annamite Cordillera to the north-east.

Area
181,040 sq km

Highest Point
Phnom Aoral in the south-west (1,810 m)

Major Rivers and Lakes
Mekong and Tonle Sap River, and Tonle Sap Lake

Climate
Tropical, with the south-west monsoon from May to November and a dry season from December to April

Natural Resources
Timber, gemstones, iron ore, manganese, silver and phosphates

Government
Since the 1993 UN-sanctioned elections, Cambodia is a constitutional monarchy with a democratically-elected government. The chief of state is King Norodom Sihamoni, and head of state, Prime Minister Hun Sen. The bicameral parliament is made up of the 123-seat National Assembly and 61-seat Senate.

Cambodia's Monarchs Since 1860	
Duang	died 1860
Norodom	r. 1861–1904
Sisowath (Norodom's half brother)	r. 1904–1927
Monivong (Sisowath's eldest son)	r. 1927–1941
Norodom Sihanouk	r. 1941–1955
Suramarit (Sihanouk's father)	r. 1955–1960
Sisowath Kossomak Nirireath (Sihanouk's mother)	r. 1960–1970
Norodom Sihanouk	r. 1993–2004
Norodom Sihamoni	r. 2004–

From 1970–1993, the nation had a succession of republican-style governments with no monarch.

Administrative Divisions
20 provinces (*khaitt*, singular and plural): Banteay Meanchey, Battambang, Kampong Cham, Kampong Chhnang, Kampong Speu, Kampong Thom, Kampot, Kandal, Koh Kong, Kratie, Mondolkiri, Otdar Meanchey, Pursat, Takeo

4 municipalities (krong, singular and plural): Keb, Pailin, Phnom Preah Vihear, Prey Veng, Ratanakiri, Siem Reap, Stung Treng, Svay Rieng, Penh, Sihanoukville

Population
13,600,000 (July 2005 estimate)

Ethnic Groups
90 per cent Khmers, 5 per cent Vietnamese, 1 per cent Chinese, and 4 per cent Cham and Chunchiet

Religion
Theravada Buddhism (95 per cent)

Languages
Khmer (95 per cent), French and English. Thai is spoken in areas near the border with Thailand and indigenous people speak their own languages.

Currency
Riel (KHR)

Gross Domestic Product
US$ 25.02 billion (2004 estimate)

Produce
Rice, rubber, corn, vegetables, cashews and tapioca

Industries
Tourism, garments, rice milling, fishing, wood and wood products, rubber, cement, gem mining and textiles

Exports
Clothing, timber, rubber, rice, fish, tobacco and footwear

Imports
Petroleum products, cigarettes, gold, construction materials, machinery, motor vehicles and pharmaceutical products

Keeping cool on a hot day—four of Cambodian's 50,000 monks.

Weights and measures

Cambodia uses the standard metric system of weights and measures. For those who are used to working with imperial measurements, here are some key conversions:

1 kg	=	2.20 pounds
1 litre	=	0.22 UK gallon
1 litre	=	0.26 US gallon
1 km	=	0.62 miles
1 m	=	3.28 feet

Protected Areas and Wildlife

Cambodia has 23 designated protected areas, of which seven are national parks, ten are wildlife sanctuaries, three are protected landscapes and three are for multiple-use, which means the land is available for logging and fishing.

Cambodia was once home to large numbers of elephants, wild oxen, rhinoceroses, several species of deer, sun bears, leopards, tigers and other mammals. Many bird species and a variety of freshwater and marine fish can also be found in the country. No one has seen a Cambodian tiger in recent times; but if you bag one, it's worth over US$ 1,000 on the Cambodian market, such is the widespread belief in the curative and aphrodisiac powers of tiger parts.

Illegal logging and fishing, as well as poaching of wildlife for game and trophies, have caused much environmental degradation. Environmental laws are few and rarely enforced, and at the grass roots level, ignorance and the dire need for food and firewood prevail.

COMING INTO CAMBODIA
Arriving by Air

Cambodia has two international airports—Pochentong or Phnom Penh International Airport and Siem Reap-Angkor International Airport.

Flight Information

Information for both Phnom Penh International and Siem Reap-Angkor International Airports can be found at http://www.cambodia-airports.com/

Travelling Overland
Thailand

Travellers can enter Cambodia from Thailand at various points. The Cambodian towns of Poipet and Koh Kong are the most popular crossings. Their opposite numbers on the Thai side of the border are, respectively, Aranyaprathet in Sa Kaeo province in the central-eastern region and Hat Lek in Trat province in the far south-east.

The crossing through Poipet is the shortest route overland from Bangkok to Siem Reap. Aranyaprathet is about 3 to 4 hours by bus or train from Bangkok. The road journey between Poipet and Siem Reap is about 150 km (94 miles). At the time of writing, much of this road was bitumen with lots of potholes. A 30-km (19-mile) section east of Sisophon was unsurfaced and had even bigger potholes. Many Bailey-style floodway bridges, the detritus from someone's war, have been built in this section of the highway. The most demanding aspect of driving this road is to position the wheels of the vehicle on the bridge deck planking rather than on the equally wide gaps between the planks. (I like to credit my Cambodian driver for his skill in achieving this challenging task while enveloped in a cloud of red dust from the vehicles ahead.) This is not a good road to travel at night.

If you are taking the southerly route into Cambodia via Hat Lek and Koh Kong, you start by catching the six-hour long Bangkok-to-Trat bus. From Trat, a minibus will take you to the Thai border crossing point at Hat Lek. From Koh Kong on the Cambodian side, you have the option of taking a fast air-conditioned boat ride of about four hours to Sihanoukville, or making a road journey on the recently upgraded, but highly unreliable National Route 18. This road passes through some attractive scenery, but road conditions cannot be guaranteed. The trip, including two ferry crossings, may be advertised as four hours, but can take at least twice that long. Those who appreciate a modicum of comfort will chose the boat, although they will miss a scenic drive through the flat, lightly inhabited south-west corner of Cambodia. The road from Sihanoukville to Phnom Penh is another three-hour journey along a smooth all-weather highway.

Vietnam

From Vietnam, you cross over from the border town of Moc Bai and enter Cambodia through Bavet. The road between Bavet and Phnom Penh was upgraded in 2003 and was last seen in reasonable condition. However, road conditions can vary in Cambodia. To avoid disappointment, latest bulletins should be obtained.

Laos

The land crossing is between Don Khong in Laos and Voen Khan in Cambodia. At the time of writing, this border was open, but sometimes it closes for long periods, so you should make enquiries before entering or leaving Cambodia by this route. The road to Kratie (Route 13) from Phnom Penh is in good condition. After that, between Kratie and Stung Treng is 120 km (75 miles) of rough unmade road that may be impassable even to 4WD vehicles at certain times of the year. From Stung Treng to the border, the road improves. On the Laotian side, the road is good all the way into Vientiane.

Visas and Border Checkpoints

If you are entering Cambodia from Thailand and Vietnam, you can get a visa at the border. If you are crossing from Laos, you must get your visa in advance from the Cambodian embassy. Going the other way, if you are entering either Vietnam or Laos, you must get your visa in advance. Visas into Thailand will be issued at all border crossings. Most crossing points are not open 24 hours a day, so you need to time your arrival. The precise times vary between one border crossing to another. The best time to present yourself at borders is between 8:00 am and 5:00 pm.

Arriving by Boat

River crossings into Cambodia can be made from both Laos and Vietnam. A boat journey down the Mekong from Laos is likely to be far more comfortable than the trip by road. You can boat hop all the way to Phnom Penh from this border crossing; depending on the season and depth of water, boats run from the border down to the river port of Stung Treng and from there, to Kratie, if water level and the state of the rapids at various points permit. Another boat from Kratie will get you to Sisowath Quay, in downtown Phnom Penh.

From Vietnam, boats on the Bassac River or its various tributaries in the Mekong delta, run from the Vietnamese river port of Chau Doc. The border point is about 45 minutes away at the small Cambodian town of Tonle, where you will need to change to another boat to continue onto Phnom Penh. Though a road trip from Chau Doc to Phnom Penh is theoretically possible, the road is often pretty much impassable. For this trip, the river is a far better option. Visas are issued for travelling from Vietnam to Cambodia at this point, but not from Cambodia into Vietnam.

SIGNIFICANT CAMBODIANS
Norodom Sihanouk

Norodom Sihanouk, the quiet young prince selected by the French in 1941 to take over the Cambodian throne, has become one of the most remarkable political figures of contemporary history.

At first, young King Sihanouk showed little of the passion for politics that would consume him in his later life. At the time he ascended the throne, Japan's conquest of Indo-China was under way and Cambodia was a nominal French colony in reality controlled by the Japanese army. To amuse himself in his early years as monarch, Sihanouk took an interest in movies and theatre, wrote film scripts that no one took seriously and composed music. He became an adept horseman, played the saxophone and clarinet most proficiently, pursued amorous affairs with beautiful women and signed whatever political documents the French placed in front of him.

Sihanouk's interest in affairs of the state developed at about the same time French influence in Indo-China declined. After the war, the young King began to enjoy his role on centre stage. As a self-styled actor, he developed a talent for rousing the passions of audiences to his speeches, which became longer and more theatrical over time.

He toured Europe and North America lobbying for his country's independence. Internationally, there was little resistance to the idea. The United States was preoccupied with the spread of communism and prepared to embrace Cambodia as an anti-communist ally in South-east Asia. France was growing weary of its recalcitrant Indo-Chinese colonies and other European powers were indifferent to their fate.

Inside the country, getting rid of the French received almost total support. When independence was proclaimed on 9 November 1953, Sihanouk found himself a national hero. He had shaken his country free of French rule nearly two years ahead of his self-imposed deadline.

Since then, Sihanouk has remained near centre stage in Cambodian politics for decades. His strengths are his special relationship with the rural people, who regarded him almost as a god-king in the tradition of the ancient Angkor rulers. His weaknesses were his massive ego, his sensitivity to insults and his inability to delegate. His personal characteristics governed his behaviour, and thereby his country's policies. Important strategic decisions were determined by how other leaders treated him rather than by political advantage to his country. In particular, the habits of the 1950s US ambassador to Cambodia, Robert McClintock, influenced Sihanouk's view that Americans were uncultured barbarians. McClintock was a misfit in the diplomatic corps with no sensitivity to the mores of his client nation. The manner of his dress, speech and behaviour all offended Sihanouk and his Cambodians. While on duty in Cambodia, McClintock attended official functions in the company of his pet dog and regularly strode around the streets of Phnom Penh dressed in shorts and holding a baton.

Americans outside Cambodia also treated Sihanouk dismissively. When Sihanouk went to Washington on a state visit, President Eisenhower's aides couldn't find the time to grant him an appointment. To fill in his time in Washington, the minor diplomat appointed to organise Sihanouk's itinerary suggested he visit a circus! By contrast, when Sihanouk visited China, Chou En-lai laid on banquets for an honoured guest, organised meetings with Chairman Mao and had a cheering Chinese rent-a-crowd of 100,000 line the streets. Sihanouk developed an affection for the Chinese and a dislike of the US that lasted his whole life and greatly affected Cambodia's contemporary history.

Sihanouk was prime minister for 15 years. Perhaps his key error in government was to discontinue US aid in 1963 on the grounds that Cambodia was a neutral country or as Sihanouk put it, 'an oasis of peace'. In 1960s Indo-China, by US definition, there was no such thing as a neutral country. Sihanouk was seen by the anti-communist alliance to be on the side of communists he had brutally suppressed a few years before. As the second half of the 1960s unfolded, a rift also widened between town and country. This rift was one of the key factors that the Khmer Rouge later exploited.

Loss of US aid removed most of the country's foreign exchange, and the means of paying the Cambodian armed forces. Life became more difficult for all. Sihanouk's popularity with key groups such as his generals, plummeted, though the rural population still supported him.

Sihanouk's reaction to the increasing pressures of government was to retreat into fantasy. As communists from North Vietnam rampaged through his country and his own army was in foment, Sihanouk renewed his interest in the movie industry. While Sihanouk was appropriating helicopters from his army to serve as extras for his movie sets, and casting generals in the roles of lead characters, the army was unable to buy boots and ammunition for its troops

After the 1970 coup d'état, Sihanouk was condemned to death in absentia by Lon Nol. He then took refuge in China and formed a government-in-exile. Five months after the Khmer Rouge took over in 1975, Sihanouk returned to Phnom Penh at the prompting of the Chinese. Upon arrival, Pol Pot put him under house arrest.

Sihanouk and his wife were confined to an outbuilding in the Royal Palace grounds in Phnom Penh. What saved Sihanouk from execution was his immense popularity within Cambodia and the support of the Chinese. Pol Pot, instead, executed various members of Sihanouk's extended family.

For much of his term in office, Pol Pot ignored Prince Sihanouk languishing in captivity just a few city blocks away. But on almost his last day in power, with the Vietnamese army at the city gates, Pol Pot requested Sihanouk plead Cambodia's case in the UN that the Vietnamese had violated Cambodia's sovereignty. To accomplish this chore, Sihanouk was put on a plane to Beijing one day before Phnom Penh fell to the Vietnamese. By then it was all too late. The regime had only hours to live.

During the 1980s, while overseas in virtual exile, Sihanouk founded the FUNCINPEC Party, now Cambodia's main opposition party to the ruling Cambodian Peoples Party (CPP). Under his leadership, FUNCINPEC formed a government-in-exile aligned with the Khmer Rouge.

After the 1993 UNTAC elections, in which he played a leading role, Sihanouk's life came the full circle. A constitution was adopted, defining Cambodia as a democratic monarchy, and Sihanouk was crowned king, thereby regaining the throne he had abandoned 38 years earlier.

Thereafter, Sihanouk remained delightfully inconsistent and enigmatic. People of Cambodia still hold strong opinions of him. Even now, in the twilight of his life and having abdicated once again, he is loved by some in the community, and despised by others. Which is the true Sihanouk? Prince of Light, or Prince of Darkness? was the title used for one of his unauthorised biographies. Opinions on which style of prince he might have been vary from one end of the spectrum to the other

But love him, or hate him, there is unlikely to be another quite like him.

Pol Pot

Rarely in contemporary history has a leader had such a devastating effect on his own country as Pol Pot. In per capita terms, Pol Pot's atrocities ranked him ahead of Hitler and Stalin as a contender for the mantle of the most bloodthirsty tyrant of the 20th century.

Born Saloth Sar to a middle-class rural family in a small village near Kampong Thom, a provincial capital 150 km (93 miles) north of Phnom Penh, his family was connected to the Royal Family in various ways: his sister Saroeun was consort to King Monivong; and his brother worked in the palace. These connections drew Saloth Sar to Phnom Penh and enabled him to win a scholarship to study in France, where he performed without distinction, failing to collect a degree in his chosen subject, electronics.

In Paris, Saloth Sar and various other revolutionary colleagues on Cambodian scholarships joined the French Communist Party, which was then at its most potent. When this group returned to Cambodia, they formed the nucleus of the Cambodian communist movement. Upon his return, Saloth Sar got a job as a teacher, one of life's ironies since under his ideology all knowledge was dangerous (at least to him personally), and he later executed nearly the entire teacher population of Cambodia.

Those who recall Saloth Sar from this early period described him as easy-going, unremarkable, quiet and charming. Outwardly, he projected a calm demeanour. He was always in control of his emotions and never raised his voice. His friendly manner and self-control earned respect and inspired obedience. He was particularly remembered as a persuasive, even mesmerising, speaker.

In the early 1960s, the CIA cooperated with the Cambodian government to collect information on communist party members. Saloth Sar initially managed to avoid notice. As a minor party functionary, he was inconspicuous to the point of near invisibility, and this proved a sound survival strategy. But as higher-ranking members of the party were assassinated around him, management positions became vacant and he was promoted to more important posts.

As he advanced through the party hierarchy, despite his best intentions, Saloth Sar started to gain attention. In 1963, when he learnt his name had been added to Lon Nol's hit list, he went into self-exile. For the rest of the decade, Saloth Sar was constantly on the move in Cambodia's remote rural areas, hunted unsuccessfully by Lon Nol's agents. While in hiding, Saloth Sar helped the party build up a political network of disaffected peasants.

Around this time, he changed his name to Pol Pot. In his 25 years as a student of the revolution, Pol Pot had studied the works of Stalin and Mao and was to adopt many of their methods when he finally took control of the country. According to the biography Brother Number One written by one of Cambodia's leading contemporary historians, David Chandler, Pol Pot was at least as bad as he has been portrayed in movies such as The Killing Fields.

Chandler relates that Pol Pot had a wonderful warm smile, which he employed to great effect to confuse his enemies. A favoured strategy was to lull his opponents into a false sense of security prior to moving against them. Most of the few photos taken of Pol Pot show him smiling from what seemed like a kind, amiable face.

Pol Pot was the epitome of a self-controlled, even-tempered, smiling assassin.

He maintained his shadowy existence even after coming into power. No one, not even his own family, knew he was Brother Number One. As Saloth Sar, he had dropped out of contact with his circle of acquaintances upon his self-exile in 1963, and for 15 years his family thought him dead. When the revolution came, Pol Pot's family, evacuated from towns along with the rest of the urban population, suffered alongside other similarly uprooted Cambodians. It wasn't until 1978, three years after he had taken over his country's leadership, that his surviving siblings happened to see one of his rare photographs and realised that their easy-going and obliging brother was the mysterious and brutal figure running the country!

Like his role model, Mao Tse Tung, Pol Pot became increasingly paranoid that his colleagues were plotting against him. He adopted ever more bloodthirsty methods to deal with these real and perceived threats. Pol Pot's political colleagues lived in constant fear of being purged. During his time in power, Pol Pot executed a third of his cabinet. The staff at Tuol Sleng who interrogated, tortured and executed people on his behalf were not spared. About half of them were themselves later interrogated, tortured and executed.

In 1977, after a Vietnamese force came within 50 km (31 miles) of Phnom Penh, Pol Pot visited his armies on the eastern borders, praising them and their leaders for their heroism. Shortly after returning to the capital, he purged their ranks down to the level of the wives and children of foot soldiers. One hundred thousand of his own supporters perished.

After the Vietnamese took over, the Phnom Penh government tried Pol Pot in absentia in 1979 and condemned him to death for his crimes. But he couldn't be captured. Human rights activists also tried to bring Pol Pot to justice in the International Court of Justice in the Netherlands. They too failed. The odd alliance of countries supporting Pol Pot at the time, principally the United States, Thailand and China, would not release him for trial.

In the 1980s, financed by illegal logging and gem-smuggling operations laundered through Thailand and supplied with Chinese arms, the Khmer Rouge regrouped with the objective, so far as the international powers were concerned, of destabilising the Vietnamese-backed government.

The departure of the Vietnamese army in 1989 encouraged the Khmer Rouge to raise their profile inside Cambodia. It seemed to some, that the Khmer Rouge's return to power was imminent. However, in 1994 that same year, the Khmer Rouge captured, held to ransom and executed three Western backpackers who had stumbled into their hands. The Khmer Rouge ambushed the train on which the backpackers were travelling en route from Phnom Penh to Sihanoukville. The three were shot when negotiations for their release failed and before the Cambodian army could arrive to save them. To the Khmer Rouge, this was merely a routine murder, but to the Western press it was a major story. The fate of David Wilson, Mark Slater and Jean-Michel Braquet (from Australia, Great Britain and France respectively), attracted worldwide interest and public outrage. The international community at last saw the Khmer Rouge as beyond the pale.

At about this time, the Khmer Rouge was further weakened by a split in the organisation. One group, centred on the town of Pailin in Cambodia's west, accepted an amnesty offer by the Cambodian government to lay down their arms. The other group—which included the hard line leaders Pol Pot and his general, Ta Mok—battled on and made its last stand in the Dandrek Mountains of northern Cambodia. By this time, the estimated fighting force of the Khmer Rouge was down to less than 1,000.

Even as the outside world was closing in, Pol Pot had one last bloodthirsty act to perform. Violent to the end, Pol Pot murdered San Sen, one of his most trusted allies from his revolutionary days in Paris. Camped on the western border with Pol Pot and his small band of cadres, San Sen was killed along with his wife, his children and relatives in a massacre that took the lives of 14 of San Sen's close and extended family.

The murder of San Sen was too much, even for the Khmer Rouge hardliners. After years of purges and senseless killings, the cadres at long last, turned on Pol Pot. He was arrested and tried by his peers in an open-air court in front of a thatched hut at a temporary border camp. Pol Pot was found guilty and sentenced to permanent house arrest. In April 1998, as the new Khmer Rouge hierarchy was negotiating to hand him over to the International Court of Justice, Pol Pot died at the age of 73 while still in Khmer Rouge territory.

Officially, Pol Pot died of natural causes, though the rapid disposal of his corpse suggests he may have been murdered. His body was hurriedly cremated on a pyre of tyres in front of his house in Anlong Veng, in northern Cambodia. No autopsy could be conducted since no body was available. The life of this violent man remains an enigma. So does his death. Pol Pot's cremation mound has since become a minor tourist attraction.

Hun Sen

The other enduring character in contemporary politics is the equally enigmatic Hun Sen who, at the time of writing, was still the prime minister of Cambodia.

Hun Sen was born to a rural family in Kampong Cham province in 1952. His family was too poor to enrol him in school. At 13, he entered a monastery where an education was provided free of charge. As the Indo-Chinese wars raged about him and the United States laid waste to Cambodia through its bombing offensive, Hun Sen threw his lot in with the communists. He quit the monastery at 18 and became a full-time Khmer Rouge revolutionary. Rising quickly through the ranks, he became regimental commander of 2,000 guerrillas. He participated in the battle of Phnom Penh in 1975, losing his left eye to a shrapnel wound. The damaged eye was removed and replaced by a glass eye that he still wears today.

Though he had served the regime well, after the revolution, ten of Hun Sen's uncles and nephews were executed on Pol Pot's orders. In 1977, having heard that he was about to be picked up for interrogation, which would have meant torture and certain death, he decided to defect. With four companions, he walked across the border into Vietnam.

At the time of his defection, relations between Cambodia and Vietnam were cool. Suspecting he was a spy, the Vietnamese interrogated him for the best part of a month. Gradually, Hun Sen won the confidence of his captors, convincing them he was really was a disillusioned guerrilla who wished for a change of regime in Cambodia. In 1978, he played a leading part in Vietnam's invasion of Cambodia.

After the Vietnamese forces assumed control of Cambodia in January 1979, Heng Samrin, a fellow Khmer Rouge deserter, was appointed prime minister and Hun Sen the foreign minister. In 1985, Hun Sen himself became prime minister.

Since then, he has survived continual political turmoil, including the presence of the Vietnamese army in his country, its later withdrawal, the rearming of the Khmer Rouge by the Western alliance, the transition to democracy and three elections. Accused of corruption, answering to the Vietnamese, rigging elections and assassinating political opponents, Hun Sen has been a controversial figure. In one of its issues, Time magazine dubbed Hun Sen the 'Strongman of Cambodia' and compared his rule to that of Indonesia's Suharto.

Whatever his faults, Hun Sen has dominated the Cambodian political scene since the end of the Pol Pot era, and continues to do so today.

Sam Rainsy

Sam Rainsy is a passionate and driven man prone to delivering fiery speeches at impromptu political rallies across the country. For over a decade, he has made anti-corruption the main plank of his electoral platform, campaigning for an honest, open government.

Sam Rainsy was born in 1949 in Phnom Penh. His father was a deputy prime minister in Sihanouk's government in the 1950s and his mother was the first Cambodian woman to complete high school. Rainsy received much of his education abroad, in Paris. He holds degrees in economics, political science and business administration, and was a former investment manager with various banks and financial institutions in Paris.

Sam Rainsy returned to Cambodia in 1992 and was a founding member of FUNCINPEC, alongside Sihanouk. He became finance minister between 1993 and 1994. But his strong anti-corruption stance and campaigns against government mismanagement of the economy made him unpopular. In October 1994, Sam Rainsy was fired from his ministerial post and in May 1995, he was expelled from FUNCINPEC. A month later, he lost his seat in the National Assembly.

In late 1995, Sam Rainsy established the Khmer Nation Party. However, the 1997 coup d'état by the ruling CPP forced KNP members to go into hiding. Looters, with the apparent blessing of the authorities, ransacked KNP's headquarters and his home.

Later that year KNP members, including Sam Rainsy, regrouped. But the government continued to make life difficult for Rainsy and his followers. It managed to persuade a small group of KNP members to break away and counterclaim the party's name in court. The government hoped the dispute would weaken Sam Rainsy's political ambitions. The government-appointed court refused to hear the case before the 1998 elections, on the basis that the parties involved should resolve the dispute on their own. Rainsy had no choice but to change the KNP's name. This time he chose a name that would be hard to steal—the Sam Rainsy Party.

In the most recent election of 2003, his party polled 22 per cent of the votes. Persecution of Sam Rainsy continues—he and two fellow parliamentarians were stripped of their parliamentary immunity in early 2005. They faced charges of defamation for claiming the government was plotting to kill its political rivals and that Prince Ranariddh took bribes to join the government. If found guilty, they may receive fines or even a spell in jail. At the time of writing, Sam Rainsy was in exile abroad and soliciting support from international governments to regain his National Assembly seat.

SAFETY AND SECURITY

In recent years, Western nations, particularly the US, have developed a high level of concern regarding the safety of their citizens in other countries. The US State Department issues cautions from time to time regarding South-east Asia generally, including Cambodia.

The main focus of the Western world in recent times has been on Islamic fundamentalists. Cambodia has a small Muslim minority—the Cham. But it is fair to say that the Chams stick to themselves and pose no threat to anyone. On the contrary, the Chams themselves have faced persecution from various factions in Cambodia's recent history.

While those of the Islamic faith have done little to terrorise Cambodia, the same cannot be said of the international community who have sent their armies and bombers across the borders. But the Cambodians seem to bear few grudges. Despite the thousands of tonnes of ordinance that the first world has rained down on Cambodia, there is little evidence of a simmering resentment against people from the west that you sometimes find in Vietnam. A certain level of racial intolerance is sometimes directed against Cambodia's Vietnamese and to a lesser degree, the French. US citizens and other non-French Westerners should, in general, be well received

Tee for an Apology

Cambodians, more than most, recognise that citizens of most countries are not really responsible for the actions of their leaders. For Americans who might feel like making their own personal apology to the Cambodians for the actions of the Nixon administration in bombing their country to bits in the early 1970s, T-shirts are available in the Khmer language to enable you to do just that. They can obtained from Womyn's Agenda for Change (WAC) at 1 Sisowath Quay, Phnom Penh. The Internet address is www.womynsagenda.org.

DRUGS

Official attitudes towards drug use are more lax in Cambodia than in neighbouring countries, but not as free and easy as a few years ago. Possession and use of drugs is illegal and, at least in theory, can attract a lengthy jail sentence to be served in some of South-east Asia's least salubrious jails. But action by authorities is rare.

Marijuana, otherwise known as ganja, is widely available in Cambodia and, said by connoisseurs in this field, to be of respectable quality. Ganja is grown quite openly on riverbanks close to Phnom Penh and sold freely at markets around town at cheap prices. Point of contact is just about any moto driver. Amongst the Cambodian drug community, ganja is seen as an 'old man's' drug. Its use is so widespread, ganja is no longer considered 'cool'. The younger generation in Cambodia have moved onto newer and more exciting forms of substance abuse. Drugs that would be difficult to get in most places in the world are readily available. Heroin can be bought as easily as candy, and for a comparable price. Pharmacists (a mixture of qualified and unqualified) dispense morphine over the counter without a prescription.

Despite the easy availability of drugs, Cambodians themselves do not appear to be heavily into the drug culture. The same cannot be said of some of Cambodia's long term visitors, for whom the easy drug culture in Cambodia is a major drawcard.

ABBREVIATIONS & ACRONYMS

APSARA	Authority for Protection and Management of Angkor and the Region of Siem Reap
ASEAN	Association of South-east Asian Nations
CPP	Cambodian Peoples Party
FUNCINPEC	Front Uni National pour un Cambodge Indépendent, Neutre, Pacifique, et Coopératif
NGO	Non-Governmental Organisation
UNESCO	United Nations Educational, Scientific and Cultural Organisation
UNTAC	United Nations Transitional Authority in Cambodia

CULTURE QUIZ

SITUATION 1

Many Cambodians are keen to improve their English as a way to get ahead in life. You are an English-speaking male attracted to a Cambodian girl and wish to know her better. Should you:

Ⓐ Ask the girl for a date?
Ⓑ Offer to help the girl with her English as a way to get to know her better?
Ⓒ Apply for an English-teaching position at a local language school so that you can meet more Cambodian girls?

Comment

Certain aspects of Cambodian society will probably remain closed to you. Cambodian girls from traditional family backgrounds will not normally become romantically involved with foreigners. **Ⓐ** will probably fail. The girl is unlikely to get her family's approval to go on a date with you. **Ⓑ** may work out. The girl would be unlikely to visit your apartment for classes, but may take the offer at face value, insisting that classes be conducted at a public venue. So far as **Ⓒ** is concerned, local language schools are always looking for English-language teachers. But you may have to sign a contract with a clause that requires you to refrain from fraternising with students in the manner you envisage.

SITUATION 2

You are a non-Buddhist walking along the street and your Buddhist companion stops to *sompeyar* and offer a short prayer to a Buddhist icon. Should you:

Ⓐ *Sompeyar* at the Buddhist icon as well?
Ⓑ Wait for your companion to complete paying his respects?
Ⓒ Carry on walking?

Comment

Buddhism is a tolerant religion. You won't offend anyone by taking any of the three courses of action. But **Ⓐ**, while not impolite, might be thought of as meaningless, at least by yourself, since you are not a Buddhist. **Ⓑ** is somewhat impolite if you walk too far ahead. But **Ⓒ**, if you walk a few paces, then stop, allowing your companion increased personal space, is perhaps the best option of the three.

SITUATION 3

On entering a temple, a vendor at the doorway tries to sell you some joss sticks. You decide to accept and carry the joss sticks into the temple. Inside the temple, you see groups of people praying in front of various statues of Buddha. You see these people push lighted joss sticks into the sand boxes in front of the Buddhist icons. Should you:

Ⓐ Offer your joss sticks to someone else?
Ⓑ Place your joss sticks in the sand box like everyone else, ignite them and pray in front of them?

Ⓒ Hang onto your joss sticks and take them out with you?

Ⓓ Discreetly leave your joss sticks somewhere in the temple for someone else to find?

Comment

None of the above is a fatal error. Anyone can enter a Buddhist temple and anyone can pray. Monks conduct services from time to time, but services are unstructured and informal. People come and go as they please. Offering joss sticks to someone who is not well off (**Ⓐ**) would be considered meritorious. Lighting the joss sticks and praying (**Ⓑ**) would be the trickiest course of action to perform correctly. Normally you would light your joss stick from the open flame of a candle or an oil lamp. You may need to know which is the correct flame for this purpose. A Westerner praying in a Buddhist temple would probably attract a glance or two. Neither of the other two answers **Ⓒ** or **Ⓓ** will cause offence.

SITUATION 4

You are wearing an expensive pair of brand-name running shoes. You know you are meant to take your shoes off upon entering a home and a temple. If you were entering a beauty salon, a shop, a bank or immigration office, should you:

Ⓐ Keep your shoes on because you don't want to get your feet dirty?

Ⓑ Keep your shoes on because you think someone might steal them?

Ⓒ Take your shoes off and leave them at the door?

Ⓓ Take your shoes off and stuff them in your carry bag (because you think someone might steal them)?

Comment

At some commercial establishments, it is proper to remove your shoes. At others, people leave them on. Whether there is a pile of shoes at the front door of the establishment is the vital clue. Take a look also at the feet of the person answering the door. The complexity of later finding your shoes increases greatly with the number of people in the building. Temples attended by many people have numbered shoe racks near the entrance, so that shoes can be readily located on leaving. The concern for the security of your shoes is valid. Many cases have been reported of brand-name shoes going missing. If you are concerned for the safety of your shoes it is fine to carry them in your bag (**D**), rather than leaving them on (**B**) or at the door (**C**).

SITUATION 5

You are out to dinner and out to impress. You know that in some cultures it is considered polite to leave some food on the plate after eating. In others, leaving food on the plate can be interpreted as a statement on the quality of the dishes. In Cambodia, when you have finished eating, should you:

A Clean every morsel off the plate?
B Leave some food behind?

Comment

You may find that in Cambodia, people serving food and drinks seem to hover at your shoulder forever topping up your glass and refreshing your plate with what you might need. Calorie-counting is quite difficult in this culture. If you have a clean plate in front of you, it is a sign that you are still hungry. You may find more food added to the plate, whether you want it or not. If you are done eating, **B** may be a better option.

SITUATION 6

You are in a restaurant. Your order arrives first and no one else seems to be getting theirs. Your food sits in front of you steaming, and getting cold. Do you:

A Wait until everyone is served before eating?
B Start eating when the food arrives?
C Offer to share your food with others?

Comment

Food in Cambodian restaurants is served as it is prepared. Rarely will everyone at the same table receive their courses at the same time. It is quite in order to start eating as soon as the food arrives (**B**), rather than wait for everyone else's food (**A**). If you wait, you could be waiting a long time. With regard to **C**, sharing dishes in Cambodia is much more common than in Western cultures. Usually a common bowl of rice is provided at the start of the meal. It is polite to offer others some of your food. If so, your offer will be reciprocated. You should not be embarrassed to start eating, but no one is likely to suggest you do.

SITUATION 7

Your taxi driver suggests you should visit the Tuol Sleng Genocide Museum and the Choeung Ek Killing Fields. You are unsure if you want to see this bit of Cambodian history, and are concerned that doing so will suggest a touch of ghoulishness on your part. Should you:

A Refuse?
B Feel embarrassed, but accept?
C Accept without embarrassment?

Comment

A or **C**. There is no need to feel embarrassed (**B**), but accept only if you feel comfortable with what you are likely to see. Scenes at Tuol Sleng are both harrowing and graphic. For the most part, Cambodians want visitors to see the Genocide Museum and the Killing Fields, and have turned them into a tourist attraction for the purpose.

SITUATION 8

You are the manager of a joint venture company, working for a group of Chinese businessmen. You have just completed building a factory. Your partners tell you they are preparing an opening ceremony where Buddhist monks from the local monastery will bless the factory in the appropriate manner.

At the ceremony, to be held on the factory floor, you will be the centre of attraction. After making enquiries, you realise this will involve your sitting for a long period on the floor at the feet of the monks. You doubt your knees are up for it. Should you:

Ⓐ Stand during the ceremony?
Ⓑ Get a chair?
Ⓒ Go through with the lotus position
Ⓓ Leave town on the vital day?

Comment

Regarding **Ⓐ**, the rule is that you are not allowed to have your head above the level of the monk's head. The monks will be sitting side by side facing you. They will expect to be seated on a cushion or a rug. Your best course of action, whatever option you take, is to construct a low platform for the monks, thereby elevating them. Regarding **Ⓑ**, you can sit on a chair provided your head is not too high. Going through with the lotus position **Ⓒ** is not a good idea. You can either sit lotus style for long periods or you can't. An alternative, which some people find easier, is to sit with your legs to the side. This is quite acceptable if you can manage it. Going AWOL **Ⓓ** could cost you your job. The proper blessings are a very serious matter in this part of the world. Your absence would assuredly earn bad karma for the enterprise.

SITUATION 9

You are travelling by boat from Siem Reap to Phnom Penh. You are carrying a rucksack and a bag. You make your way up a rickety gangplank and are gratified to find yourself on a substantial craft. You choose to seat inside the enclosed air-conditioned lounge instead of the roof. As you are about to enter the lounge, a young boy appears at your side and offers to relieve you of your rucksack. He explains that rucksacks are stored in a hold at the stern of the boat and offers to deposit the rucksack there for you. Should you:

A Accept the offer of help?

B Decline the offer of help and deposit the rucksack in the holding area yourself

C Decline the offer of help and keep the rucksack with you in the lounge, thinking that if you let the pack out of your sight someone will steal it.

Comment

Maintaining ownership of one's possessions is the bane of travellers everywhere. In parts of South-east Asia, transport operators are decidedly casual about luggage security. Luggage consigned to the safety of luggage handlers frequently goes missing, along with the handlers themselves. Luggage lost is rarely found. In fact, it is difficult to get travel providers even slightly interested in locating a lost bag. Against that, given the level of poverty, Cambodians are extraordinarily honest. The bag incident actually occurred to me on a trip down Tonle Sap Lake to Phnom Penh. At the time I adopted **A**. Shortly afterwards the boy reappeared in the lounge sans rucksack, insisting I pay him a dollar for his service in removing the rucksack from my care. After the boat had left the wharf and we were underway, I didn't see the boy around and spent the trip wondering if the boy had got off the boat before it left with both my rucksack and dollar. He hadn't. At the end of the trip, I was able to retrieve the rucksack from the hold. But if it were to happen to me again, I would adopt **C**. When travelling, I am never comfortable being separated from my possessions unless, as in travelling by plane, there is no alternative.

SITUATION 10

You have been reading your Cambodian history and are curious about your companion's experiences during the Khmer Rouge years. Should you:

ⓐ Ask outright for your companion's experience at that time?

ⓑ Lead the conversation generally in that direction and see what happens?

ⓒ Avoid the subject entirely?

Comment

Occasionally I have adopted **ⓐ** and found that almost everyone will talk about the Khmer Rouge years. They will describe quite dispassionately and without apparent grief and resentment precisely what happened to members of their family. However, it is entirely possible your companion could have been on the other side of the transaction as a young Khmer Rouge cadre. **ⓑ** is probably the best approach. People are generally happy to talk about the Khmer Rouge, and often raise the subject themselves. There seems to be no sense of national shame on the issue. It's as if the Khmer Rouge was some outside invading force, rather than the fellow Cambodians they actually were.

DO'S AND DON'TS

DO'S

- Respect all aspects of the Buddhist faith.
- Respect the elderly.
- Speak slowly and clearly.
- Dress conservatively.
- Keep cool in stressful situations.

DON'TS

- It is rude to point at people or things with your feet.
- Never sit on the floor of a temple with your feet pointing at the Buddha icon!
- Do not touch the heads of anyone, including children.
- It is frowned upon to be too familiar with another person in public.
- Do not shout in public (to anybody) including your spouse and your children.
- It is considered bad form to punish your children in public.
- Do not shoot video camera sequences of hill tribe areas
- It is dangerous to flaunt your possessions as in opening a wallet full of credit cards.

GLOSSARY

This is a short list of useful Khmer words and phrases for those who didn't get round to buying a language guide. Many Khmer words are composites of simpler words. For example, the word for aeroplane is composed of two words: fly and ship, thereby 'flying ship'. The word airport thus becomes 'a station for flying ships'. I find the easiest way to learn vocabulary is to build from the short root words. Their combinations come reasonably naturally. If you know the root words, the compound words are far easier to remember.

COMMONLY USED WORDS AND PHRASES

Chum Ree eubp Soo-a	Hello
Chum Ree eubp	Goodbye
Baat (spoken by male) / *Jaas* (spoken by female)	Yes
Dtay	No/Not
Sabai	Well (as in health)
K'nyom	I
Neeak (varies, but this is a general all-purpose word)	You
Som	Please
Aagon	Thank you
Lahoor	Good
A way	What?
Ayr na dinna	Where?
Bpayl naa	When?
Hait-ay	Why?
Nayuk naa	Who?
Nee ak sok sa bai gee a dtay?	How are you?
K'nyom sok sabai	I am well
K'nyom sok dtay sabai	I am not so well

Your moto awaits.

NAVIGATING AND TAXI PHRASES

Psar	Market
Tornee-a gee-a	Bank
Sondtakee-a owhtel	Hotel
Sontakee-a owtel Hilton	Hilton Hotel
Jom-nort/Setanee	Station
Ho	Fly
G'bul	Ship
G'bul ho	Aeroplane
Jom-nort g'bul ho	Airport
Laan	Car
Ch'noo-ul	Rent (as in lease)
Laan ch'noo-ul	Bus
Setanee laan kerong	Bus station
Ra-dtay	Cart
Pleung	Fire
Ro-dtay Pleung	Train
Setanee ro-dtay pleung	Train station
Plow	Street

Bon dtoa-up	Next
Plow bon dtoa-up	Next street
Dtoa	Go
Dtoa dtrong	Go straight
Ch'wayng	Left
S'dum	Right
Bot	Turn
Bot ch'wayng	Turn left
Bot s'dum	Turn right
Choap	Stop
Groam	Under
Ler	Over
S'bpee'un	Bridge
Tee Nee	Here
Yeut	Slow
Leu-un	Fast
Leu-un	Point of the compass
Dteu khang jeung	North
Dteu khang tb'ong	South
Dteu khang keat et	East
Dteu khang le	West
Dtak-see	Taxi
Dto naa	Where are you going?
K'nyom dto	I am going…
K'nyom dto psar	I am going to the market
Groam/leu s'bee un	Under/over the bridge

SHOPPING

Dtoom-hoom	Size
Dtoa-ich	Small
Tom	Big

Bpoa-a	Colour
Bpoa a gra-horm	Red
Bpoa-a kee-o	Blue
Bpoa-a bai-dtorng	Green
Bpoa-a leu-ung	Yellow/orange
Bpoa-a k'mao	Black
Bpoa-a sor	White
Bpoa-a t'naot	Brown
Naa	Very
Telay	Expensive
Telay naa	Very expensive
Johs bon-tick baan dtay?	Can you reduce the price?

ACCOMMODATION AND DINING

Bon-dtop	Room
Grai dayk	Bed
Bon-dtop grai/dayk	Bedroom
Bong-goo un	Toilet
Bon-dtop teuk	Bathroom
Bon-dtop n'ym bai	Dining room

Bai	Food (also means rice)
Peuk	Drink
Bun-na-rai mook m'hoap	Menu
Dteuk	Water
Dteuk gork	Ice
Bee-yair	Beer
Dorp	Bottle

EMERGENCIES

Bpai et	Doctor
P'dtay-ah llo-uk t'num bpai eti	Pharmacy
Moo-un dtee bpai	Hospital
T'num bpai et	Medicine

RESOURCE GUIDE

EMERGENCY NUMBERS

- **Police**: 117 or (023) 724-016
- **Siem Reap Tourist Police**: (023) 722-067
- **Fire**: 118 or (023) 723-555
- **Ambulance**: 119 or (023) 723-840

LOCAL AND INTERNATIONAL PHONE CALLS

Cambodia has reasonable mobile phone coverage. Mobile phones are usable within major towns and over a fair percentage of the rural areas, particularly on the western side of the country. If your mobile phone is set up with the GSM 900 and 1800 system used in Europe, Australasia or the rest of South-east Asia, you can substitute the SIM card in your phone after you arrive. Mobile phone set-ups for operation in North America are less likely work in Cambodia. Check with your service provider before leaving home. Alternatively, you can hire a phone inside Cambodia.

Network operators include:
Samart (website: http://www.hello016-gsm.com)
Cambodia Shinawatra (website: http://www.cam shin.com)
CamGSM MobiTel (website: http://www.mobitel.com.kh)

INTERNET FACILITIES

Internet connections are widely available through **Speednet**, a superior Internet access service based on Asynchronous Digital Subscriber Line (ADSL).

HOUSING AND FAMILY

People coming to Cambodia for extended periods are likely to rent a house. Cambodia has many private realtors. Many can be accessed on the Internet, one of which is **Bonnarealty**. com (19AE Street, 282 Corner 63, Sangat Boeung, Keng Kang, Phnom Penh; website: http://bonnarealty.com)

HOSPITALS/CLINICS

Medical facilities in Cambodia are below international standards. Larger cities like Phnom Penh and Siem Reap have facilities to handle basic emergencies. For anything more serious, you should consider making the trip across the border into Bangkok, Thailand. The best hospital in Bangkok, in my experience, is the **Bumrungrad Hospital** (website: http://www.bumrungrad.com/). Attention and medication are top quality and reasonably priced. For less serious health problems, where you require English-speaking doctors and medical staff, you can try:

- **AEA/SOS International Clinic**
  No 161 Street 51, Sangkat Boeung Peng; tel: (023) 216-911, fax: (023) 215-811 (it's right across the road from the US embassy in Phnom Penh)

For dental treatments, you can get more detailed information on available services in Phnom Penh through the **Cambodian Dental Association** at the Faculty of Dentistry [tel: (016) 911-205; fax: (023) 211-338].

SCHOOLS
International Schools

- **International School of Phnom Penh (ISPP)**
  website: http://www.ispp.edu.kh
- **Northbridge International School Cambodia**
  website: http://www.northbridgecommunities.com/
- **British International School of Phnom Penh**
  No 213 Street 51, Phnom Penh; tel: (023) 213-056, fax: (023) 210-724; email: mbschool@online.com.kh

For more schools, you can look up this website at http://www.shambles.net/pages/countries/.

Language Schools

- **The Khmer School of Language at Phnom Penh**
  Website: http://www.cambcomm.org.uk/ksl

MANAGING YOUR MONEY

The three main currencies in circulation in Cambodia are the Cambodian riel, the US dollar and the Thai baht. No ATMs in Cambodia are linked to foreign banks. Credit cards are not widely accepted, though some banks in Phnom Penh will advance cash on the strength of a VISA card. The easiest way to generate cash in Cambodia is to carry traveller's cheques, which cost about 2 per cent of their face value to cash. The two most widely accepted traveller's cheques are those issued by **Thomas Cook** and **American Express**. Both these companies have offices in Phnom Penh where loss of traveller's cheques can be reported. Given the high incidence of pilfering in Cambodia, it's worth making photocopies of traveller's cheques prior to travelling and carrying the copies separate from the cheques themselves. For those who want to wire funds, there are three **Western Union** offices in Phnom Penh and one in Siem Reap.

POSTAL

Cambodia offers a postal box service, but does not deliver mail door to door. There are five post offices in Phnom Penh as well as post offices in major towns. Mailboxes are available and postal services are quite reliable. Post office hours are Monday to Friday, from 7:30 am to 12 noon, and from 2:30 pm to 5:00 pm. The cost of a stamp is around 2,000 riel to most destinations. For those who like to check their prices, a notice of standard postage to various destinations is posted on notice boards of post offices. Mail is consolidated in Phnom Penh and sent out about twice a week. Delivery time for airmail is around five to eight days. Parcel post is also available from Phnom Penh, but it is expensive. The main post office (website: http://www.mptc.gov.kh/) in Phnom Penh is open until 9:00 pm. It is located on the western side of Street 13 between Street 98 and Street 102.

TOURIST INFORMATION

The Cambodia Ministry of Tourism's official website is at http://www.mot.gov.kh. Your own government would also operate websites with up-to-date advice on the pleasures and perils of touring Cambodia. Three worth checking out are:

- United Kingdom Foreign Office
  (website: http://www.fco.gov.uk/travel)
- Australian Department of Foreign Affairs
  (website: http://www.dfat.gov.au)
- US Department of State
  (website: http://travel.state.gov/travel)

The *Lonely Planet* offers excellent tourist information at its website: http://www.lonelyplanet.com/destinations/south_east_asia/cambodia. One of many website offering details of entertainment and restaurants is http://www.bongthom.com.

EXPAT CLUBS

For those who wish to meet up with people from their home countries, or partake in activities from home, try checking with your embassy if they have a list of expat associations and clubs.

RELIGIOUS INSTITUTIONS

As Cambodians are predominantly Buddhist, temples catering to the Buddhist faith are plenty. For Buddhists, Christians and those of other faiths, you can look up the *Yellow Pages* at http://yellowpages-cambodia.com/Community/Churches-and-Religions-Services-2.html for places of worship. For those with an interest in learning Buddhist culture, the Cambodian government formed the **Ministry of Culture and Fine Arts** in 1997. Details can be found on http://www.moi-coci.gov.kh/culture/default.htm.

HOTELS

Publications such as the *Lonely Planet* and other excellent tourist guides on Cambodia offer a full range of hotels from five-star to backpacker class. Prices of all standards of accommodation are reasonable by most standards. Prices at the lower end of the market are really cheap. Most of the upmarket hotels and many of the budget hotels in the tourist centres of Phnom Penh, Siem Reap and Sihanoukville can be pre-booked over the Internet. Rates vary between the high season (November to February) and the rest of the year. Electricity is expensive in Cambodia. Air-conditioned rooms cost US$ 8–10 more per night than rooms with an overhead fan. Air-conditioned rooms also offer hot water. Rooms with an overhead fan don't.

HANDICAPPED FACILITIES

Cambodia has the highest rate of disabilities in the world per capita, a result of its turbulent recent history. Assisted by various NGOs, Cambodia has gone flat out to try and find its disabled useful employment and provide prosthetics. Unfortunately, it has not provided much in the way of infrastructure to assist those with disabilities. Cambodia has not been able to fill the potholes in its streets and footpaths, let alone install ramps. If you are disabled and want to visit Cambodia, you are advised to contact a disability organisation in your country for specific advice. The one possible advantage of Cambodia as a destination for the disabled is that hired help is cheap; the rate for hired help is about US$ 10–15 a day.

MUSEUMS

For Phnom Penh, the genocide museum at **Tuol Sleng** has already been mentioned, while the **National Museum** just off Sisowath Boulevard takes a broader sweep of history, focusing on Cambodia's early history—it contains numerous exhibits from Angkor. The **Royal Palace**, home of Cambodia's kings for a few centuries, is open to the public in the day. Next door to the Royal Palace, the **Silver Pagoda** (Wat Preah Keo) is so named for its floor, covered with 5,281 silver tiles, each weighing just over 1 kg. Central to the Silver Pagoda is a pure gold Buddha encrusted with nearly 10,000 diamonds.

MEDIA
Newspapers/ Magazines
These days, Cambodia has about 200 printed media publications of various sorts. The two best-selling Khmer-language papers, *Reaksmei Kampuchea* and *Kaoh*

Santepheap are sensationalist in style. Reporting by both papers is pro-government. Published twice weekly is the French language *Camboge Soir*. English newspapers are *The Cambodia Daily* (website: http://www.cambodiadaily.com)—published Monday to Saturday, and the *Phnom Penh Post* (website: http://www.phnompenhpost.com) published fortnightly. Both English papers give a reasonable mix of national and international news. Other news websites include http://www.cambodianews.com and http://www.gocambodia.com.

One interesting aspect of buying a paper in Cambodia is that a newspaper can effectively be leased for a short period. After the paperboy sells you a newspaper, should you linger at a café table, he will return to reclaim it (at no cost to himself) to sell to someone else, at its original purchase price. Recycling newspapers between readers is another example of the Cambodian way of obtaining the maximum use of whatever they have and throwing little away. Apart from that, the practice is a nice little earner for the paperboy.

Movies

The entertainment genre, presently popular in Cambodia, might be politely termed as 'action movies'. Along the streets of Phnom Penh, hand-painted ads for movies depict bloodletting by vampires and similar lurid themes. Films are typically sourced from Thailand, where the tastes in entertainment run along similarly bloodthirsty lines. Thai films carry Khmer subtitles. Chinese action films are also popular in Cambodia and also carry subtitles. Movies are typically screened four times a day.

Television Stations

Cambodia has seven TV channels:

- **TV 3**—operated by the Phnom Penh municipality and KCS Cambodia
- **TV Channel 5**, also known as TV Fark—operated by the Royal Cambodian Air Forces

- **TVK** (National Television of Cambodia), or TV CH 7—ostensibly the government's television station, it is owned by Hun Sen's Cambodian Peoples Party (CPP)
- **Cambodian TV Station Channel 9**, or TV 9—owned by the main opposition party, FUNCINPEC
- **Apsara TV**—operated by Apsara Media Group, an organisation with close ties to the CPP
- **Cambodian Television Network** (CTN)—run by the Royal Group of companies and Modern Time Group
- **Bayon TV**—another station with close ties to the CPP

French TV via channel CFI is transmitted locally in Phnom Penh by the French Cultural Centre. Cable television is also available in Phnom Penh. Programs offered include Star TV, HBO, Cinemax, the Cartoon Channel, ESPN, BBC News, the Discovery Channel, the National Geographic Channel, MTV and CNN. Other channels are available for those who install a satellite dish.

Cambodian TV has adopted the European PAL system. Televisions and VCRs formatted for the US NTSC system will not work in Cambodia. For VCR and DVD movie watchers, Phnom Penh has a couple of video rental store offering movies in English and French.

Radio Stations

Phnom Penh has two English-language radio stations, both broadcasting on the FM band: 97.5 MHz plays pop music interspersed with current affairs and news; 99 MHz plays light entertainment. A number of short-wave international radio English-language broadcasts can be received in Cambodia, including BBC (website: http://www.bbc.co.uk/worldservice), Voice of America (http://www.voa.gov) and Radio Australia. The French-language view of the world can be picked up from Radio France International on the FM band. Frequencies may change from time to time.

LANDMINE INFORMATION

Various NGOs are working on clearing landmines in Cambodia. The Landmine Museum (*refer to* Chapter 7: Sights and Sounds of Cambodia *on page 169*) is a purely Cambodian operation run by Mr Aki Ra. He personally clears the landmines in his area of interest around Siem Reap. More details can be found on the Landmine Museum website at http://www. landmine-museum.com. Donations to this effort can be sent to Western Union Bank, Siem Reap Branch, Account Name: Aki Ra, Account Number: 0100-20-127260-1-5.

A SELECTION OF NGOS IN CAMBODIA

Listed below are just a small percentage of the numerous NGOs working in Cambodia. NGOs work on an enormous range of tasks, from agriculture, education, health, and interpersonal relationships.

- **American Friends Service Committee**
  1501 Cherry Street, Philadelphia, PA 19102
  Tel: (1-215) 241-7154;
  Website: http://www.afsc.org/intl/asia/cambodia.htm.
  It addresses the issue of widespread violence in everyday life through non-violence training and weapons reduction. Other programmes include food production, health education, literacy and more.

- **Church World Service**
  475 Riverside Drive, New York, NY 10115
  Tel: (1-212) 870-2008
  Website: http://www.churchworldservice.org/cambodia/ 2000annualreport/overview.html.
  Partners a local organisation called Buddhism for Development to raise awareness about land issues and to organise people to protect the forests. Other programmes include self-help credit groups, sustainable agriculture, education, income generation, health care, problem solving, emergency response and more.

- **Maryknoll**
  PO Box 305, Maryknoll, NY 10545
  Tel: (1-914) 941-7590
  Website: http://www.maryknoll.org/join/want/mm_aids_
  cam.htm.
  Offers care for children living with HIV/AIDS. Cambodia
  has the highest HIV rate in Asia. Other programmes
  include literacy, help for landmine victims and more.

- **Mennonite Central Committee**
  PO Box 500, Akron, PA 17501
  Tel: (1-717) 859-1151
  Website: http://www.mcc.org/areaserv/asia/cambodia/
  index.html.
  Health education for villagers includes common illnesses,
  nutrition, maternal and child health, domestic violence and
  AIDS. Other programmes include emergency assistance,
  income generation, education, tree planting and more.

- **World Education**
  44 Farnsworth Street, Boston, MA 02210
  Tel: (1-617) 482-9485
  Website: http://www.worlded.org/projects_region.
  html#cambodia.
  Sponsors the Cambodian Master Performers Programme
  (website: http://www.cambodianmasters.org) which
  supports the relatively few performing artists who survived
  Cambodia's genocide in teaching their art and in preserving
  the unique Khmer cultural heritage. Other programmes
  include AIDS education, mine risks, and more.

- **Cambodian Community Mental Health Services** in
  Siem Riep
  Ms. Svang Tor
  c/o Harvard Program in Refugee Trauma, 22 Putnam Ave.,
  Cambridge, MA 02139
  Tel: (1-617) 876-7879
  Email: stor@partners.org.
  Treats mental health patients and the severely traumatised.

- **Southeast Asia Development Programme**
  36 Pondview Drive, Amherst, MA 01002
  Tel: (1-413) 253-3197
  Email: sadp@bigpond.com.kh
  Website: http://www.sadpc cambodia.org.
  Helps villagers learn to use non-violent direct action to
  reclaim, defend and manage their community's forest,
  fishery and land resources against logging concessions,
  illegal fishery and land confiscation.

- **Cambodian Educational Network**
  3774 Castro Valley Boulevard, Castro Valley, CA 94546
  Tel: (1-510) 881-5977
  Email: shoeumsok@excite.com (look for Mr Khoeum Sok)
  Khmer-Americans working to stop trafficking of women
  and children for labour and sexual exploitation and to
  address illiteracy in Cambodia.

- **Village Focus International**
  2327 SE Main Street, Portland, OR 97214
  Email: vfilao@laotel.com.
  Provides technical assistance in drafting and implementing
  natural resources protection legislation in Cambodia.
  Addresses trafficking of women and children.

- **Cambodian Volunteers for Community Development**
  #416 Street 310, Sangkat Boeung Kang Kong III, Phnom
  Penh, Cambodia
  Tel: (855) 023 216 615
  Email: cvcd@forum.org.kh.
  A Cambodian organisation addressing literacy, skills
  training, health issues, and environmental awareness.

- **Seva Foundation**
  1786 Fifth St, Berkeley, CA 94710
  Tel: (1-510) 845-7382
  Website: http://www.seva.org/cambodia.html
  Sets up eye care and blindness prevention programmes.
  In 2002, Cambodia only had two ophthalmologists.

FURTHER READING

HISTORICAL

A History of Cambodia. David P Chandler. Chang Mai, Thailand: Silkworm Books, 1998.

- This book describes the history of Cambodia from its earliest beginnings to about 1996. A standard academic book, it is nevertheless an easy-to-read, comprehensive account of the influence and personalities of the Cambodian historical panorama, including explanations for Khmer Rouge policies during the convulsive period in Cambodian history from 1975–1979.

KHMER ROUGE

Brother Number One: A political biography of Pol Pot. David P Chandler. Chiang Mai, Thailand: Silkworm Books, 1999.

- This book, from Cambodia's leading contemporary historian, tries to find the answer to the elusive question— why did he do it? How did Pol Pot, born Saloth Sar, once a mild-mannered schoolteacher end up as a paranoid homicidal maniac in charge of his country? The questions raised are tough to answer. One of the difficulties in writing this biography was Pol Pot's excessive secrecy, before, during and after living a shadowy life while on the run for 12 years before he came to power. From the scanty evidence and interviews with Pol Pot's associates, David Chandler pieces together a fascinating account.

And First They Killed My Father: A Daughter of Cambodia Remembers. Loung Ung. New York, New York: Perennial, 2001.

- An incredible and harrowing autobiography of a very young girl and her family who were uprooted from a middle class upbringing in Phnom Penh by the Khmer Rouge and sent to labour in the fields. The book describes how she survived four years of harsh labour and ultimately, having reached the age of nine, escaped from Cambodia by boat.

Stay Alive, My Son. Pin Yathay. New York, New York: Touchstone Books, 1988.

- Similar in account to Loung Ung's book and just as gripping. The story is told from the point of view of an educated man who struggled to keep his family together after being uprooted from a comfortable middle-class city lifestyle in Phnom Penh and sent to labour in the fields. There they lived a life of constant harassment, starvation under threats of execution. Pin Yathay was one of the few Cambodians to escape from the Khmer Rouge's internment camps. He made his way across the rugged Cardamom mountains, finally finding freedom in Thailand. His wife, who went with him, did not survive the journey.

GEO POLITICS AND CAMBODIA

Cambodia 1975-1982. Michael Vickery. Seattle, Washington: University of Washington Press, 2000.

- Vickery provides an alternative viewpoint by questioning the more widely accepted view of the Khmer Rouge's tyrannical rule. He suggests that the reported brutality was exaggerated and that the actual casualties were far fewer than was reported. He explains that much of the motivation for the revolution was the exploitation of the rural peasant class by an elite middle class in Phnom Penh and other cities. Studies after the book was published dismiss the low casualty count Vickery offered, though Pol Pot himself declared the revolution only took 'a few thousand' lives instead of the millions frequently quoted. The true casualty count will never be known since population statistics are too scanty.

INDO-CHINESE WARS

Sideshow: Kissinger, Nixon, and the Destruction of Cambodia. William Shawcross. New York, New York: Cooper Square Press, 2002.

- A painstakingly researched and detailed book explaining the war in Cambodia from the US administration's point of view. Even as US strategy in Indo-China was falling apart, US President Richard Nixon and Secretary of State Henry Kissinger ordered bombing raids to continue. Thousands of civilian casualties on the ground meant nothing to these two strategists who saw progress in terms of mega-tonnage of destruction, not in hearts and minds won. Ironically, Henry Kissinger—the man who, as much as any other, brought to Cambodia the horrors of war, and did much to create the conditions for the subsequent Khmer Rouge genocide—went on to receive the 1973 Nobel Peace Prize for his part in bringing the curtain down on the Vietnam War.

The Quality of Mercy: Cambodia, Holocaust, and Modern Conscience. William Shawcross. New York, New York: Simon and Schuster, 1984.

- Shawcross's follow-up to Sideshow describes what happened in Cambodia after the Vietnamese army threw out the Khmer Rouge in 1979. The departure of the Khmer Rouge did not end the Cambodian people's suffering; they continued to be denied the aid they needed. Shawcross details the duplicitous nature of the participants in the continuing struggle for Indo-China. The heroes in the book are the Cambodians themselves, and the aid groups trying to get help to people left desperate by a decade and a half of civil war with its attendant deprivations. The villains are the politicians and bureaucrats of the various parties involved: the Western alliance headed by Thailand, the Vietnamese government, the puppet regime in Phnom Penh, and worst of all, the Khmer Rouge. Like Sideshow, The Quality of Mercy is a compelling read.

QUESTIONING AID RELIEF

The Lords of Poverty: The Power, Prestige, and Corruption of the International Aid Business. Graham Hancock. New York, New York: Grove Press/Atlantic Monthly Press, 1992.

- This book describes the downside of the government aid business. Says Hancock, 'An entire library of worthy books describes at best the uselessness at worst the serious harm, brought about by aid agencies. Some of the books are personal accounts, others are scientific and scholarly. The findings are the same.' Hancock's book focuses on the large government-related agencies that provide non-specific aid to the governments of recipient countries. He suggests the main beneficiaries of government aid are powerful elites in the recipient country who siphon off the cash before it reaches the needy. In some cases, this may well be true of present-day Cambodia. Other NGO's work directly with the needy, keeping bureaucrats at arm's length.

BIOGRAPHY

Sihanouk: Prince of Light, Prince of Darkness. Milton Osborne. Sydney, Australia: Allen & Unwin Pty Ltd, 1996.

- A 'warts and all' unauthorised biography of Prince Sihanouk, by an author who lived in Cambodia during some of the more traumatic years of Sihanouk's reign as prime minister. On the one hand, Sihanouk is portrayed as a true patriot with a genuine love for his country. On the other, he is portrayed as an egoist with an even greater love for himself. The underlying theme is that while Sihanouk wanted the best for his people (whom he termed his 'children'), he felt that only he could deliver them the goods. The Sihanouk that emerges is an enigmatic mixture who, at times, led a life of self-indulgence and, at others, worked tirelessly for his country. Whatever his motives, and whoever he supported during a lifetime of shifting allegiances, Sihanouk, according to most accounts, has been his country's most powerful unifying force in the last 50 years.

Hun Sen, Strongman of Cambodia. Harish and Julie Mehta. Singapore: Graham Brash, 1999.

- This book displays Hun Sen as an almost flawless individual guiding his country with a firm but fair hand. Hun Sen, one-time Khmer Rouge military leader, is found innocent of culpability in any of the Khmer Rouge atrocities. He is described as a persuasive, intelligent, forceful man and the main character in the liberation of his country. The accounts of Hun Sen's overwhelming desire to serve his fellow Cambodians is at odds with Shawcross's account that Hun Sen, acting under instructions from Hanoi, was the principal roadblock impeding aid to his countrymen during the 1979–1982 relief operation of international agencies. The authors cast Hun Sen as the victim, not the perpetrator of the 1997 coup in which he wrested control of government from the then joint-prime minister, Prince Ranariddh. The book also discounts CPP involvement in assassination attempts on leaders of rival parties. The authors skate over the increasing number of allegations of corruption being levelled against the Phnom Penh government. The source of information for much of this book is Hun Sen himself.

Off the Rails in Phnom Penh: Into the Dark Heart of Guns, Girls, and Ganja. Amit Gilboa. Singapore: Graham Brash, 2000.

- This irreverent account tells of the author's time in Asia fraternising with a bunch of male, Western dropouts whose interest in life had reduced to two things: girls and ganja. This group divided much of its time between the red light district, where they had sex with prostitutes, and their guest house where they got stoned. To get the small amount of money needed to support this lifestyle, they taught English now and then at local language schools.

Cambodian Interlude. Tom Riddle. Bangkok, Thailand: Orchid Press, 2000.

- A delightfully written book, full of amusing insights of the life and times of a UNTAC officer working on the United Nations project preparing Cambodia for its transition to a democratic country. The book describes the foibles of the UN as a large unwieldy organisation, the political environment at the time, the difficulties of establishing the electorate, and the unremitting interference of the Khmer Rouge in the state of affairs. On a more personal level, the book tells of the author's own love affair with a Cambodian woman working for the UN on the same project. This side of the story offers some wonderful insights into the cultural divide between Cambodia and the West.

ABOUT THE AUTHOR

Peter North first started living and working in Asia about 25 years ago. He has spent time in the Middle East, Thailand, Cambodia, and now lives in Kuala Lumpur, Malaysia. He started writing for Marshall Cavendish about eight years ago and has now contributed five titles to the *CultureShock!* and business reference series. Peter is also a frequent contributor of magazine articles, in particular *Pacific Ecologist*. He spends his time pursuing various interests in environment, science and engineering. Peter's titles include *Succeed in Business: Australia, CultureShock! Success Secrets to Maximize Business in Australia, Culture Shock! Success Secrets to Maximize Business in Britain, Countries of the World: Australia* and *CultureShock! Saudi Arabia*—all published by Marshall Cavendish, and *Growing for Broke* published by Tomorrow Press.

268

INDEX

Titles in the CULTURESHOCK! series:

Argentina	Hong Kong	Paris
Australia	Hungary	Philippines
Austria	India	Portugal
Bahrain	Indonesia	San Francisco
Barcelona	Iran	Saudi Arabia
Beijing	Ireland	Scotland
Belgium	Israel	Sri Lanka
Bolivia	Italy	Shanghai
Borneo	Jakarta	Singapore
Brazil	Japan	South Africa
Britain	Korea	Spain
Cambodia	Laos	Sweden
Canada	London	Switzerland
Chicago	Malaysia	Syria
Chile	Mauritius	Taiwan
China	Mexico	Thailand
Costa Rica	Morocco	Tokyo
Cuba	Moscow	Turkey
Czech Republic	Munich	Ukraine
Denmark	Myanmar	United Arab
Ecuador	Nepal	Emirates
Egypt	Netherlands	USA
Finland	New York	Vancouver
France	New Zealand	Venezuela
Germany	Norway	Vietnam
Greece	Pakistan	

For more information about any of these titles, please contact any of our Marshall Cavendish offices around the world (listed on page ii) or visit our website at:

www.marshallcavendish.com/genref